Cambridge Introductions to Music
Gregorian Chant

What is Gregorian chant, and where does it come from? What purpose
does it serve, and how did it take on the form and features which make it
instantly recognizable? Designed to guide students through this key topic,
this introduction answers these questions and many more. David Hiley
describes the church services in which chant is performed, takes the reader
through the church year, explains what Latin texts were used, and, taking
Worcester Cathedral as an example, describes the buildings in which chant
was sung. The history of chant is traced from its beginnings in the early
centuries of Christianity, through the Middle Ages, the revisions in the
sixteenth and seventeenth centuries, and the restoration in the nineteenth
and twentieth. Using numerous music examples, the book shows how
chants are made and how they were notated. An indispensable guide for
all those interested in the fascinating world of Gregorian chant.

David Hiley is Professor in the Institute of Musicology at the University
of Regensburg, Germany.

Cambridge Introductions to Music
Gregorian Chant

DAVID HILEY

CAMBRIDGE
UNIVERSITY PRESS

CAMBRIDGE UNIVERSITY PRESS
Cambridge, New York, Melbourne, Madrid, Cape Town, Singapore, São Paulo, Delhi

Cambridge University Press
The Edinburgh Building, Cambridge CB2 8RU, UK

Published in the United States of America by Cambridge University Press, New York

www.cambridge.org
Information on this title: www.cambridge.org/9780521690355

First published 2009

Printed in the United Kingdom at the University Press, Cambridge

A catalogue record for this publication is available from the British Library

Library of Congress Cataloguing in Publication data
Hiley, David.
Gregorian chant / David Hiley.
    p.   cm. – (Cambridge introductions to music)
Includes bibliographical references and index.
ISBN 978-0-521-87020-7 (hardback)
1. Gregorian chants–History and criticism.   I. Title.   II. Series.
ML3082.H53   2009
782.32′22–dc22   2009035294

ISBN 978-0-521-87020-7 hardback
ISBN 978-0-521-69035-5 paperback

For Meg and Cathy

Contents

Illustrations

The author and publisher are grateful to be able to include the following illustrations.

Musical examples

Note on the musical examples

Notes are named according to a modification of the Guidonian system, with capital letters for the lower octave, small ones for the upper octave:

Guidonian:

In this book:

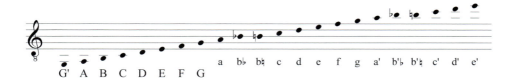

Notes are given in the main text in italic.
Liquescent notes are printed small and joined to the main note with a slur:

The note-groupings of the original manuscripts are reflected in the transcriptions, without the use of slurs.
Sign for *oriscus*: 𝑛
Sign for *quilisma*: 𝑤

Tables

Text boxes

Preface

This book tries to answer some of the questions which are often raised about Gregorian chant: what is it about and why is it the way it is? where does it come from, who composed it, and for whom? These are questions about its history, and the book is orientated towards historical matters. Thinking about the nature of Gregorian chant may nevertheless help explain why so many are interested in it and like to listen to it. For it may very well be that more people listen to Gregorian chant today, or have heard it at some time or other, in some form or other, than at any time in history. In sheer numbers, that is, not as a percentage of the population in lands with a Christian heritage. Every so often a recording of Gregorian chant climbs towards the top of the sales charts (as I write these words, the singing of the monks of the Cistercian Abbey of Heiligenkreuz in Austria is making the running). No beat, no harmony, such simple note patterns! Sung quietly, free from tension, it is far removed indeed from modern music of almost every kind, and a welcome respite from the haste and clamour of everyday life. Its 'other-worldly' character appeals to esoteric movements, and it has been thoroughly exploited in branches of the entertainment industry.

By contrast with this popularity of Gregorian chant outside the church, things are less happy in the original home of chant, the worship of the Christian church. Church attendance and the numbers of those entering holy orders fall. The changes brought about after the Second Vatican Council (1962–5) led to a drastic decline in the use of Latin, the language of Gregorian chant, in the services of the Roman Catholic Church. Those in the church who regard chant as a relic of the past, inappropriate for the modern church and best forgotten, are by no means few in number. Nevertheless, there are strong movements in many countries today to cultivate chant in church worship, and singing courses are popular. There seems little danger that chant will sink into oblivion.

As well as occupying these spaces in modern life, plainchant is of great interest to anyone with a feel for history. It is, after all, the earliest substantial (very substantial!) body of music preserved in written form. So it has a regular place in the syllabus of institutions of higher education, not least in inter-disciplinary courses in medieval studies.

The reasons why so many are interested in, or listen to chant, outside its original context are certainly important, but they should be the subject of a different book. This one concentrates on the time when chant was created. For it is a fact that nowadays we do not compose chant, just as we do not build medieval cathedrals. In the Middle Ages singing chant dominated the lives of very many men and women, including many of the leaders of medieval society. To understand chant we need not only to look at it note by note but also to think about the circumstances in which it was made and performed. We need to get a sense of the purpose and shape of the religious services, of the places of worship, and of how medieval men and women might have thought about chant.

There are plenty of musical examples in this book, and it is my earnest hope that readers will take the time to sing them through, at least in their minds, or even pick them out on a musical instrument. Then they can test their reactions against my descriptions. Some, however, may well wish to keep to the more general information and pass over the discussion of particular pieces of chant, which are accordingly set off in appearance.

I have written about the music fully aware of the well-known problem that music is something which happens in time. Looking at a string of marks on a page in musical examples is very far removed from experiencing chant in a medieval church service. But that is what I would wish readers to try and imagine, in their mind's ear and eye. Hence the decision to relate some of what is explained to a specific church, Worcester Cathedral, and to transcribe most of the musical examples from Worcester manuscripts.

My view of chant is naturally shaped by my own experience of it, the way I have come to know it, what I have read and learned, what I should like to believe about it. The experience of others is inevitably different. But that is the chance any writer on things of the past has to take. Faced with the miraculous beauty of the music and the sheer size of the achievement – nothing less than creating Latin chant to be sung most of the day (and part of the night) throughout one's whole life – it seems well worth taking that chance. For the ultimate point is not to describe the patterns made by those marks on the page but to understand and appreciate the creative achievement of which men and women are capable. I am also convinced that music is such a complex phenomenon, and our powers of appreciating it so infinitely various, that the distance in time between then and now is relatively insignificant, and no more of a hindrance for chant than it is for any great music of the past.

As its place in the series of Cambridge Introductions suggests, this book is not intended to be as comprehensive as some previous reference books on chant. In keeping with this, the 'Further Reading' paragraphs and Bibliography are mostly restricted to publications basic to the study of chant, although some citations will take readers into more specialized research.

The book is also different in character from another one with a similar title, Richard Crocker's *An Introduction to Gregorian Chant* of 2000. This is the right place to acknowledge a debt to Richard Crocker. Helping his volume in the New Oxford History of Music towards publication in 1989 was one of the most valuable formative experiences of my early career. That we write quite differently about chant would have become clear when my own *Western Plainchant: A Handbook* appeared in 1993. Now history has repeated itself, once again in the shape of two very different books.

I am grateful to Vicki Cooper of Cambridge University Press for commissioning this book, and both to her and to Rebecca Jones, Rosina Di Marzo and Ann Lewis for their expert help in guiding it into print. Special thanks go to Nicolas Bell of the British Library, Christopher Guy of Worcester Cathedral, Ute Engel and Jill Atherton for their help and generosity over the illustrations. My wife Ann saved me from many egregious errors and persuaded me to smarten up many points of presentation.

As a music historian I have learned most of all from what has been written by the glorious company of chant scholars, past and present, not least those of the Research Group 'Cantus Planus' of the International Musicological Society, whose meetings over more than two decades have been such pleasant and profitable occasions. If their words and ideas appear to have fallen on stony ground here, I beg their forgiveness. Teaching for ten years at Royal Holloway College, University of London, and for over twenty at Regensburg University, has certainly benefitted me as much as my students. I hope future students will find something in these pages to spur their imagination. In a similar way, I am sure I have learned more from my daughters than they have from me (though not about Gregorian chant) and so this book is dedicated affectionately to them.

Note on front cover illustration

London, British Library, Cotton MS Caligula A.xiv, from fol. 26r: The Annunciation to Joachim

The first part of the manuscript Caligula A.xiv is an eleventh-century troper probably made in Winchester for Worcester. In this illustration an angel announces to Joachim that his wife Ann will bear a child. This will be a daughter, Mary, mother of Christ. The illustration appears amid the trope verses to chants for Mass on the feast of the Nativity of the Blessed Virgin Mary, 8 September. Joachim is depicted as a herdsman with a flock of animals. The story of Joachim and Ann is not biblical but is related in the Greek Protevangelium of James, then in the Latin apocryphal gospel of Pseudo-Matthew. Like all the pictures in MS Caligula A.xiv, this one is framed by Latin verses in Leonine hexameters (that is, with internal rhyme, so named after Leoninus, *optimus organista* of Notre-Dame in Paris *c.*1200):

> *Credidit angelico   Ioiachim per nuntia verbo*
> *credens foecundam   conceptu germinis Annam*
> *Christum glorificat   inopi qui semper habundat*
> [Joachim believed the angelic word through the (divine) message, believing Ann to be fertile by the conception of an child. He glorifies Christ, who is always generous to one in need.]

(Translation based on that by Elizabeth C. Teviotdale, 'The Cotton Troper (London, British Library, Cotton MS Caligula A.xiv, ff. 1–36): A Study of an Illustrated English Troper of the Eleventh Century,' Ph.D. dissertation, University of North Carolina at Chapel Hill, 1991, p. 309.)

Chapter 1

Gregorian chant in the service of the church

1.i Singing music in church in the Middle Ages; the function of Gregorian chant; levels of musical elaboration in the declamation of sacred texts; sacred sound for sacred space

Gregorian chant is the single-voice ('monophonic') music sung in the services of the Roman church. It was first recorded in writing, that is, with musical notation, in the ninth century. A great number of its Latin texts can be traced back for another century before that, but the melodies first become tangible, so to speak, in the ninth century. Gregorian chant is the earliest music preserved in such quantities – for we are talking about thousands of items. Much of the medieval corpus has dropped out of use, but it is still the music with the longest reconstructible history sung today. It is an inspiring thought that we can not only stand in an early medieval church like Charlemagne's Palatine chapel at Aachen (Aix-la-Chapelle), built 792–805, but also perform the chant sung at the time the chapel was built or soon after. Inspiring in more ways than one: most obviously because something embedded deep in our history becomes audible. Admittedly, music does not survive in notation alone and there is, alas, no unbroken line of performance practice between then and now. When we sing Gregorian chant today we cannot ultimately be sure how close we are getting to the way it was done in Charlemagne's time. Nevertheless, the written link between then and now is longer than a millennium.

The function of Gregorian chant

Gregorian chant is liturgical chant. 'Liturgy' is a word used very often in this book. It is the usual word for the cycle of services as a whole in the worship of the Christian churches. Liturgical chant is therefore chant sung during Christian services. The term comes from the Greek word *leitourgia*, late Latin *liturgia*, meaning simply 'service' in the public good, without restriction to religious worship. The modern English term 'service' is to be understood here as 'the service of God', things done in his service. Compare the German term 'Gottesdienst'; while French 'office' and Italian 'ufficio' relate to the term 'office' in the sense of the performance of a duty. 'Office' is usually restricted in Latin Christian worship to refer to the Office hours, that is, the services other than Mass. Liturgy usually refers to everything performed, in both the Mass and the Divine Office. In the Eastern churches the term 'liturgy' is restricted to the Eucharist, the part of Mass where bread and wine are given to the believers. (The Greek word *eucharistia* means 'thanksgiving'.) The word 'liturgy' can be used in conjunction with other terms to refer to something more specific. So the 'Good Friday liturgy' refers to the services performed on Good Friday.

Chant functions principally as a vehicle for the ceremonious declamation of sacred Latin texts, whether by a single soloist, a small group or a choir. Chanting the texts in a measured, disciplined manner is a good way for the group of worshippers to act together; the more harmonious the singing, the more inspiring the communal act. When soloists exert their full powers in singing, say, a tract or offertory at Mass, they add a dimension to the religious experience commensurate with all those other things beyond the Latin text that enhance worship, such as the ceremonial actions, the vestments of the participants, and the architectural setting, including such features as stained-glass windows. Music is one of many non-verbal elements in worship, none the less essential for being difficult to describe in words.

In the liturgy mankind gives thanks and praise to God, who is present during the liturgy. Moreover, through the liturgy God acts to bestow his grace on mankind. He is praised because he is above all things, transcendent, distinct from the universe. He is thanked for creating the world and saving mankind through the gift of his son, Jesus Christ. Praising, thanking and asking for God's mercy are done in prayers, while lessons (readings) recall important events in the history of salvation. In chants, selected sentences are given a special musical setting which enhances their spirituality. This is especially appropriate because God is a spirit, not material.

Over the centuries since Christianity was declared the state religion by the Roman Emperor Constantine the Great (324–37) a complicated cycle of services was developed in which the praises of God were sung and the death and resurrection of Jesus Christ were commemorated. Each day had its round of services, and each service had its own particular form and content; and the services were performed each day throughout the year. Some days were more important than others. Sundays were more important than ordinary weekdays, and so too were special days in Christ's life, and days when holy men and women of particular significance for the history of the church were commemorated. What was sung, and how much, depended on the importance of the day. But even on an ordinary weekday with no special occasion to be commemorated, the full cycle of services took up most of the day and part of the night.

Text box 1.1 Gregory the Great on the Eucharist

The role of Gregory the Great, pope from 590 to 604, in the creation of 'Gregorian' chant is not as clear as one would like, but his status as a theologian, the last of the four Latin 'Doctors of the Church', is unchallenged. His *Dialogues* tell of the lives of St Benedict and other early saints.

What right believing Christian can doubt that in the very hour of the sacrifice, at the words of the Priest, the heavens be opened, and the quires of Angels are present in that mystery of Jesus Christ; that high things are accomplished with low, and earthly joined to heavenly, and that one thing is made of visible and invisible.

From *The Dialogues of Gregory the Great*, trans. P. W., ed. Edmund Gardner (London, 1911), 4.58. Original text in J.-P. Migne, *Patrologia latina*, vols. 75–78 (Paris, 1878–1903).

Levels of musical elaboration in the declamation of sacred texts

There are four basic categories of sacred text. Readings from the Bible and other chosen literature (such as the sermons and homilies of the Church Fathers), and prayers addressed to the Almighty, are two of these categories. Both are performed by intoning the texts on a single note with slight inflections at the ends of clauses. During the performance of the Office (the cycle of services other than Mass), a large number of psalms are sung, each and every day; these are performed by a choir using simple intonation formulae not very different in principle from the way prayers and lessons are intoned. The fourth category is made up of verses for more elaborate singing.

Even the very simple intonation of lessons and prayers lends to them a special quality, compared with plain reading. It sets them apart from everyday speech and 'depersonalizes' them, since the same formula is used over and over again regardless of the semantic content of the text, regardless of whether it is joyful or sorrowful, narrative or hortatory. The priest praying or the deacon or other official intoning the lesson is a vehicle, an instrument whereby the words become audible, rather than an actor delivering a personal statement.

Much of this holds good for the more elaborate forms of Gregorian chant as well. They have a much more varied melodic vocabulary than the formulae for intoning prayers and lessons, and can therefore respond in infinitely subtle ways to the text being sung. However, this subtlety is not a matter of more 'expressive' singing, of the sort we know from romantic and modern music. That would bring the chant down to the personal level when it should partake of the divine. But the elaborate musical style reflects the syntactic structure of the text in a great variety of ways, giving it musical shape at the level of the sentence, the clause, down to individual words.

Sacred sound for sacred space

Gregorian chant creates a sacred sound to match the sacred space in which it is sung. This is something which religious music of many kinds, outside Western Christian society as well, has always done. Therefore, while Gregorian chant is undoubtedly a means of making the sacred Latin text audible, it does so in ways whereby the text sometimes seems almost secondary. The sacred sound is more important than the sense. It is part of a ritual where most of what is done has symbolic significance, far removed from the mundane actions of everyday life. Gregorian chant contributes in its own special way to the quality of the ritual experience.

What do we mean by 'ritual'? Ritual is here understood as a system of traditional actions to be carried out in the presence of what is sacred, following established rules. Such systems are active in all human societies where the 'sacred' has any meaning. They typically comprise actions of symbolic significance, a special form of language and a special body of texts to be recited or sung. The rituals attached to the Christian religion are particularly rich in form and content, not least in their musical components. When trying to understand the ritual of which Gregorian chant is a part, it should be remembered that music is not its only non-verbal component. There are others: church architecture and stained-glass windows, images and church furniture, the dress of the performers and the objects they hold and use, the bells and the incense. It is fair to say that these things have a stronger cumulative impact than the Latin texts being recited.

Words and music

Much depends on the degree of musical elaboration. Simple antiphons, which frame the Office psalms, enhance the text quite delicately, in a concise and restrained manner, so that the words are perfectly audible. In other sorts of chant, such as the gradual or offertory at Mass, the proportion of notes to syllables is much greater, and the melody transcends its role as a vehicle for the text. As far as understanding the text is concerned, this musical richness might be thought an obstacle to comprehension, but that is actually a minor consideration. The great majority of the texts were excerpted from the Book of Psalms, known by heart in its entirety and sung more or less complete every week. The chants themselves were performed from memory. It is important to understand that the Latin texts are not being presented to an audience, as a story-teller might address a group of listeners. They are more like a reference point for a religious musical experience, for a reaching out to the deity, who is no more to be comprehended in words than is music itself.

It might be objected that ordinary people in the Middle Ages did not know the Latin Psalter by heart, that in fact they did not understand Latin at all. But a religious community performed the liturgy in the manner (including the language) established as the right way for praise and commemoration. The religious community did this both for itself and on behalf of the rest of mankind, for those who had mundane occupations and no time for praise and commemoration but who needed to know that the religious were acting for them, in the proper manner.

Many of us come to Gregorian chant from the standpoint of classical music. At school and university, chant is often presented as Chapter One, as it were, in the long story of the History of Western Music, probably in a programme of required reading and listening. We might easily gain the impression that chant, monophonic music, is hardly more than a primitive forerunner of more sophisticated and interesting polyphonic music, in a progression moving steadily onward and upward. Or we may simply have heard a lot of classical music in our formative years. It may take some time to realize that chant does not 'work' in the same way as music from at least the sixteenth century onwards. When William Byrd writes a motet on the text *Defecit in dolore* (*Cantiones sacrae*, 1589), or Schubert a song such as *Erstarrung* ('Ich such' im Schnee vergebens', *Die Winterreise*, 1827), they match words and music (to varying degrees, of course) in such a way that the music only makes expressive sense with that particular text; there would be no reason to write this particular music if the text were a different one. The relationship between melody and text in Gregorian chant, on the other hand, is much more like that of a motet of the thirteenth century, or a chanson of the fourteenth century by Guillaume de Machaut. In many of these chansons the same music carries different verses of text because of the strophic form or repetition scheme. Individual words will not be matched by a unique melodic gesture, and individual turns of phrase in the music have none of the expressive connotations they were later to carry.

This has two obvious implications for Gregorian chant. The first is that the same text could be delivered in different ways according to the liturgical context, and the same music could be used for different texts.

Here is an example:
'Eripe me de inimicis meis, Deus meus' is the start of Psalm 58 (Psalm 59 in the King James Bible): 'Deliver me from mine enemies, O my God'. The whole psalm will be chanted to a simple tone, with the same melodic formula for every verse, on Tuesday each week during the Night Office (if not displaced by the different selection of pieces needed for a special feast day). The first verse of the psalm alone is sung as the central section of some of the great responsories of the Night Office, such as *Adiutor et susceptor* and *Ne perdas cum impiis* on Passion Sunday. In this context *Eripe me* is sung to a more elaborate tone than a simple psalm. These tones, one for each of the eight modes, are used hundreds of times in the course of a year. Elsewhere in the Office hours, *Eripe me* turns up in some manuscripts as the beginning of a simple antiphon sung at

Lauds on Friday each week. Turning to the Mass, we find it as a gradual, coupled with other phrases of similar import from Psalm 17. Here it is sung on Passion Sunday to an elaborate mode-3 melody, which shares melodic phrases with other mode-3 graduals. But this is by no means all. An alleluia in mode 2 sung on one of the summer Sundays of the year has *Eripe me* as its verse, and two offertories also begin with the same phrase, one in mode 7 for the Wednesday of Passion Week, and one in mode 3 for the Monday of Holy Week. All these very different ways of declaiming the text are appropriate for their liturgical purpose. It goes without saying that none of the melodies, from simple psalm tone to ornate offertory, express in a modern, personal way the feelings of a man oppressed by his enemies.

The other side of the coin, so to speak, is a matter of compositional technique. Many turns of phrase in Gregorian chant are associated with particular modes (that is, tonalities) and particular types of chant (responsory, gradual, etc.). The opening melodic phrase of the gradual *Eripe me* is used for at least four other graduals in mode 3, the next phrase in three others, while two graduals besides *Eripe me* use the same final phrase. The second part of the chant, the verse, has more examples of this sharing of melodic phrases. Recognizing this technique is of crucial importance for understanding how it was possible to learn, perform and pass on thousands of melodies to many generations of singers, largely without written aids. The traditional melodies, many composed of the same well-known phrases, were fixed in a framework made up by the structure of the text and the norms of melodic movement (established ways of starting and ending a chant, how to get to and from important points in between, and how to halt the musical motion in order to deliver lengthier passages of text). Knowing how graduals like *Eripe me* were sung as a type was more than half way to knowing how to sing *Eripe me* as an individual piece.

Just as phrases from sacred texts recur again and again, setting up a network of associations across all of sacred history, so also musical phrases recur. Just as the Latin texts are drawn again and again from the inexhaustible riches of holy writ, so the chant seems to be drawn out of a divine well of music, eternally renewed, ever present, resonating in the sacred space from one end of the year to the other.

Further reading

The study of religious worship in its wider sense, and not restricted to Christianity, involves the very large subject areas of anthropology and theology, waters too deep to enter here. Christian worship is treated in a wider context in Eliade, *Patterns in Comparative Religion*. See also the opening chapters in Senn, *Christian Liturgy:*

Catholic and Evangelical, and *The Study of Liturgy*. Dictionaries which contain at least brief information on many aspects of liturgy are *The Oxford Dictionary of the Christian Church* and *The New SCM Dictionary of Liturgy and Worship*.

1.ii Where chant was sung, and by whom

Chanting the round of services each day was a major, indeed the most important activity in the life of religious communities in the Middle Ages. These communities were of several types, the most notable being those of cathedrals and collegiate churches, on the one hand, and of monasteries and convents for monks and nuns on the other.

Gregorian chant is performed today both by trained church musicians and in religious groups and communities whose members have learned to sing chant not as professional singers but as worshippers. In the Middle Ages this was also more or less so, with two general differences. The trained singers in, say, a medieval cathedral choir would perform very little music other than Gregorian chant, whereas today's singers are expected to master a great deal of polyphonic music of widely differing types and styles, from several different centuries. Furthermore, in the Middle Ages the singers' duties would take up much more time than today, when it is usual for a cathedral singer to have other part-time employment. Something approximating more closely to the medieval system can be found today in English cathedrals with a choir school, where a singing man (choral vicar, lay clerk, or whatever he is traditionally called) may be a member of the teaching staff for the boys attending the school (who will also be singing in the cathedral choir). For those who follow a contemplative life as monks or nuns circumstances have not changed as much since the Middle Ages, although the performance of the Divine Office does not take as much time. The Night Office was already being shortened in the fifteenth century, and since then has rarely been performed with its full sung complement of lessons and great responsories.

As just said, in the Middle Ages those chiefly responsible for singing chant were members of an ecclesiastical community. They were attached either to a cathedral, collegiate church or parish church, where they were free to interact with the non-ecclesiastical population, or they belonged to an order of monks or nuns and lived withdrawn from the world. The different forms of liturgy which these two types of community follow are referred to as 'secular' and 'monastic', respectively. When the order of the services is set out in more detail in section 1.iii below a distinction is therefore made between two models. On the one hand we have the secular or 'Roman' arrangement, for which the practice of the Roman papal chapel was the ultimate model. On the other hand there is the monastic or 'Benedictine' arrangement; the

Benedictine monastic order, following the Rule of St Benedict, was one of the oldest orders and the largest.

Cathedral and collegiate church

The term 'collegiate church' refers to a church with a large staff who lived together in a community (*collegium*) and were bound by rules of conduct for their common life. The Greek word for rule is *kanōn*, taken up in Christian Latin in several senses, giving rise to the word *canonicus*, a canon, one who lives by a rule or rules of conduct. The chief purpose of the collegiate church was that of prayer and praise. Pastoral care of the population was left to the priests of parish churches, which did not usually have the resources to perform the liturgy in its full musical splendour. Cathedrals are, in effect, large collegiate churches; their special importance derives from the presence of a bishop, who is the spiritual leader of an ecclesiastical diocese and has a throne (*cathedra*) in the church. The administrative head of the collegiate church (or cathedral) was the dean (*decanus*), his chief support in liturgical matters being the cantor or precentor (*praecantor*). The duty of directing and performing the liturgy was often shared with an assistant cantor, the succentor (*subcantor*). Many members of the college would be in holy orders, in descending order: bishop (*episcopus*), priest (*presbiter*), deacon (*diaconus*), subdeacon, and the minor orders of porter, lector, exorcist and acolyte. The term *clericus* (cleric, clerk, hence the collective term 'clergy') could refer to anyone in holy orders but usually meant those from subdeacon downwards. (Since training for the clerical life invariably involved learning to read and write, it became common to call 'clerk' someone employed as a writer of documents, a scribe, whether in holy orders or not.) An important official of the church was the sacrist, who would be in holy orders and who had care of the sacred vessels, vestments and other objects needed for the services.

The prayer and praise which was the chief business of the college followed the liturgical round of the Office hours and Mass (outlined in section 1.iii below). All members took part, the better singers being appointed to sing chants (or parts of them) reserved for soloists or small groups. Many important churches had a school where boys received an education fitting them for a religious life or administrative work in the service of the crown or the local lord; but performance of the liturgy was the most important part of their lives, and particular chants (or parts of them) were assigned to them as well.

Monastery and convent

Monks and nuns spent most of their lives enclosed within the walls of their monasteries and convents, leading a life of prayer and contemplation which was dominated by the performance of the liturgy. St Benedict called this the *opus Dei*, 'the work of God'. Their way of life also followed a 'rule'. The most important of these was the Rule of St Benedict; those who followed it thus belonged to the Benedictine Order (the Black Monks). Two other important orders were the Carthusians and Cistercians (White Monks), both to a large extent conceived as reformed Benedictines. Another important rule was that of St Augustine, but this was less specific in many ways, so that a number of groups evolved within the Augustinian order, the Premonstratensians being one tightly knit congregation. Augustinians are usually referred to as regular canons (Black, or Austin Canons) rather than monks; the designation 'regular' indicates that they followed a *regula*, a rule.

The head of a monastery was the abbot (derived from Aramaic *abba*, Greek and Latin *abbas*, 'father'), elected by his brethren, the election being approved by the bishop of the diocese. (The influence of secular powers on elections, particularly in monasteries endowed by them with lands and wealth, was a recurrent problem.) Since the abbot of an important monastery was often called away on ecclesiastical or other business, one or more priors deputized for him in the administration of the monastery. The cantor or precentor was responsible for the performance of the liturgy, hence also the training of the monks in singing chant. Very often he had charge over the liturgical books and therefore the scriptorium (writing room) of the monastery. The fabric of the church, especially its valuable relics, was the province of the sacrist.

Friars (from Latin *frater*, a brother) and sisters in the orders of the Franciscans (the Grey Friars), Dominicans (Black Friars), Carmelites (White Friars) and Augustinians (Austin Friars), among others, had important work in the secular community as preachers, teachers and pastors. They, too, were committed to strict rules of conduct, including a life of poverty (hence their collective denomination as 'mendicant' or begging orders), and the performance of the liturgy.

The liturgies observed by the monastic and mendicant orders had the same basic structure as that in secular churches, while differing to a greater or lesser extent in detail. This might involve differences in the structure of individual Offices, including the number of pieces to be sung, as may be seen in Table 1.3 in the next section, where the Roman or secular 'cursus' (order of services), observed in cathedrals and collegiate churches, is compared with the Benedictine cursus. While the Cistercians followed the Benedictine cursus, Augustinian monasteries used the secular form, as did the mendicant orders.

The celebration of the Mass was different for nuns, because no woman could be admitted to holy orders. An ordained priest had to administer the Eucharist, and other ministers might be required to perform other liturgical functions. This did not much affect the singing of the chant, which could obviously be performed just as well by nuns as by monks.

Text box 1.2 The Benedictine Rule

Although the form of the Mass can be traced back over many centuries, few of the exact texts
used are precisely documented before the seventh century. It is therefore all the more
astonishing that in the Rule of St Benedict of *c*.530 the form and much of the content of the
Office is already set out, and has remained unaltered to this day. The following extracts are
(1) part of the order for singing the Night Office in Chs. 8–10, (2) the order of the other Office
hours in Ch. 16, and (3) an exhortation to sing in the right spirit in Ch. 19. (References to the
'prophet' are to David as composer of the psalms, regarded in this context as a prophet.)

1

Chapter VIII Of the Divine Office at Night
In winter time, that is, from the first of November until Easter, the brethren shall rise
at what may reasonably calculated to be the eighth hour of the night; so that having
rested till some time past midnight, they may rise having had their full sleep. And let
the time that remains after the Night-Office be spent in study by those brethren who
still have some part of the Psalter and lessons to learn. But from Easter to the first of
November let the hour for the Night-Office be so arranged that, after a very short
interval, during which the brethren may go out for the necessities of nature, Lauds,
which are to be said at day-break, may follow without delay.

Chapter IX How many Psalms are to be said at the Night Hours
In winter time, after beginning with the verse, 'O God, come to my assistance; O Lord
make haste to help me' [Ps. 69:2], with the *Gloria*, let the words 'O Lord, Thou wilt
open my lips, and my mouth shall declare Thy praise' [Ps. 50:17] be next repeated
thrice; then the third Psalm, with a *Gloria*, after which the ninety-fourth Psalm is to
be said or sung, with an antiphon. Next let a hymn follow, and then six Psalms with
antiphons. These being said, and also a versicle, let the Abbot give the blessing: and,
all being seated, let three lessons be read by the brethren in turns, from the book on
the lectern. Between the lessons let three responsories be sung – two of them without
a *Gloria*, but after the third let the reader say the *Gloria*: and as soon as he has begun
it, let all rise from their seats out of honour and reverence to the Holy Trinity. Let the
divinely inspired books, both of the Old and New Testaments, be read at the
Night-Office, and also the commentaries upon them written by the most famous,
orthodox and Catholic Fathers. After these three lessons with their responsories, let
six more psalms follow, to be sung with an *Alleluia*. Then let a lesson from the Apostle
be said by heart, with a verse and the petition of the Litany, that is, *Kyrie eleison*. And
so let the Night-Office come to an end.

Chapter X How the Night-Office is to be said in Summer Time
From Easter to the first of November let the same number of Psalms be recited as
prescribed above; only that no lessons are to be read from the book, on account of the
shortness of the night; but instead of those three lessons let one from the Old
Testament be said by heart, followed by a short responsory, and the rest as before laid
down; so that never less than twelve Psalms, not counting the third and ninety-fourth,
be said at the Night-Office.

2

Chapter XVI How the Work of God is to be done in the day-time
As the prophet saith: 'Seven times in the day have I given praise to Thee' [Ps. 118:164].
And we shall observe this sacred number of seven if, at the times of Lauds, Prime,
Tierce, Sext, None, Vespers and Compline, we fulfil the duties of our service. For it
was of these hours of the day that he said: 'Seven times in the day have I given praise
to Thee'; just as the same prophet saith of the night watches: 'At midnight I arose to
give Thee praise' [Ps. 118:62]. At these times, therefore, let us sing the praises of our
Creator for the judgements of His justice; that is, at Lauds, Prime, Terce, Sext, None,
Vespers and Compline; and at night let us arise to praise Him.

3

Chapter XIX Of the Discipline of saying the Divine Office
We believe that the Divine presence is everywhere, and that the eyes of the Lord behold
the good and evil in every place. Especially should we believe this, without any doubt,
when we are assisting at the Work of God. Let us, then, ever remember what the
prophet saith: 'Serve the Lord in fear' [Ps. 2:11]; and again, 'Sing ye wisely' [Ps. 46:8];
and, 'In the sight of Angels I will sing praises unto Thee' [Ps. 137:1]. Therefore let us
consider how we ought to behave ourselves in the presence of God and of His angels,
and so assist at the Divine Office, that our mind and our voice may accord together.

From *The Rule of St Benedict*, edited with an English translation and explanatory notes by
D. Oswald Hunter Blair (Fort Augustus, 1886, 5th edn 1948), pp. 55–9, 67, 75.

In both collegiate churches, cathedrals and monasteries, boys were educated in singing the liturgy and received a more general education to fit them for ecclesiastical or civil life. Their numbers were often limited to six in monasteries, whereas in the bigger choirs of collegiate churches there might be many more. Their duties included carrying candles, a cross or a censer, for example in the procession to the lectern where the Gospel was intoned. But they were also trained for important musical duties, such as singing the start and verse of responsories, intoning the Lamentations in Holy Week, and singing the antiphon to the Blessed Virgin after Compline and the weekly or daily Mass of the Blessed Virgin.

The interior layout of churches

The celebration of Mass is centred on the main altar of the church, for it is here that the bread and wine of the communion are brought during the offertory chant, blessed and consumed. Relics of the patron saint of the church were kept in the altar. The area around the altar is called the sanctuary. Lessons were recited at another place in the church, from a pulpit (*pulpitum*, desk) or from a raised platform known as the ambo, the book of scriptures being placed on a lectern. When the Gospel, the most important lesson, was to be recited by the deacon, a small procession was formed to conduct him to the pulpit, and likewise for his return to the sanctuary. The choir stood or sat apart in its own area. Sometimes it sang during the performance of some ritual action, as when the introit was sung during the entrance of the ministers, the offertory when the bread and wine are brought to the altar, or the communion during the final actions of the communion ceremony. The gradual and alleluia (or tract), on the other hand, form a group with the lessons, and were started by soloists from the pulpit, to be continued by the choir in its own place.

The Office hours, by contrast, are purely meditative, consisting primarily of psalms with framing antiphons, and, in the Night Office, of alternating lessons and responsories.

This simple scenario was much amplified and elaborated in larger churches, principally because of the presence of multiple relics of saints and corresponding altars, often placed in recesses at other points in the church or in chapels of their own. The need to place the altars of more and more saints in a worthy setting was indeed one of the reasons for the increasing dimensions of medieval churches. A striking development in church architecture from the thirteenth century onwards was the building of chapels dedicated to the Blessed Virgin Mary, or 'Lady Chapels', often at the east end of the church or cathedral. Masses would be celebrated at these supplementary altars on the appropriate day each year, and some would be used more frequently, either for 'private' Masses (spoken by a priest alone) or on the route of a liturgical procession. Special veneration of the Blessed Virgin Mary led to the custom of singing a Mass weekly or even daily in her honour and celebrating a cycle of Office hours parallel to the canonical round.

Processions took place within the largest churches every day, with regular routes to particular shrines, sometimes taking in the cloisters (which often contained further shrines). The processions from a cathedral led into the cathedral close, where a parish church was often to be found, or to other churches in the town. Monastic processions, though just as regular in occurrence, did not leave the monastery grounds except on Palm Sunday and the Rogation Days.

An example: Worcester cathedral

To give some idea of the spaces in which the liturgy was performed, a ground plan of the cathedral at Worcester in the West Midlands of England is given here. Following that comes a sketch of the cathedral precinct as it existed in the Middle Ages, and finally the town and its churches as it used to be. (Figs. 1.1–3.) The reason for choosing Worcester, apart from the splendour of the cathedral, is that almost all the chant sung in the course of the year, at Mass and during the Divine Office, has survived in a manuscript of the thirteenth century, still preserved in the Chapter Library of the cathedral (manuscript F 160). Two other chant books with Worcester connections survive, now bound together with a book of the lives of saints (in Anglo-Saxon), kept in the British Library in London (manuscript Cotton Caligula A.xiv). These manuscripts have been used for some of the musical examples in the present book, and the oldest has provided the illustration for the front cover. Another Worcester chant book with large numbers of Office chants, now in Corpus Christi College, Cambridge (manuscript 391), is traditionally known as the 'Portiforium of St Wulstan', a book small enough to be carried around by the famous bishop of the eleventh century.

Interestingly, Worcester was one of nine cathedrals in the reorganization of the English church after the Norman Conquest which were monastic, with a community of Benedictine monks, not staffed by secular clergy. Their liturgy followed the Benedictine cursus. Head of the monastic community was thus the prior, not an abbot, hence the name of Worcester Cathedral Priory for the institution as a whole. The bishop of the diocese had his throne in the church and certain items in the annual liturgy were reserved for him, apart from his episcopal functions of the baptism, ordination of priests, and so on. The present cathedral, built with stone from Highley, superseded a previous, smaller building, and was dedicated in 1218.

Worcester Cathedral Priory is dedicated to the Blessed Virgin Mary and St Oswald (Bishop of Worcester 961–92, also Archbishop of York from 972). The high altar (6) is dedicated to them. In the wall behind the high altar are the shrines of St Wulstan (Bishop of Worcester 1062–95) and St Oswald (7 and 8). The area with the sanctuary in the east and the choir in the west (12) is commonly referred to as the chancel. It forms a sort of inner church within the great cathedral, partly separated from it by dividing walls. At the west end of this inner church was a substantial stone screen (the 'choir-screen') with an opening leading west into the rest of the church, the screen being strong enough to support an organ in later times. (In the Middle Ages the separation of the choir was completed by further stone screens at the sides, since removed.) It was here, in the chancel, that the liturgy was for the most part chanted. The choir-screen played an important part, for up on the screen was the pulpit (13) from which the lessons were intoned on major feast days, and the chants between them were sung, the gradual, tract or alleluia and sequence. This is a ceremonial element quite missing in modern worship. Now we can see the sense of approaching the pulpit in procession for the reading of the Gospel.

In the middle of this area stands a subsidiary altar ('medium altare') dedicated to St Peter and St Wulstan. St Peter was the patron saint of the former principal church of Worcester, before it was superseded by the abbey church dedicated to St Mary, the

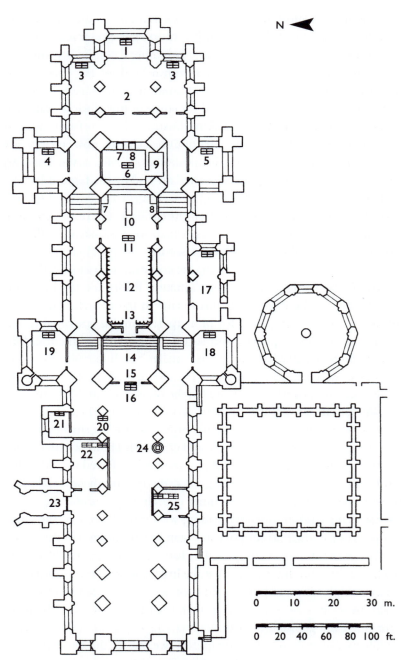

N ◄

1 Altar of the Blessed Virgin Mary; 2 Lady Chapel; 3 Altars of Sts Philip and James, Sts Simon and Jude; 4 Altar and chapel
of St John the Baptist; 5 Altar and chapel of St John the Evangelist; 6 High altar of the Blessed Virgin Mary and St Oswald;
7 Shrine of St Wulstan; 8 Shrine of St Oswald; 9 Chantry chapel of Prince Arthur († 1502); 10 Tomb of King John († 1216);
11 Middle altar ('medium altare'); 12 Choir; 13 Choir screen and pulpit; 14 Lower choir ('chorus minor'); 15 Rood screen;
16 Altar of the Holy Cross; 17 Sacristy; 18 Altar and chapel of St Thomas of Canterbury; 19 Altar and chapel of
St Mary Magdalene; 20 Altar of St Edmund of Canterbury; 21 Chantry chapel of Bishop Thomas Cobham († 1327);
22 Altar and chapel of the Blessed Virgin Mary 'at the red gate'; 23 North porch ('red gate'); 24 Font; 25 Altar and chapel of
Sts George and Christopher

Figure 1.1 Ground plan of Worcester Cathedral Church

forerunner of the present cathedral. While the main Mass of the day was celebrated at the high altar, the morning Mass was held at the *medium altare.*

There are other, later shrines in the sanctuary, but they are not of such liturgical importance. Nevertheless, the presence of the tomb of King John of England (1199–1216) (10) and the chantry chapel where Masses were said for the soul of Prince Arthur († 1502), eldest son of Henry VII of England (9), underlines the importance of cathedral churches to the royal families of England.

Beyond the sanctuary to the east is the chapel of the Blessed Virgin Mary, again architecturally self-contained. Here stood a large statue of the Virgin, bedecked with rich robes and precious jewels. Her altar (1) is flanked by those of Sts Philip and James to the north and (possibly) Sts Simon and Jude to the south (3). More large chapels are to be found north and south of the sanctuary, dedicated to St John the Baptist (4) and St John the Evangelist (5). Further along to the south is a large room of mostly practical use, the sacristy (17), equipped with chests and cupboards for vestments and other objects, and a large table for laying out the vestments. Here liturgical vessels (cups, plates and so on) and books would be kept. A crucifix was also preserved here and formed the object of liturgical processions.

At the centre of the great edifice four massive pillars support the central tower of the cathedral. Steps lead down from the choir into this square, which forms an extension of the choir, known in Worcester as the 'chorus minor' (14). We know that in some English monastic cathedrals old and infirm monks would sit on benches in this lower choir to hear the services in which they could no longer play an active part. The west of the lower choir is dominated by the main cross of the cathedral, set up on a screen, the 'rood screen' (15), beneath which is the altar of the Holy Cross (16). This is outside, in other words to the west of, the minor choir, so that when Mass is celebrated here the priest will still face east. To the north and south, respectively, are two more large chapels, dedicated to St Mary Magdalene (19) and St Thomas of Canterbury (18), respectively.

The western half of the cathedral, the nave, is brought into the liturgical scheme by processions, which will sometimes leave or enter the cathedral through the north portal, or 'red gate' (23), near to which is another Lady Chapel (22). The great font of the cathedral is placed in the nave (24), since baptisms concern the bishop and laity rather than the daily liturgy of the clergy. Processions also go into the quadrangular cloister on the south side of the church and to other parts of the cathedral close. Unfortunately, many buildings which originally formed part of the priory have not survived. The round chapter house still exists. Here the community would meet each day on administrative business, and also to hear readings from the martyrology, the record of saints to be commemorated, and to recite a number of prayers and psalms. The refectory on the south side of the cloisters is now part of the King's School. As to the rest, the monks' dormitory, kitchens and buttery, infirmary and various chapels, and so on, they are long gone, although archaeological research has made possible a fairly complete sketch of the medieval groundplan (see Fig. 1.2). Within the church again, many altars mentioned in the medieval service books are also no longer extant.

One more sacred space should be mentioned, not possible to display on Figure 1.1. This is the crypt underneath the east end of the cathedral, with further tombs.

Relics

The veneration of relics was an essential feature of medieval worship. The saints had been temples of the Holy Spirit while on earth, miracles had taken place through the agency of their mortal remains, and they might intercede before God on behalf of mortal men. An interesting event which illustrates their importance and their passage from one church to another took place in Worcester in 1218. At the dedication of the new Gothic cathedral and the Translation of the relics of St Wulstan to a new shrine, Bishop Sylvester gave relics of the saint to the bishops of Salisbury and Norwich who were present. Wulstan's feast day was duly observed at these churches thereafter. A rib was sent to the Abbot of Waltham Abbey. Durham, Exeter, Glastonbury, Tewkesbury and Walbrook also possessed relics of the saint.

The presence of altars dedicated to various saints, each containing their relics, has obvious consequences for the liturgy, for these are the saints whose feast day will be celebrated with particular solemnity. This means, to put it very simply, more chanting than usual and in many cases the singing of chants special (the usual word is 'proper') to the saint in question. The composition of cycles of new Office chants for local saints is in fact one of the most interesting developments in the history of chant from the tenth century onward, for the new pieces often differ quite markedly in melodic style from the older, 'classical' Office chants. (This is discussed in section 3.ii below.)

The important feast days in the Worcester calendar

A general account of the structure of the church year is given below, in section 1.iii. A church such as Worcester Cathedral Priory will follow the general pattern but will also have a few special priorities about the ranking of feast days in order of importance and about the local saints of special significance for Worcester.

The fourteen highest feast days of the year at Worcester were as follows:

- Christmas Day, Easter Sunday, and Whitsunday, to which Ascension Day was eventually added;
- the Nativity of St Wulstan (19 January – the day he died, regarded as the day of his birth, 'nativity', into eternal life);

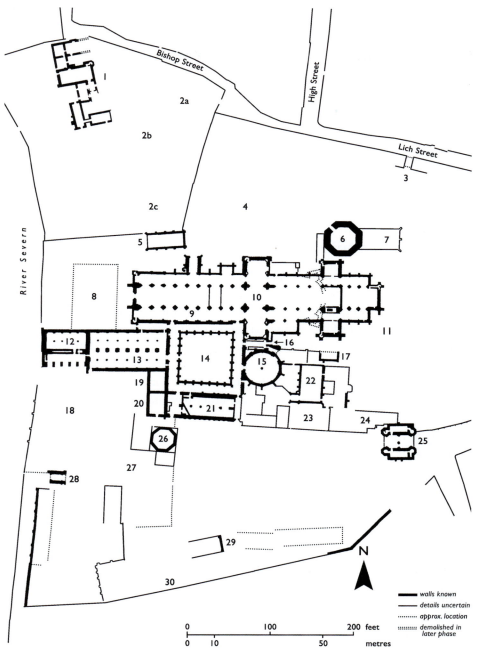

Figure 1.2 Ground plan of Worcester Cathedral Priory

1 Bishop's Palace; 2 Grounds of Bishop's Palace; (2a) Gatehouse, stables; (2b) Green Court, with bowling alley;
(2c) bakehouse, brewhouse; 3 Cemetery gate; 4 Lay cemetery; 5 Charnel chapel; 6 Bell tower; 7 Church of St Michael in
Bedwardine; 8 Infirmary; 9 Library over south aisle of cathedral; 10 Cathedral priory church; 11 Monk's cemetery;
12 Infirmary with chapel above; 13 Great dorter (dormitory); 14 Great cloister; 15 Chapter house; 16 Parlour over passage;
17 Chapel; 18 Garden and bowling alley; 19 Subprior's lodgings; 20 Cellarer's lodgings; 21 Frater (refectory) upstairs;
22 Guest hall; 23 Buttery and pantry; 24 Almonry; 25 Priory gate; 26 Kitchen; 27 Cook's lodgings; 28 Water gate;
29 Stables, barn, granary, bakehouse, brewhouse, etc.; 30 Priory wall

- the Translation of St Wulstan (7 June) fell on the same day as the anniversary of the Dedication of the cathedral church, so the saint was specially commemorated again a week later (14 June); 'translation' means the solemn transferring of the relics of a saint to a new resting place;
- the Deposition (burial) of St Oswald (28 February) and his Translation (8 October);
- the Assumption (15 August) and the Nativity (8 September) of the Blessed Virgin Mary;
- Sts Peter and Paul (29 June)
- the Translation of St Benedict (11 July – the day his body was brought to Fleury on the Loire);
- All Saints (1 November).

Processions in medieval Worcester

Processions, as already mentioned, brought ever wider areas of sacred space into the liturgical life of the community. On each day that a particular saint was commemorated, a procession went from the heart of the cathedral, the sanctuary and choir, to the saint's altar. (Some of these altars have now disappeared and their original place is unknown, for example those for Andrew, Bartholomew and Matthew.) These processions took place after Lauds and again after Vespers. Every Saturday there was a procession to the cross in the sacristy. This was also done after Lauds and Vespers on Thursday in Whitsun week, but on the other days in that week the procession went to the altar of the Holy Cross.

The days immediately preceding Easter Sunday involved numerous special ceremonies of great solemnity. One of these was the Blessing of the New Fire and the lighting of the Paschal Candle on Holy Saturday, which at Worcester took place in the cloisters, followed by a solemn procession into the choir. On the same day a procession was made to bless the font, and the font was the goal of the procession before Mass on the first three days of Easter week, and on the eve of Pentecost. On the other days of Easter week the procession went to the altar of St Thomas of Canterbury.

A procession went down to the crypt on 8 September, the feast of the Nativity of the Blessed Virgin Mary. This was because St Wulstan had been consecrated bishop on that day in 1062 and had built and consecrated the crypt. So an antiphon from the dedication festival and another for All Saints, together with prayers and a psalm, were used in the processional ceremony. In the crypt was an altar to Sts Peter and Paul, where the Requiem Mass was recited daily in the late Middle Ages.

On the highest feast days of the year (listed above) a procession called St Wulstan's procession ('quae Sancti Wulstani vocatur') was made after Compline. Its destination is not clear, since the Wulstan altar in the middle of the choir is of no great distance and a descent into the crypt would be unusual. To judge by the example of other cathedral priories in England, this procession would have gone through the church and round the cloister, and, remembering the souls of the departed, round the monk's cemetery as well.

On Palm Sunday the procession went out into the cathedral close. After the distribution of the palms the procession went from the cloisters through the monks' cemetery to the church of St Michael in Bedwardine, by the bell tower at the north-east corner of the cathedral (see Fig. 1.2), and thence round to the north door for a solemn re-entry. Elaborate instructions are given for everything that has to be done at the various 'stations', the places where the procession pauses. A final station is made at the altar of the Holy Cross, before the final return to the choir. Among the many things to be sung are the great antiphons such as *Pueri Hebreorum* ('The Hebrew children carrying olive branches met our Lord, crying out and saying: "Hosanna in the highest"') as the palms are distributed, *Occurrunt turbe* ('The multitude go out to meet our Redeemer with flowers and palms') as the company assembles at the stational church, and *Ingrediente Domino in sanctam civitatem* ('As the Lord entered the holy city') at the re-entry.

In many places, though not at Worcester, the Palm Sunday procession would go out into the city. This happened at Worcester on St Mark's Day (25 April), the day of the Great Litanies, and on the Rogation Days, Monday, Tuesday and Wednesday before Ascension Day (which is a Thursday). On these days special antiphons asking for God's mercy and practical help – good weather, or rain, for example – are sung, as well as the litanies invoking the aid of a long series of saints. As the procession leaves the cathedral close and enters the city, the antiphon *Deprecamur te* is sung, the antiphon famously reported to have been sung by St Augustine and his companions as they landed in England in 597: *ut auferetur furor tuus et ira tua a civitate ista* ('that your fury and anger may be taken away from this city'). (See Ex. 1.1.) The procession took place after Sext. Bells were rung at the churches passed on the way. Where a station was made, an antiphon was sung in honour of the patron saint of the church and Mass was celebrated and the litanies sung. The stational churches were St Helen's, St Peter's, St Andrew's, All Saints, St Nicholas, St Martin's and St Swithun's. (The thirteenth-century manuscript indicates that others were visited but does not name them.) St Helen was the mother of the Roman emperor Constantine the Great, who made Christianity an official religion of the empire. In Jerusalem in 326 Helen discovered the Cross on which Christ had been crucified. Appropriately, the special antiphon to be sung at St Helen's is *Crux fidelis inter omnes*, taken from the cycle of Office chants for the feast of the Exaltation of the Holy Cross (14 September – see Ex. 1.1).

On the Rogation Days the procession might even go outside the city. There is a record of payments to a boatman of a ration of bread for his services in ferrying

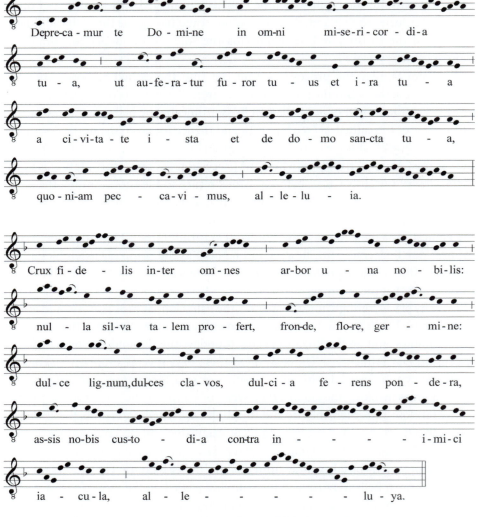

Ex. 1.1 Antiphons *Deprecamur te Domine* and *Crux fidelis inter omnes*

A. Deprecamur te Domine

We entreat thee, O Lord, in thy great mercy, that thy wrath and thy anger may be laid aside from this city and from thy holy house, for we have sinned, alleluia.

A. Crux fidelis inter omnes

Faithful cross, above all other, the one noble tree:
no other tree offers such foliage, blossom, or fruit:
sweet wood, sweet nails, bearing so sweet a burden,
be to us a safeguard against the darts of the enemy, alleluya.
(Venantius Fortunatus)

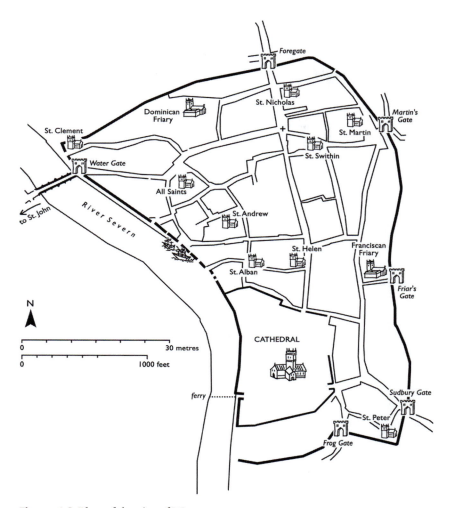

Figure 1.3 Plan of the city of Worcester

monks across the River Severn on festival days, perhaps for a service in the church of St John to the west of the city.

Figure 1.3 sketches the location of the cathedral, the city and its churches, and the Severn.

Like all medieval cathedrals, Worcester would have echoed to the constant sound of services being sung and said. Apart from the full sung cycles for Mass and the Divine Office outlined in the next section, extra Masses and Offices were constantly being recited, very often by a single priest in fulfilment of the terms of a benefaction, whereby Masses were to be said for the soul of the benefactor. This might be done at an altar specified for the purpose, or a special chantry chapel might be erected within the cathedral (in Worcester, see nos. 9 and 21 on Fig. 1.1). Little more will be said about these solemnities, because many did not call for singing.

Further reading

Harper, *The Forms and Orders of Western Liturgy from the Tenth to the Eighteenth Century*, as well as being an excellent guide to the liturgical forms summarized in section 1.iii below, has a lot of information about the institutions which performed them. The opening chapter of Harrison, *Music in Medieval Britain*, is a fine survey of the situation in England, to which British scholars have since added even more. Wright, *Music and Ceremony at Notre Dame of Paris*, describes the organization and practice of one particular and very important institution, much of which is typical of other cathedrals. There are numerous good books on monasticism, such as the handy accounts by Knowles, *Christian Monasticism*, and Lawrence, *Medieval Monasticism*. An excellent new survey with liturgical information is Davril and Palazzo, *La vie des moines au temps des grandes abbayes X^e–XIIIe siècles*.

The layout of medieval Worcester has been reconstructed in Baker and Holt, *Urban Growth and the Medieval Church: Gloucester and Worcester*. The book by Engel, *Worcester Cathedral: An Architectural History*, is an excellent, very detailed account. Doig, *Liturgy and Architecture*, is a general survey of the relationship between the liturgy and medieval church architecture.

The antiphoner (with chants for the Office hours), the processional and the hymnary from the thirteenth-century Worcester compendium (but not the gradual with Mass chants) were published in facsimile with a valuable introduction Dame Laurentia McLachlan, in *Paléographie musicale* vol. 12 (Solesmes, 1922). *St Wulfstan and his World* is a collection of essays about early medieval Worcester, including an essay by Susan Rankin on its chant.

1.iii The structure of the church year and the daily services. Mass and Office, processions

The daily acts of worship in which chant was sung follow a cycle, repeated each year, articulated by seasons, periods and days commemorating events or persons of particular significance.

The forms presented in simple outline here are those prevalent in the central Middle Ages. If one compares the practice of churches at different times and places one will inevitably find differences in detail. Medieval ecclesiastical ritual was full of elaborate detail and, understandably, this was often adapted to suit local circumstances.

The services each day (and night) consist of the Mass, on one hand, and the hours of the Divine Office on the other. Mass is an act of thanksgiving of a very special type, with many unique components, whereas the services of the Divine Office are contemplative and share most components with each other. Beside their chants, all services include prayers and readings from the Bible or other texts of special authority.

Mass

The service which is still most familiar (though much in it has changed since the Second Vatican Council, 1962–5) is the Mass (Latin *missa*, also known as the Eucharist), which commemorates and gives thanks for the Christ's institution of the Last Supper. This was the last time Christ ate with his disciples before his arrest, trial and crucifixion. The account in St Matthew's gospel reads: 'And as they were eating, Jesus took bread, and blessed it, and brake it, and gave it to the disciples, and said, Take, eat; this is my body. And he took the cup, and gave thanks, and gave it to them, saying, Drink ye all of it; For this is my blood of the new testament, which is shed for many for the remission of sins' (Matt. 26:26–8; cf. Mark 14:17–26; Luke 22:14–20; 1 Cor. 11:23 *et seq.*). The act of communion which perpetuates this event is the most important part of Mass and is special to it. There is nothing like it in the other services. It is preceded by a number of preparatory and other ceremonial items. In Table 1.1 the important items are listed vertically, numbered 1–21, divided into two columns for the chants and one column each for prayers and lessons. The chants are divided between two columns because of the distinction between so-called 'ordinary' chants and 'proper' chants. 'Ordinary' refers to items whose text remains the same at every Mass, while the texts of 'proper' items change from Mass to Mass: they are chosen to be especially appropriate to the particular occasion.

The Mass can be divided into several parts. 'Introitus' (no. 1 in Table 1.1) means 'entrance', and refers to the chant where the priest and his assistants enter the church and come to the altar. The introit begins an introductory section, after which nos. 5–10 form a second group, two readings enclosing chants. The heart of the service is reached with the offertory (no. 12), the first in a series of items leading to the communion, that is, the participation of the faithful in eating the bread and drinking the wine. (The word 'communion' can refer both to this act and to the chant which accompanies it, no. 19.) This part of the Mass, from the offertory chant to the postcommunion prayer, is sometimes called the Mass of the Faithful, since historically it was reserved for those who had been baptized.

The alleluia, tract and sequence (nos. 7–9) are not sung together at every Mass, but they are musically of such importance that they appear on Table 1.1 together.

Table 1.1 *The order of Mass*

chants		prayers	lessons
proper chants	ordinary chants	prayers	lessons
1 Introit/*Introitus*			
	2 Kyrie		
	3 Gloria in excelsis Deo		
		4 Collect/*Collecta*	
			5 Epistle/*Epistola*
6 Gradual/*Graduale*			
7 Alleluia/*Alleluia*			
8 Tract/*Tractus*			
9 Sequence/*Sequentia*			
			10 Gospel/*Evangelium*
	11 Credo in unum Deum		
12 Offertory/*Offertorium*			
		13 Secret/*Secreta*	
		14 Preface/*Praefatio*	
	15 Sanctus – Benedictus		
		16 Canon/*Canon*	
		17 Lord's Prayer/*Pater noster*	
	18 Agnus Dei		
19 Communion/ *Communio*			
		20 Postcommunion/ *Postcommunio*	
	21 Ite missa est		

The alleluia was sung outside Lent, the tract during Lent, the sequence followed the alleluia (therefore outside Lent) only on the most important feast days.

The lessons (nos. 5 and 10) are 'proper', being different for each Mass, and so also are three of the prayers (nos. 4, 13 and 20). The preface (no. 14) also varies according to season.

It should be emphasized that Table 1.1 (like all the tables in this chapter) greatly simplifies ceremonies which in fact were highly elaborate. For example, before the introit there are preparatory prayers; the solemn reciting of the Gospel is surrounded by special ceremonial; and the consecration of the bread and wine, the

Table 1.2 *The daily cycle*

Ad vesperas	First Vespers	before nightfall
Ad completorium	Compline	at nightfall
Ad matutinas	Matins (Vigils, Night Office, Nocturns)	in the night, before Lauds
Ad laudes	Lauds	before dawn
Ad primam	Prime	at dawn
Missa matutinalis	Morning Mass	(after Terce in winter)
Ad terciam	Terce	
MISSA	MASS	(after Sext in winter)
Ad sextam	Sext	at midday
Ad nonam	None	
	*On high feast days:**	
Ad vesperas	Second Vespers	
Ad completorium	Compline	

* On days of special importance a second Vespers proper to the feast day in question would be sung instead of the ordinary Vespers for the eve of the next day

breaking of the bread ('fraction') and the distribution of the consecrated elements to the faithful in the communion are also composed of multiple ritual actions and texts.

The hours of the Divine Office

The Office hours are dominated by the singing of psalms. All 150 psalms were to be sung each week, divided between the different days and hours. The services contain a certain number of prayers. Lessons are important only in the Night Office. (The Chapter/*Capitulum* in some of the hours is a short lesson.) The hours begin with Vespers on the eve of the day in question, followed by the Compline when night falls. The Night Office (also called Matins, or Vigils) is the longest of the hours, composed of one to three Nocturns, each with a number of lessons. The most important of the day hours is Lauds, and the cycle is rounded out with the so-called Little Hours: Prime, Terce, Sext and None. The hours are listed in Table 1.2, showing the usual position of both the main Mass of the day and also the morning Mass (*missa matutinalis*, sometimes called 'Morrow Mass') often added when two feast days coincided or as an act of veneration for the Holy Trinity, the Holy Spirit, Holy Angels, and other things. (The morning Mass is not of great musical importance.)

Because of the different number of daylight hours, the timetable (*horarium*) was not the same in summer as in winter. The scheme outlined here is a fairly common one, but there were local variations.

As to the content of the services, a distinction has to be observed between the Office as celebrated in a cathedral, collegiate church or parish church and the way the hours were performed in the Benedictine and some other monastic orders. For most services the differences are not very great (so they are merely indicated in parentheses in Table 1.3 below), but to explain the differences in the Night Office parallel tables are necessary. In simple tables like these it is impossible to list all the variations in content which would occur, especially those which distinguished an important festival day from an ordinary weekday. Only the main outlines are given here.

The basic structures given in simple outline in Table 1.3 are found in a number of variant forms. For example, the number of psalms, and the different combinations of antiphon + psalm(s) + antiphon-repeat, vary not only according to the importance of the day, but also according to the customs of different places and times. Another example: the papal chapel from the thirteenth century on, and the Franciscans, who followed the same use, omitted the last responsory of the Night Office.

The Magnificat, Nunc Dimittis, Benedictus and Quicunque vult are canticles, chanted in a manner similar to the psalms. The texts of canticles are biblical but not from the Book of Psalms. Another canticle is chanted instead of a fourth psalm at Lauds, and a group of canticles are chanted (with just one framing antiphon) instead of a group of psalms in the Third Nocturn of the Benedictine Night Office.

As will be explained in section 1.v below, psalms and lessons are chanted to simple 'tones', formulae for recitation. The Office chants of chief musical interest are the antiphons, the short responsories of the lesser hours, the great responsories of the Night Office and hymns. A very large number of these were sung during the year. Even on a single, ordinary weekday more than twenty antiphons and four or five each of the great and short responsories were required. As already stated, all 150 psalms from the Book of Psalms in the Old Testament were to be sung during each week. (Their distribution is different in Benedictine use from Roman use, but the principle is the same.) The Divine Office as a whole was correspondingly organized first and foremost on a weekly basis. A basic stock of antiphons, short responsories and hymns was allocated to each day of the week. The great responsories of the Night Office were allocated in a different way, since each Sunday and feast day had its own set. Sunday responsories could be repeated during the week, but there was no set which belonged specially to Monday, Tuesday, etc. like the sets of antiphons for the different days of the week. Medieval manuscripts commonly provide a week's supply of about 140 different antiphons, up to thirty great responsories and eight short responsories.

Table 1.3 *The hours of the Divine Office*

VESPERS

Deus in adiutorium, etc.
Antiphon/*Antiphona* – 5 Psalms – Antiphon-repeat, or 5 × [Antiphon–Psalm–Antiphon-repeat]*
  (4 Psalms in Benedictine use)
Hymn/*Hymnus*
Chapter/*Capitulum*
Responsory/*Responsorium* (on feast days)
Antiphon – Magnificat – Antiphon-repeat
Benedicamus Domino

COMPLINE

Deus in adiutorium, etc.
Antiphon – 4 Psalms – Antiphon-repeat (3 Psalms in Benedictine use)
Hymn
Chapter + Short Responsory/*Responsorium breve*
Antiphon – Nunc dimittis – Antiphon-repeat (not in Benedictine use)
Benedicamus Domino
Antiphon of the Blessed Virgin Mary / *Antiphona de Beata Maria Virgine*

NIGHT OFFICE (VIGILS, MATINS)
on ordinary weekdays

Roman use	**Benedictine use**
Domine labia mea aperies, etc.	*Deus in adiutorium meum intende*, etc.

Invitatory/*Invitatorium*-Antiphon +
  -Psalm (Ps. 94 *Venite exsultemus*)
	Invitatory/*Invitatorium*-Antiphon and -Psalm (Ps. 94
	  Venite exsultemus)

Hymn	Hymn
1 Nocturn, consisting of	First Nocturn, consisting of
6 × [Antiphon + 2 Psalms + Antiphon-repeat]	Antiphon + 6 Psalms + Antiphon-repeat
Versicle and Response	*or* 3 × [Antiphon + 2 Psalms + Antiphon-repeat]
3 × [Lesson + Responsory]	*or* 6 × [Antiphon + Psalm + Antiphon-repeat]
	Chapter + Short Responsory in summer
	3 × [Lesson + Responsory] in winter
	Second Nocturn, consisting of
	Antiphon(s) and Psalms as in First Nocturn
	Chapter
	Benedicamus Domino

on Sundays and feast days

Roman use	**Benedictine use**
Domine labia mea aperies, etc.	*Deus in adiutorium meum intende*, etc.
Invitatory-Antiphon + -Psalm	Invitatory-Antiphon + -Psalm
(Ps. 94 *Venite exsultemus*)	(Ps. 94 *Venite exsultemus*)

(*cont.*)

Table 1.3 (*cont.*)

Hymn	Hymn
3 Nocturns, each consisting of	2 Nocturns, each consisting of
3 × [Antiphon + Psalm +	6 × [Antiphon + Psalm + Antiphon-repeat]
Antiphon-repeat]	Versicle and Response
Versicle and Response	4 × [Lesson + Responsory]
3 × [Lesson + Responsory]	Third Nocturn, consisting of:
	Antiphon + 3 Canticles/*Cantica* + Antiphon-repeat
	Versicle and Response
	4 × [Lesson + Responsory]
Te Deum laudamus (outside Advent and	Te Deum laudamus
Lent)	Gospel/*Evangelium*
	Te decet laus

LAUDS

Deus in adiutorium, etc.
Antiphon + 5 Psalms + Antiphon-repeat
  or 5 × [Antiphon + Psalm + Antiphon-repeat]
  (At Lauds the fourth Psalm is a Canticle/*Canticum*)
Chapter
Short Responsory (in Benedictine use)
Hymn
Antiphon + *Benedictus* + Antiphon-repeat
Benedicamus Domino

PRIME

Deus in adiutorium, etc.
Hymn
Antiphon + 3 Psalms + Antiphon-repeat (4 Psalms on Sunday in Benedictine use)
Antiphon + Quicunque vult + Antiphon-repeat (not in Benedictine use)
Chapter + Short Responsory
Benedicamus Domino

TERCE, SEXT and NONE

Deus in adiutorium, etc.
Hymn
Antiphon + 3 Psalms + Antiphon-repeat
Chapter + Short Responsory
Benedicamus Domino

---

* This complicated sequence should be explained more specifically. Either the antiphon is repeated either after all five (four) psalms have been sung, or each psalm is enclosed within its own antiphon, so that the performance is: Antiphon 1 – Psalm 1 – Antiphon 1; Antiphon 2 – Psalm 2 – Antiphon 2; Antiphon 3 . . . etc.

However, that is still only a small fraction of the number of chants sung in the course of a year. Firstly, all through the penitential season of Lent, Passiontide (the two weeks before Easter) and Easter week, each day had its own special set of prayers, lessons and chants. In Holy Week, on Maundy Thursday, Good Friday and Holy Saturday, even the order and form of the services is partly different. During four other weeks in the year, Wednesday, Friday and Saturday also had their own proper chants and other items. These are known as the Ember Days, in the weeks following St Lucy (13 December), Ash Wednesday, Whitsunday, and the feast of the Holy Cross (14 September). Secondly, if an important feast day fell on one of the ordinary days, all its proper items (chants, prayers and lessons, even psalms, according to the nature of the feast day) would supersede the ordinary ones. Almost no week passes without an interruption of this sort. So many are the days with their own proper chants that an enormous number, over 2,000 antiphons and over 800 responsories, not counting repetitions, was required in the course of a year. Performing this great corpus of music – not forgetting the several hundred chants sung during the same year at Mass – required remarkable powers of memory and a well-functioning system of training.

Service books

Service books of the Middle Ages usually set out the chants, prayers and lessons in several sections. Office books may begin with the weekly cycle, the services for ordinary Sundays and weekdays. There is no Ordinary section of this sort in books for the Mass, since each Sunday had its own proper Mass. The section containing the Sundays through the year, the weekdays which have their own proper services in Lent, Passiontide, the Ember Days and so on, and the services at Christmas and Easter is referred to as the 'Temporale' (or 'Proper of the Time'). The cycle of saints' days (except for St Stephen and St John, who are usually included straight after Christmas Day) is referred to as the 'Sanctorale' (or 'Proper of the Saints'). A further section will include items for those saints not important enough to have their own proper pieces, chants for a Martyr (or several Martyrs), a Confessor, a Virgin, and so on. This section is referred to as the 'Commune Sanctorum' (or 'Common of the Saints').

The different types of medieval service book are described briefly in section 4.iv below.

The ranking of different days

A great deal of knowledge and expertise was required to manage the correct performance of the complex annual cycle. The cantor, or whoever had this task, had to know precisely which chants were sung every day, which Sunday chants were repeated during the week, which rotated on a weekly basis, and so on. It was especially important to know how much dignity was to be accorded to the numerous feast days, resulting in a greater or lesser degree of replacement of the 'normal' chants. Feast days thus came to be graded according to their relative importance. In many churches they were accorded the status of 'simple/*simplex*' or 'double/*duplex*', with subdivisions in the latter such as '*semiduplex*' and '*principale duplex*'. In the calendars at the front of many service books, where the feast days to be celebrated at a particular church are entered, the more important feasts are usually noted in red ink (hence our expression 'red-letter day'). There may also be a note 'iii lectiones' (three lessons, that is, only one Nocturn in the Night Office, not an important day) or 'ix lectiones' (nine lessons, so three Nocturns, more important). The number of candles to be lit on the high altar may be given: seven, nine, fifteen, or whatever, according to the custom of the place. Other ways of differentiating among the various degrees of importance were the robes to be worn by the minister and his assistants (for example, a white alb for many feasts, a coloured cope on more important ones), and the number of singers detailed to perform certain chants (or parts of them). Very high feasts called for a special procession, and liturgical items from the highest feasts of all would be repeated through the octave, that is, each day of the following week through to the eighth day, a week after the feast day.

The church year

Many of the feast days celebrated in these special ways were fixed on a particular date in the year. Such are Christmas Day (25 December) and the days following: St Stephen (26 December), St John the Evangelist (27 December), Holy Innocents (the children killed on the orders of Herod, 28 December), New Year's Day (1 January, a week after Christmas, celebrated as the Feast of the Circumcision of Christ) and Epiphany (6 January). Into this category come the numerous feast days of the Blessed Virgin Mary and other saints. Many saints were celebrated all over Europe, while others were important only in a particular region, or city, or perhaps only for a single church, where the relics (bones or other mortal remains) of the saint were preserved.

The most important feast days of the Blessed Virgin Mary in the Middle Ages were her Purification (2 February), Annunciation (25 March), Assumption (15 August) and Nativity (8 September). (Purification was also known as Candlemas, because of the special ceremony of blessing and processing with lighted candles. This commemorates the day when the child Jesus was presented in the temple in Jerusalem and was called by the aged Simeon 'a light to lighten the Gentiles'.

All of Simeon's words, beginning 'Nunc dimittis servum tuum' [Luke 2:29–32], were sung as a canticle during the procession.)

The greatest saints' days were those of John the Baptist (24 June), Peter and Paul (29 June), Laurence (10 August), Michael (29 September), All Saints (1 November), Martin (11 November) and Andrew (30 November). Some saints profoundly venerated in earlier centuries receded in importance, others came to the fore, such as Mary Magdalene (22 July) and Nicholas (6 December) from the eleventh century onward, Thomas of Canterbury (29 December) from the late twelfth century, and Francis (4 October) from the thirteenth.

Clearly, these days will fall on different days of the week from year to year, and will take precedence even over Sundays, which has more of its own chants and other items than the rest of the days of the week. But a number of Sundays (and sometimes the succeeding weekdays) were also of special importance, being part of a cycle governed by the most important Sunday of all, Easter Sunday, when Christ rose from the dead. As is well known, the exact calendar date of Easter varies from year to year, actually falling anywhere between 23 March and 26 April (one day earlier since the seventeenth century). Since Easter is related to the Jewish Passover, it was calculated in the same way, in conjunction with lunar months. The precise method to be used was often a matter of controversy. The one eventually employed universally takes its bearings from the spring equinox, 21 March. The next point of reference is the lunar cycle, beginning with a new moon, and, after that, the fourteenth day of the lunar cycle. The first time this fourteenth day falls on or after 21 March gives the cue for Easter Sunday, which will be the first Sunday after that fourteenth day. The Sundays and other days whose liturgy is governed by Easter are set out in Table 1.4.

A smaller number of Sundays are cued to Christmas Day. Their actual calendar date will not vary as much as those in the Easter cycle, because the room for variance is only one week (Christmas Day can fall on any day of the week). These are listed in Table 1.5.

Liturgical processions

As explained in section 1.ii above, most services were celebrated in the sanctuary and choir of the church or in a special chapel (such as the Lady Chapel, for services in honour of the Blessed Virgin Mary) or at a special altar. A number of processions were also made to particular altars, chapels or churches, which also involved the recitation of prayers and the singing of chants. Many of these processions moved around within the church, some within the cathedral close or monastery walls. Others went outside into the town or city. The clergy of one of the great medieval cathedrals might be on the move several times a month, processing to one or other of the churches in the city or even outside the city walls. Monasteries interacted

Table 1.4 *The Easter cycle*

Septuagesima Sunday	nine weeks before Easter Sunday
Sexagesima Sunday	eight weeks before Easter Sunday
Quinquagesima Sunday	seven weeks before Easter Sunday
Ash Wednesday	start of Lent, a period of penitence and fasting
Ember Days after Ash Wednesday	
First to Fourth Sunday of Quadragesima	six to three weeks before Easter Sunday
Passion Sunday	two weeks before Easter Sunday, the start of Passiontide
Palm Sunday	one week before Easter Sunday, the start of Holy Week
Maundy Thursday	
Good Friday	
Holy Saturday	
EASTER SUNDAY	Eastertide extends to the Saturday after Whitsunday
First to Fifth Sunday after Easter	
Ascension Day	Thursday forty days after Easter Sunday, in the sixth week after Easter
Sunday after Ascension	
Whitsunday (Pentecost Sunday)	fifty days after Easter Sunday
Ember Days after Whitsunday	
Trinity Sunday	one week after Whitsunday (from the ninth century)
Corpus Christi	Thursday after Trinity Sunday (from 1264)

Twenty-two to twenty-seven Sundays after Trinity, until the First Sunday of Advent stops the series.
The Ember Days after the feast of the Holy Cross (14 September) will fall within the Sundays after Trinity.

Table 1.5 *The Advent–Christmas–Epiphany cycle*

First Sunday of Advent	the nearest Sunday to St Andrew's Day (30 November). There will always be four, starting at the earliest on 27 November, ending at the latest on Christmas Eve (24 December), when the Fourth Sunday in Advent will be more or less totally superseded by the services proper to Christmas Eve.
Second to Fourth Sundays in Advent	
The Ember Days after the feast of St Lucy (13 December) will fall within Advent	
Christmas Eve (24 December)	
Christmas Day (25 December)	
First Sunday after Christmas	
New Year's Day (Feast of the Circumcision)	
Epiphany (6 January)	
One to six Sundays after Epiphany, until Septuagesima Sunday stops the series	

less frequently with the population. Monasteries such as those of the Cistercians and Carthusians, who particularly valued seclusion, were deliberately situated away from urban settlements. The older Benedictine monasteries, frequently founded on the edge of cities, did not often make religious processions out into town. Nevertheless, on Palm Sunday and the days of penitence on St Mark's Day (25 April) and the Monday, Tuesday and Wednesday before Ascension Day all religious communities would make processions. These are known as the Rogation Days (from Latin *rogare*, to ask, beg or pray for), when litanies are sung asking for the aid of God, Mary, the angels and all the saints, named one after another in a long repetitive chant.

Most chants sung during the daily processions inside a church, and many of the longer ones, were antiphons or responsories borrowed from the Office hours. But a number were special to the processions. The most important of these are the antiphons sung during the Palm Sunday procession, when Christ's entry into Jerusalem was celebrated, and those sung on the Rogation Days. Some are long, elaborate chants quite different in character from the great majority of Office antiphons.

Days with special liturgies

The procession on Palm Sunday, which usually took place between Terce and Mass, is one of the special ceremonies observed in Holy Week. Later in the week, on Maundy Thursday, Good Friday and Holy Saturday, other ceremonies of great antiquity and solemnity were observed and much of the daily pattern of the rest of the year was set aside. There is space here to mention only a few important occasions.

Maundy Thursday commemorates the Last Supper and Christ's institution of the Eucharist, after which he washed the feet of his disciples. When this ceremony was repeated in the Middle Ages, its first antiphon quoted the words of Christ, *Mandatum novum do vobis* ('A new commandment I give unto you'), hence the word 'maundy'. The ceremony would be performed either in the evening or during Mass. The Night Office and Lauds were called 'Tenebrae' (shadows) because after each psalm (nine for the Night Office, five for Lauds) one of the fifteen candles on the altar was extinguished. The last candle was then concealed behind the altar. This was done during the Night Office and Lauds on Good Friday and Holy Saturday as well. On these three days the Night Office has only three readings, taken from the Lamentations of Jeremiah (passages which are well known today in polyphonic settings by composers of the sixteenth century).

Good Friday witnessed the ceremony of the Adoration of the Cross, a crucifix with an image of Christ crucified, veiled in purple. An ancient, short form of Mass was celebrated after None, with the Adoration ceremony at the beginning. Its most striking feature is the singing of the Improperia ('Reproaches'). Here, words of Christ in which he reproves his ungrateful people, sung by soloists, are answered with refrain verses in Greek and Latin, sung by two choirs in alternation: *Agios o Theos. Sanctus Deus. Agios ischyros. Sanctus fortis*, and so on. After Mass the host (*hostia*, the communion bread) was often placed or 'buried' in a special tabernacle or 'sepulchre', from which it would be resurrected early on Easter morning in a symbolic representation of Christ's resurrection.

The special ceremonies of Holy Saturday were the Blessing of the New Fire and Lighting of the Paschal Candle, and the sacrament of Baptism. While the latter needed no special chants, the candle ceremony included a number of unique hymns and a very long prayer, chanted to a set of elaborate recitation formulae, the *Exultet*.

Alongside the main Mass and Office hours, several others were sung, or more commonly said. Practice varied from church to church. The Morning Mass usually took the form of a weekly cycle of votive Masses. A daily Mass of the Blessed Virgin would be said or (at least in the later Middle Ages) sung in her chapel. The Hours of the Virgin were said daily – often called the 'Little Office of the Virgin'. More important musically was the sung Office and Mass of the Virgin on Saturday.

Further reading

There are good sections on the church year and forms of service in the following reference works: Harper, *The Forms and Orders of Western Liturgy from the Tenth to the Eighteenth Century*, Part II: Medieval Liturgy; Harrison, *Music in Medieval Britain*, Chapter II: The Liturgy and its Plainsong; Hiley, *Western Plainchant*, Chapter I: Plainchant in the Liturgy.

Less practically orientated, and with much more historical and theological information, are the four volumes of Martimort, *The Church at Prayer, New Edition*. For an extremely detailed account which stretches even specialists to the limit, see Hughes, *Medieval Manuscripts for Mass and Office*.

1.iv The sacred word

As well as knowing about the liturgical context and the places where chant was sung, it is important to have a sense of which texts were sung and why they were chosen.

Christian worship has at its disposal an immense treasury of sacred texts, the Bible, together with commentaries by the Church Fathers. (Latin for 'father' is *pater*, hence the term 'patristic writings', the writings of the Fathers of the Church. Their teaching on doctrinal matters was held to be of especial authority. In the Latin church the writings of the four Doctors of the Church, St Augustine, St Ambrose, St Gregory and St Jerome were of particular importance.) In the two lessons of Mass and the nine of the Night Office (or twelve, in Benedictine use) the principal themes of the church year were adumbrated, setting out the written evidence, so to speak, for the events being commemorated, the reason for the prayer and praise of each day.

The other principal texts of Mass and Office, the prayers, were equally important. They were not biblical but often of great antiquity and composed by such authorities as Pope Leo I ('Leo the Great', d. 461) or St Gregory. They do not concern us here because they did not provide texts to be sung in the more advanced musical forms. The lessons, however, did just that. Alternatively, the chant texts drew upon the same sources as the lessons.

The Book of Psalms

One book of the Bible, the Book of Psalms, was particularly important as a source for chant texts. As already explained, all 150 psalms would be sung each week during the Divine Office. When feast days interrupted the weekly cycle, a different selection might be sung, but the psalms were clearly omnipresent. Nearly all the chants of Mass were settings of psalm verses. (Only the communions form an exception here: all have biblical texts, but about half come from the New Testament, and about a dozen from the Old Testament, with one from the Apocrypha. So less than half have psalm texts.) In the Mass, psalm verses are sung in both a simple form and in more complex chants. The main part of the introit is an ornate type of antiphon, after which a psalm verse is sung to a simple tone. (In early times as much of the psalm was sung as was necessary until the officiating priest and his assistants had reached the sanctuary.) The communion also had at least one psalm verse, largely obsolete by the central Middle Ages. That is a simple use of a psalm verse or verses. But nearly all the principal chants also have psalm verses for their text.

For example, on Quadragesima Sunday, the first Sunday in Lent, all the principal chants of Mass take their texts from Psalm 90:

Introit *Invocabit me, et ego exaudiam eum* (v. 15: 'He shall call upon me, and I will answer him')

Introit verse *Qui habitat in adiutorio* (v. 1: 'He that dwelleth in the secret place of the most High')

Gradual *Angelis suis Deus mandavit de te* (v. 11: 'He shall give his angels charge over thee')

Gradual verse *In manibus portabunt te* (v. 12: 'They shall bear thee up in their hands')

Tract *Qui habitat in adiutorio* (vv. 1–7, 11–16: the tract has thirteen verses)

Offertory *Scapulis suis obumbrabit tibi* (v. 4: 'He shall cover thee with his feathers')

Communion *Scapulis suis* (as the offertory)
It is true that such concentration on a single psalm is uncommon. And tracts do not usually have so many verses. But the principle is clear enough.

The two lessons at Mass, the Epistle and Gospel, were chosen to reflect the event or season of the church year. In a lot of instances the choice was clear, but there are also many Sundays (and weekdays) of a less obviously topical nature. Many parts of the Old Testament, especially the books of the prophets, looked forward to the coming of the Messiah. Several psalms are also referred to as the 'Messianic' psalms in this sense. Other Old Testament stories were understood to foreshadow events in Christ's life. For example, Daniel in the lions' den, whose story is read as the Epistle on Tuesday of Passion Week, is a figure of Christ, Daniel's release prefigures Christ's resurrection. Such texts were obviously of importance when the cycle of readings took shape. The desire to use only the Bible for lessons at Mass, and only the psalms for chant texts, relied on a powerful sense of the associations inspired by the sacred word. This was important when non-biblical saints or events were being celebrated.

For example, early martyrs from the time of the persecutions under Diocletian and other Roman emperors do not appear in the Bible. Of the four great feasts of the Blessed Virgin Mary, two relate to New Testament events (Purification and Annunciation), but two do not (Assumption and Nativity). How can the feast days of these saints and the Blessed Virgin be associated with the Bible? Let us take the examples of the Assumption of the Blessed Virgin Mary. Table 1.6 gives a common choice of lessons and chants. (Medieval sources are not unanimous. This selection is taken from the use of Salisbury, very widespread in England in the Middle Ages.)

Several chant texts are excerpted from Psalm 44, a psalm for the wedding of a king, with frequent references to the beauty of the king's daughter. (Other sources have even more, such as the introit *Vultum tuum* and the communion *Dilexisti quoniam*.) The lessons draw upon associations with Wisdom, in the Epistle, and Mary the sister of Martha in the Gospel.

Chant texts for the Mass, as we have already seen, were drawn almost exclusively from the Psalter. Not surprisingly, objections were raised when from the ninth century onward non-biblical texts were added in the form of sequences (after the alleluia) and trope verses (supplementing the introit in particular).

The greatest quantity of material for lessons was required in the Night Office. Once again the Bible provided the largest number. Many were related directly to the topic of particular days, while cycles for the groups of 'neutral' Sundays were built up mostly from the Old Testament, including the Apocrypha.

Table 1.6 *Texts for Mass of the Assumption of the Blessed Virgin Mary*

Introit	*Gaudeamus omnes*	non-biblical	'Let us all rejoice in the Lord, celebrating . . . Mary' (also used, with the appropriate name inserted, for St Agatha and for All Saints).
Introit verse	*Eructavit cor meum*	Ps. 44:1	'My heart is inditing of a good matter.'
Epistle	*In omnibus requiem quesivi*	Wisdom 24:11–20	'Likewise in the beloved city he gave me rest, and in Jerusalem was my power.' The passage continues with Wisdom likening herself to beautiful and sweet-smelling plants and trees.
Gradual	*Propter veritatem*	Ps. 44:4	'Because of the word of truth.'
Gradual verse	*Audi filia*	Ps. 44:11	'Hearken, O daughter, and consider.'
Alleluia	*Alleluia. Hodie Maria virgo celos ascendit*	non-biblical	'Alleluia. Today the virgin Mary has ascended into heaven.'
Gospel	*In illo tempore, Intravit Iesus in quoddam castellum . . . Maria optimam partem elegit.*	Luke 10:38–42	'He entered into a certain village: and a certain woman named Martha received him into her house . . . Mary hath chosen that good part, which shall not be taken away from her.'
Offertory	*Diffusa est gratia*	Ps. 44:3	'Full of grace are thy lips.'
Communion	*Beata viscera Marie virginis*	non-biblical	'Blessed is the womb of the Virgin Mary.'

Although these cycles for Mass and Office obviously fall far short of reading the whole Bible in the course of the year, they constitute a practical selection, touching all the main types of book. The main point of the selection is, of course, to show through the sacred word how human history is shaped by God, culminating in the birth, death and resurrection of Christ and the redemption of mankind.

Lessons in the Night Office also included other types of text: sermons on the theme of the day and commentaries ('homilies') on passages of scripture, by the Church Fathers. In the three Nocturns of the Night Office (when there are three), the readings in the First Nocturn are from the Bible, in the Second Nocturn from a sermon, and in the Third Nocturn from a homily. On special days in the year this pattern is changed: for example during Eastertide, when there is only one Nocturn (and Old Testament lessons are in any case inappropriate) only homilies are read.

Adapting biblical verses for chant and making new ones

All these lessons were potential sources of chant texts, either by direct quotation or by paraphrasing. And here some very interesting techniques emerge, particularly in the responsories which follow each reading. Firstly, chant texts do not often take up the sermon or homily, but continue with the biblical narrative or paraphrase. To this extent they form little narrative cycles of their own, and indeed a set of responsories was often known as a 'historia'. In spite of what one might think from its name, the responsory does not necessarily respond directly (by quotation or paraphrase) to the lesson immediately preceding it. Furthermore, the biblical verses may be excerpted, recombined and paraphrased, sometimes resembling a short meditation on a biblical verse.

Here are some examples, taken for convenience from the Salisbury use.
   The lessons of the Night Office on the feast of the Epiphany are as follows:

   Lessons 1–3 from the prophecy of Isaiah 55:1–5 and 6–12, and Isaiah 60:1–7.
   Lessons 4–6 from the Epiphany sermon of Leo the Great.
   Lessons 7–9 from the homily of Gregory the Great on Matt. 2:1–12.

   Gregory expounds a passage from Matthew which tells of the coming of the Magi to worship Jesus. This event is of course mentioned in Leo's sermon. But it is the responsories which provide the most direct references to the theme with scriptural quotations (see Table 1.7).
   Two of the responsory texts may be singled out. The fifth responsory reads:

   Interrogabat magos Herodes, Quod signum vidistis super natum regem? Stellam magnam fulgentem, cuius splendor illuminat mundum. Et nos cognovimus et venimus adorare Dominum. V. Vidimus stellam eius in oriente. (Repeat: Et nos cognovimus et venimus adorare Dominum.)

   [Translation: Herod questioned the Magi: 'What sign of the newborn king did you see?' 'A great shining star, whose splendour lights up the world. And we knew it and are come to worship the Lord.' Verse: 'We have seen his star in the East.']

This is a paraphrase of the biblical narrative. The initial announcement by the Magi of their reason for coming is made into a reply to Herod's questioning. Matthew's gospel reads: 'Behold, there came wise men from the east to Jerusalem, saying, Where is he that is born King of the Jews? for we have seen his star in the east, and are come to worship him . . . Then Herod, when he had privily called the wise men, inquired of them diligently what time the star appeared.'
   The sixth responsory is written in rhyming prose, that is, the six lines are of varied length and irregular rhythm, but they all end in '-a', two of the six in '-ia'.

Tria sunt munera preciosa,	The precious gifts are three,
que obtulerunt magi Domino in die ista	which the Magi offered on this day to the Lord
et habent in se divina mysteria.	and which have in them a divine mystery.
In auro ut ostendatur regis potentia,	In gold the power of the king is shown:
in thure sacerdotem magnum considera,	in frankincense contemplate the great priest,
et in mirra Dominicam sepulturam.	and in myrrh the burial of the Lord.

Table 1.7 *Responsory texts for Epiphany*

responsory	biblical source	theme
R1. *Illuminare, illuminare, Hierusalem,*	Is. 60:1	These verses take up the passage recited in the Third Lesson, with the emphasis
V. *Et ambulant gentes*	Is. 60:3	on the 'great light' which will shine on Israel and the kings which will come to it. This is understood as the star seen by the Magi.
R2. *Omnes de Saba veniunt*	Is. 60:6	The respond says that 'they from Sheba shall come: they shall bring gold and
V. *Reges Tharsis et insule*	Ps. 71:10	incense'. Then the cantor turns to Psalm 71, which foretells that 'kings of Tharsis and of the isles shall give presents: the kings of Arabia and Saba shall bring gifts'.
R3. *Reges Tharsis et insule,*	Ps. 71:10	(as previous)
V. *Et adorabunt eum*	Ps. 71:11	
R4. *Magi veniunt ab oriente,*	Matt. 2:1–2	Gospel text
V. *Cum natus esset Iesus*	Matt. 2:1	
R5. *Interrogabat magos Herodes,*	cf. Matt. 2:1–2 and 7	Gospel text
V. *Vidimus stellam eius*	Matt. 2:2	
R6. *Tria sunt munera preciosa,*	–	A poetic meditation on the three great signs associated with Epiphany (see
V. *Salutis nostre auctorem magi*	–	below).
R7. *Hodie in Iordane baptizato,*	Matt. 3:16–17	Christ's baptism by John in the river Jordan, the descent of the dove, the
V. *Celi aperti sunt*	Matt. 3:16–17	voice of God acknowledging Christ as his son, the second sign.
R8. *Dies sanctificatus illuxit,*	–	Prose meditation on the light and the Trinity: 'The Father was heard in the
V. *Pater enim auditur*		voice: the Son was manifested in the man: the Holy Spirit was recognized in the form of a dove'.
R9. *In columbe specie,*	Matt. 3:16–17	The theme of baptism prompts an inspired reference to Ps. 28: 'It is the Lord that
V. *Vox Domini super aquas*	Ps. 28, 3–4	commandeth the waters: it is the glorious God that maketh the thunder. It is the Lord that ruleth the sea'.

The three gifts are named in Matt. 2:11, but the significance attributed to them is non-biblical and comes from the mystery-literature of the early centuries.

Three signs are associated with Epiphany: the 'manifestation' (Greek *epiphaneia*) of Christ to the Gentiles in the person of the Magi, Christ's baptism, and a third, not mentioned so far. This was Christ's first miracle, when at the marriage at Cana he turned water into wine. No lessons refer to this, but in the antiphon for the Benedictus at Lauds all three 'mysteries' are brought together in virtuoso and typically medieval fashion:

Hodie celesti sponso	Today the church
iuncta est ecclesia,	is joined to the celestial husband,
quoniam in Iordane	since in the Jordan
lavit Christus eius crimina:	Christ washed away her sins:
currunt cum muneribus magi	the Magi hastened with gifts
ad regales nuptias:	to the royal marriage:
et ex aqua facto vino letantur convive.	and the guests rejoiced over the wine made from water.

The chant is transcribed as Example 1.2.

Ex. 1.2 Antiphon *Hodie celesti sponso*

A. Hodie celesti sponso

Today the Church is joined to the heavenly Bridegroom, for Christ washed away her sins in the Jordan; the Magi hastened with gifts to the royal wedding; and the guests rejoiced when wine was made from water, alleluia.

From all this we can see that the chant texts were not wholly dependent on the liturgical lessons but contributed independently to the contemplation of the themes of the church year. They did this by introducing biblical texts other than those of the lessons, but also by paraphrase and, in some cases, new and individual thought.

Further reading

The only studies of the origins of liturgical chant texts are highly specialized. Among them McKinnon's justly celebrated *The Advent Project* should be cited as a superb attempt to explain how the chant texts of Mass were selected and organized in cycles.

1.v The principal forms and styles of Gregorian chant

The previous sections have tried to give an impression of the numerous different ceremonies and circumstances in which chant was performed. There were frequent references to simple or ornate chants, things sung by soloists or by the choir, recitations, repetitions and refrains, and plenty of other indications that chant, far from being primitive and monotonous, is a musical repertory of remarkable variety. This is quickly apparent if we attend a fully sung plainchant Mass. There are also various levels of musical complexity and clear distinctions of musical form in the Office hours (although today we are unlikely to be able to hear the Night Office, where the rich variety is most audible). When we turn now to consider these forms and styles in more detail, we should not forget that they have evolved – or, better, singers over centuries have developed them – to serve a particular ritual purpose at a particular point in the liturgical cycle.

Most accounts of Gregorian chant in reference books begin from the simplest chants and work through to the most complex, and that is what I shall do here. From this one might gain the impression that chant actually developed in that way, from simple beginnings through to ornate and sophisticated masterpieces in the nth century. But there lies a problem. As we shall see in Chapter 2, there is a great deal of uncertainty about when specific pieces were composed, or how soon they reached the form in which we know them. In fact, there is no reason to believe that expert singers could not have developed sophisticated techniques of declaiming the sacred texts at a very early time, say, the sixth century or even earlier. (Gregory the Great, whose name is used to dignify the chant repertory, died in 604.) As far as the notes are concerned, we cannot see further back than the ninth century, when musical notation shows us how complex and sophisticated many of the melodies are. It can certainly be argued that the melodies would have been sung in much the same way decades or even centuries earlier. For present purposes it is undoubtedly right to imagine the simple and the complex as having come into use at more or less the same time. (The Menuet of one of Haydn's London symphonies is not as complicated as the first movement, but both were composed by the same genius.)

Describing melodies

In the next paragraphs there are attempts to describe several different types of chant. What features are important when we try to define the character of the melodies? What would have been important to those who made these melodies? What was the 'right' way to sing this ritual music?

Clearly the starting point was the Latin text, chosen for its appropriateness to the day and hour when it was to be chanted. But the text should also be suited to the type of music required at this point. The two are interdependent.

The chant respects the syntactic structure of the text. Ends of phrases in the text will be matched by a musical cadence of some sort. The cadences are therefore the points of repose toward which the melody will move, and the singer/composer will have a clear idea of which cadence notes are appropriate for the piece in question. These will be determined by the choice of mode for the piece. As we shall see, some types of chant prefer some modes above others, that is, it was conventional for a particular category of chant to be performed in a particular mode. The system is not water-tight, and we can only speak of preferences and tendencies, not absolute rules. Each mode favours a particular tonal space, within which the melody can move, and particular points of repose. In the older layers of the chant repertory phrases normally occupy a restricted space of just a third, a fourth or a fifth. After the millennium they frequently range more widely.

Another decision has to be made, about the degree of solemnity required. How simply or with how much elaboration should the text be delivered? Roughly speaking, there are two extremes: syllabic text-setting and melismatic style. Syllabic text-setting means that each syllable of text is set to a single note. Some simple hymns and antiphons approach this extreme, and it was a standard technique in sequences and prosulas, new chants of the ninth century. (In fact many of these were made by putting new texts to pre-existing, textless melodies, so they are a special case.) A long vocalization sung on a single syllable of text is called a 'melisma', hence the designation melismatic style for melodies where such melismas are a prominent feature. Many chants occupy a middle ground, somewhere between (a) simple but not completely syllabic, and (b) moderately ornate but not strikingly melismatic. Near the simple end are chants where a lot of syllables carry two or three notes, as in many Office antiphons. More ornate are some the antiphons for Magnifi-cat and Benedictus, where several syllables may well carry four or five notes, and the introit and communion of Mass, where some syllables with six to eight notes may be expected. After that we are approaching the melismatic end of the scale, with the Great Responsories of the Office, and the gradual, tract and offertory of Mass.

Another stylistic feature to look out for is the presence or absence of recitation on (or around) one note. In the simplest recitation a text is intoned on a single note. In practice the reciting note is usually reached through a few notes leading up from below, and at the end there is usually a closing cadence (from Latin *cadere*, to fall, as indeed most chants do). These methods of recitation are particularly useful when musical elaboration is inappropriate. So they are used for prayers, lessons, and the numerous psalms chanted during the Office hours. But many more ornate chants also make use of recitation techniques, perhaps for whole sections, perhaps for shorter passages, and beneath a florid surface a simpler recitation pattern may often be discerned. On the other hand, many chants do not rely on recitation techniques. Their melodic phrases move more freely within a wider tonal space. Some are quite short, and for that reason alone need no recitation to accommodate long passages of text. Strophic hymns and very many Office antiphons can be placed in this category.

The singer/composer may also bring into play not only a repertory of small motifs and turns of phrase but also longer phrases covering a whole syntactic unit of text, appropriate for the text and the type of melody. There are numerous ways of beginning and ending phrases, ways of decorating a basic melodic skeleton, of dwelling upon a tonal centre, of moving to a new one. Many of these conventional turns of phrase or standard melodic elements are characteristic of particular chants in particular modes.

The eight modes

The tonal system of chant was organized according to the eight modes. (There will be more discussion of the modes in section 4.i on music theory below, but we need to grasp some of the basics here.) At least in theory, and for the most part in practice, chants were classified in one of eight modes, according to their range and their final note. The great majority of chants could be comfortably notated ending on *D*, *E*, *F* or *G*. These four tonalities (the term 'tonality' is modern but convenient) were known as the *protus*, *deuterus*, *tritus* and *tetrardus* respectively. If the chant moved mostly or completely in the range above the final note (*finalis*), it was assigned to the 'authentic' (*authentus*) division of the tonality; if it moved mostly or completely

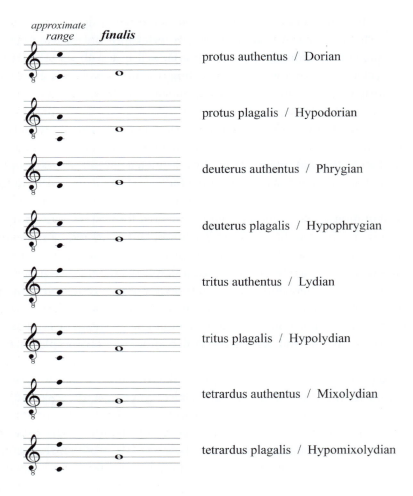

approximate range   **finalis**

protus authentus / Dorian

protus plagalis / Hypodorian

deuterus authentus / Phrygian

deuterus plagalis / Hypophrygian

tritus authentus / Lydian

tritus plagalis / Hypolydian

tetrardus authentus / Mixolydian

tetrardus plagalis / Hypomixolydian

Ex. 1.3 The eight modes

in the range around the final note, that is, down to the fourth below the *finalis* and up to the fifth above the *finalis*, more or less, it was assigned to the 'plagal' (*plagalis*) division. Another set of names for the eight modes was adapted from classical Greek music theory, though these were not commonly used in the Middle Ages. Example 1.3 gives the *finales*, general ranges and names of the eight modes.

Different types of chant prefer different modes. When each of the major categories of chant is discussed below, its 'modal profile' is indicated, that is, what proportion of its pieces are assigned to which of the eight modes. At the back of the book there is a table summarizing this information (see p. 223).

Tones for prayers, lessons and psalms

A simple way of declaiming a biblical or other liturgical text with many verses was recitation to a simple musical formula. A suitable pitch is chosen for reciting most of the text on a single note, with inflections at the appropriate grammatical points: comma, colon, full stop. There may be a lead into the principal reciting note from below. Prayers and lessons are recited by a single person, the sets of psalms in the Office are sung by the choir, divided into two sides singing alternating verses. The psalm tones differ from the tones for prayers and lessons in that they always include a subsidiary cadence after the first half verse. This reflects the normal structure of the texts, practically every verse having a binary text structure. The texts of prayers and lessons are not as regularly constructed as this. But the principles for declaiming all three types of text – prayers, lessons and Office psalms – are basically the same.

The standard prayer and lesson tones are not uninteresting, and there are some special ones, such as the lesson tones for reciting the Genealogy of Christ at Christmas time, or for the Lamentations on the days before Easter, which are quite individual. In the later Middle Ages a certain number of new tones were composed for some churches, to increase the solemnity of the performance. But in a book of this size there is unfortunately not enough space to explore such byways. We turn to the psalms instead.

When we recollect how often the psalm tones were used, we can appreciate why the simple tonal patterns which they outline may seem to embody the very essence of plainchant. It is certainly true that there are similarities between the tonal outline of some psalm tones and that of some more ornate chant models. We can see this in the following musical examples.

Example 1.4 gives the opening verses from Psalm 138 *Domine probasti me* ('O Lord, thou hast searched me') and the *Gloria patri* (known as the doxology, from the Greek *doxa*, Latin *gloria*, 'glory'), which is sung as the last pair of verses for every psalm. It is set out here with the seventh psalm tone.

This psalm was sung during Vespers on Thursday (in Roman use) or Friday (in Benedictine use). The antiphon *Confortatus est* is one of those often assigned to frame it. This antiphon is in mode 7, and this means that the seventh psalm tone is used to sing the psalm.

The half verses are divided in Example 1.4 by a double-bar. In both half verses, *d* is the reciting note or 'tenor'. In the first verse and the *Gloria patri* the reciting note is reached from below. The end of the first half verse is marked by a leap up to *f* and fall to *e*; this intermediate ending is known as the 'mediant'. At the end of the verse, singers could choose from among three cadences for this psalm tone. The choirmaster would decide which was to be sung, according to what fitted best with the repeat of the antiphon

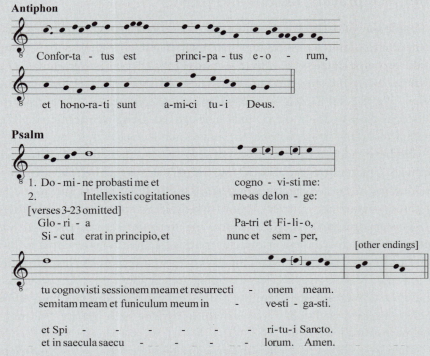

Ex. 1.4 Psalm 138 *Domine probasti me*, seventh psalm tone, with antiphon *Confortatus est*

A. Confortatus est

Their principalities were comforted and thy friends were held in honour, O God.

Ps. 138

1 LORD, thou hast searched me, and known me: Thou knowest my downsitting and mine uprising.
2 Thou understandest my thought afar off: Thou compassest my path and my lying down.

Glory be to the Father, and to the Son, and to the Holy Ghost: As it was in the beginning, is now, and ever shall be, world without end. Amen.

when the psalm was finished. Since the antiphon *Confortatus est* begins on *c*, the ending chosen in Example 1.4 ends on *c*. (Two more endings are given in brackets, to show the other possibilities for this psalm tone. They might be employed for other antiphons.)

The other verses of the psalm are sung without the initial figure, coming straight in on *d*. At the mediant and the ending, there is some flexibility in managing unaccented syllables. The accented syllables should fall on *f* and *d* at the mediant, and on *e* at the final cadence. The important thing is to know when to stop repeating notes on the reciting note and move into the mediant or final cadence. The accented syllables are one guide, though it has to be said that medieval practice was not unanimous in applying that method. The alternative was simply to count the number of syllables back from the final note, in this tone four syllables at both the mediant and the final. (Modern chant books show when to change by printing the appropriate syllables in bold type.)

This is the way all psalm tones work. Example 1.5 shows the principal notes of the eight standard psalm tones, together with an unusual ninth tone, the 'tonus peregrinus', so-called because the reciting note in the second half verse is not the same as the one in the first half. In tone 3, most medieval books give *c* as the reciting note, but some from Italy and south France prefer *b*. Some of the common alternative end notes are indicated in Example 1.5, but there is no space to include very many. It is important to notice that the psalm tone does not necessarily end on the *finalis* of the mode. The chanting of the psalm will be rounded off by a repeat of the antiphon, which does, of course, end on the *finalis* of the mode.

When antiphons are written out in medieval chant books, the psalm which they frame is indicated only by its first words, if at all. But the ending of the psalm tone to be used is given, usually with the letters 'e u o u a e', a short way of writing 'seculorum. Amen'. From this we can tell what psalm tone was to be used, with what ending, and also, in case of doubt, in what mode the antiphon was reckoned to be.

There are several other 'tones' which work like psalm tones, for other categories of chant. The tones for singing the canticles Magnificat at Vespers and Benedictus at Lauds, and for the psalm verse of the introit at Mass, are only slightly more ornate than the simple psalm tones. The invitatory Psalm 94 *Venite exsultemus Domino* at the start of the Night Office has several tones (not in all modes), which extend over each *pair* of verses, and are flexibly applied. The whole psalm is therefore usually written out in full, once for each tone, in medieval manuscripts.

In chants of many different kinds the reciting note or *tenor* of the psalm tone functions as a secondary tonal focus beside the principal note, the *finalis*, according to mode.

Responsory verses

Singing psalms with the antiphons that frame them makes up a large part of the Night Office, as well as the other Office hours. The most impressive chants of the Night Office are the Great Responsories, one following each lesson. Each responsory

Ex. 1.5 The eight psalm tones

has a main section (conveniently referred to as the 'respond') and a verse, after which the last part of the respond is repeated. The verses of responsories are also sung to one of eight tones, comparable to psalm tones in some ways, but melodically much richer. They are like psalm tones in being divided into two halves and in having standard initial gestures, mediant endings and final cadences. The second half also gets going with a standard figure. And they have reciting notes; most of the tones have a different reciting note for each half verse.

Example 1.6 gives two examples, which show how the tone for responsories in mode 7 was adapted to verse texts of different length. In some responsory verse tones, the same reciting note is used in both halves, but in other cases the two halves have different reciting notes. As may be seen, that is the case with the seventh tone shown here: the reciting note in the first half is *c*, but in the second half it is *d*, like the seventh psalm tone.

  The differences from the simple psalm tone in Example 1.4 are clear enough. There is an ornamental start, the first flourish always coinciding with the first accented syllable. After the recitation on *c*, the mediant works its way up to *d*. The beginning of the second half is also ornate, then comes the second passage of recitation, on *d*. The final flourishes are applied to the last five syllables regardless of text accent. The recitation is not as plain as in the psalm tone, since some accented syllables have a two-note lift: 'habetis', 'isti' and 'sitis'. It is interesting that the verse tone ends on *b* and not on the final note of mode 7, which is *G*. It is the repeat of the respond which will bring the

Ex. 1.6 Eighth-mode responsory verses *Dum lucem habetis* and *Nonne ecce omnes isti*

V. Dum lucem habetis
While ye have light, believe in the light, that ye may be the children of light, saith the Lord. (John 12:36)

V. Nonne ecce
Behold, are not all these which speak Galilaeans? And how hear we every man in our own tongue? (Acts 2:7–8)

chant to a final close on *G*, so the end of the verse on *b* is like an imperfect cadence. Several other responsory verse tones end, like this one, on a note other than the final of the mode. The responsory verse tone of mode 7 is decidedly 'modal' in flavour above all because of the rise to *f* at the start and the mediant. Later tonal music, in G major, would have an *f♯*. But *f♯*s rise to high *g*, which never happens here, nor in the main part of the responsory, the respond, which we shall look at in a moment.

The antiphons of the Office hours

The singing of each psalm or group of psalms was framed by the performance of an antiphon. The great majority of these are relatively short. The simplest, sung on weekdays when no feast day intervened, usually consist of only two phrases. Four phrases is an average number for antiphons as a whole, while six and more phrases are not uncommon. As a general rule, the antiphons for the Magnificat at Vespers and for the Benedictus at Lauds are longer than the psalm antiphons. Some antiphons for the Blessed Virgin Mary from the central and late Middle Ages are also longer and more ornate than average. Several long chants sung in procession on Palm Sunday and the Rogation Days, although usually labelled antiphons, are different in character, so they are discussed in the next short section.

Antiphons are real melodies in the sense indicated above ('Recitation and melody'). Both individual phrases and melody as a whole have a distinct shape. Naturally some melodies are more static and some more dynamic than others. The great majority display melodic movement which, however modest, makes a satisfying contrast to the recitation of the psalms.

The total number of antiphons to be found in all medieval chant books is very great and cannot yet be computed exactly. The research project CANTUS includes complete inventories of over 100 medieval antiphoners and by the start of 2008 had registered nearly 12,000 different antiphons. This immense number has to be sorted into manageable order if we want to get a sense of the musical nature of the antiphon repertory. The chants need to be classified in melodic families, by tonality and form, for example. Fortunately, this work has been done by László Dobszay and Janka Szendrei for a large and representative cross-section.

The edition by Dobszay and Szendrei encompasses 2,579 antiphons, divided between the eight modes as follows: mode 1 has 602 antiphons, mode 2 has 204, mode 3 has 181, mode 4 has 331, mode 5 has 151, mode 6 has 198, mode 7 has 322, and mode 8 has 590. The range of melodic types is very great and clearly impossible to summarize in a few sentences. It seems sensible to take a few examples of just one type, in order to get a sense of the basic musical character of antiphons and how melodic units function within their melodies as a whole.

Example 1.7 sets out five antiphons in mode 7. Mode 7 has been chosen to match examples 1.4 and 1.6 above.

The first antiphon, *Omnis spiritus*, is a simple antiphon like those sung on weekdays; this one actually belongs to the Office for the Dead. It simply rises from *G* up to *d* (the *tenor* of the seventh psalm tone) and returns to the *finalis*. The second antiphon, *Cito euntes*, begins similarly, and its second phrase also returns to the *finalis*, with a sort of doubling back to *d* part way. But the longer text needs two more phrases of music, so the composer adds a contrasting phrase which instead of moving between *G* and *d* emphasizes the chain of thirds *F–a–c*. This brings him up to *d* again and the descent to the *finalis* can be made as expected.

The third antiphon, *Descendit angelus Domini*, has a still longer text. What is to be done? Introduce more contrasting phrases? That would certainly be possible, but instead the composer decides to go twice over the same ground as in *Cito euntes*, compressing it where necessary. In the first phrase, 'Descendit angelus Domini' he compresses the first two phrases of *Cito euntes* into one, and then for 'ad Zachariam dicens' he uses the contrasting *F–a–c* chain before coming quickly to rest on *G*. Now is the time for the angel's words to Zacharias, for which the music rises to start on *c*. But 'accipe puerum' is actually comparable with 'euntes' near the start of *Cito euntes*, a common way of ending a phrase on *d*. And the next phrase in *Descendit angelus*, 'in senectute tua', is again like 'dicite discipulis' from *Cito euntes*. We can predict what follows. The third and fourth phrases of *Cito euntes*, with the *F–a–c* chain and descent from *d* to the *finalis*, come round again in *Descendit angelus* for 'et habebit nomen Iohannes Baptista'.

The fourth antiphon, *Non enim misit Deus*, uses similar melodic material to the first three, but introduces a new phrase rising to high *g*. This is something which could have been done in *Descendit angelus*, but wasn't. The first phrase rises to *d*, as we would expect, and since there are plenty of syllables it dwells a little on the notes around *d*. After the new phrase rising up to *g* and back there is more hovering around *d*, or perhaps we could hear it as a gentle contrasting of the *e–c* third with *d*. The final phrase is like the one in *Descendit angelus*. We could hear it as rocking back and forth between contrasting chains of thirds: *G / F–a–c / d–b / c–a–F–a / G*.

Now the way this antiphon moves up to the higher octave *g* is an indication that it is not as old as the previous ones. So also the endings from below, *cd–d*. The top *g* is reached in a similar way, *fg–g*. These are features which become increasingly common in the eleventh century, and in fact this antiphon is not found in the manuscripts before that time. But the starting point was the melodic material already tried and tested in the previous three pieces.

The last antiphon, *Apparuit caro suo Iohanni*, is more melismatic than the previous four. Two syllables carry five notes each. This and the rise to the high octave, accomplished in a fine sweep within only one phrase, are indications of a relatively recent composition. On the other hand, many phrases familiar by now reappear. (See the first and last phrases.)

Ex. 1.7 Antiphons *Omnis spiritus, Cito euntes, Descendit angelus, Non enim misit filium* and *Apparuit caro suo*

A. Omnis spiritus
Let every soul praise the Lord.

A. Cito euntes
Go quickly, and tell his disciples that the Lord is risen from the dead, alleluia. (Matt. 28:7)

There are very many groups of antiphons related by their melodic material in the same way as these five. In fact we have already seen another member of this group, in Example 1.4, the antiphon *Confortatus est*, framing Psalm 138. But even from the tiny selection offered here, we can get a sense of the basic features of such melodies. Repeated notes can be found, when it seems convenient to deal with a long phrase of text in that way, but they are not common. Instead most phrases move easily within a rather narrow compass, about a fourth or a fifth, making a passage from a lower to a higher note, or vice versa, or oscillating around one note. In the different modes it will be different notes that carry the melody along. But the strategies will be the same. These simple but effective procedures were repeated so often as to become instinctive, and hence an individual melody could be learned as a particular manifestation of one of the well-known types.

This is not meant to suggest that the whole melodic type grew out of a simple antiphon like *Omnis spiritus*. But it is useful to deploy examples in this way in order to demonstrate how flexible musical phrases like these could be expanded and contracted, and supplemented with contrasting material. The question of what was the 'original' form of the material does not actually make any sense. It was by nature infinitely pliable.

A number of melodies became very popular, that is, they were used again and again with little modification, if the text was of the right structure. The most popular of all (there are over a hundred in the Worcester antiphoner) is related to the examples we have just seen, but has a piquant tonal inflection which brings it to an end on *a* instead of *G*. The piquancy involves the fact that *b*♮ is sung in the third of the four phrases, but *b*♭ in the last phrase. Many manuscripts deal with this dichotomy simply by avoiding one or the other, or both. The descent through *b*♭ onto *a* means that the order of tones and semitones is like that of the fourth mode: *d–c–b♭–a* is

---

Ex. 1.7 (*cont.*)

A. Descendit angelus

An angel of the Lord came down and said to Zacharias: Receive the child in thy old age and he shall have the name John the Baptist. (cf. Luke 1:11–13)

A. Non enim misit

For God sent not his Son into the world to condemn the world; but that the world through him might be saved, alleluia. (John 3:17)

A. Apparuit caro suo

The Lord Jesus Christ appeared to his beloved John with his disciples and said unto them: Come to me, my beloved, for the time is come when thou shalt dine in my communion with thy brethren.

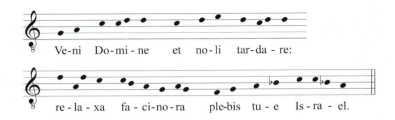

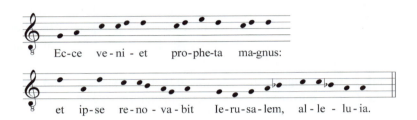

Ex. 1.8 Antiphons *Veni Domine et noli tardare* and *Ecce veniet propheta magnus*

A. Veni Domine
Come, O Lord, and tarry not: ease the wickedness of thy people Israel.

A. Ecce veniet propheta
Behold, the great prophet comes: and he shall restore Jerusalem, alleluia.

equivalent to *a–g–f–e*. So these antiphons are usually classified in mode 4. (Some early medieval theorists got quite excited about this melody and called it irregular, or worse. It was presumably the same way of thinking which led to the avoidance of the tonal clash altogether, by making 'regular' versions of the melody.) Example 1.8 shows a couple of examples.

The Great Responsories of the Night Office

In the next paragraphs we turn to the grander types of Gregorian chant, starting with the responsories, or rather the first main part of them, the respond, which is sung before and after the verse (whose music was discussed above). Stretching the reader's patience to the limit, we remain in mode 7. Two responds are given in Example 1.9. These are the responds which go with the verses in Example 1.6. To put together the complete chant we have to combine the musical examples as follows:

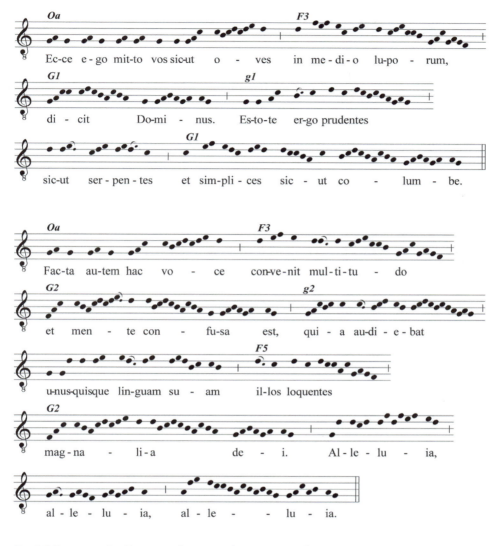

Ex. 1.9 Responsories *Ecce ego mitto vos* and *Facta autem hac voce*

R. Ecce ego mitto vos

Behold, I send you forth as sheep in the midst of wolves, saith the Lord: be ye therefore wise as serpents, and harmless as doves. (Matt. 10:16)

R. Facta autem hac voce

Now when this was noised abroad, the multitude came together, and were confounded, because that every man heard them speak in his own language the wonderful works of God, alleluia. (Acts 2:6 and 11)

Respond *Ecce ego mitto vos*, Verse *Dum lucem habetis*, repeat of Respond from 'Estote' to the end.
Respond *Facta autem hac voce*, Verse *Nonne ecce omnes isti*, repeat of Respond from 'Illos' to the end.

Ecce ego mitto vos has six phrases, while *Facta autem hac voce* has seven, plus three 'alleluia' acclamations. (The alleluias are an addition for the Pentecost season of the year and not part of the essential respond, but they are given here as in the Worcester manuscript for the sake of completeness.) Six phrases is typical for responsories, though not a hard and fast rule. Quite often one can observe a division into three periods, so that the basic structure is of three periods divided into two phrases each. In the text of *Ecce ego mitto vos* there is an obvious break after the third phrase. It would then have been possible to sing right through to 'serpentes', but the level of musical elaboration is such that the composer/singer sets a very obvious cadence at 'prudentes' as well. There is the same slight ambiguity about the second part of *Facta autem hac voce*, but the composer/singer opts for divisions very much along the same lines as in *Ecce ego mitto vos*. So for the most part both responsories bring their phrases to an end on the same cadence notes, that is, the same 'tonal strategy', as we may call it, operates in both.

Ecce ego mitto vos	d–F–G–G–c–––G
Facta autem hac voce	d–F–G–G–b–F–G

What about the musical phrases and motifs which are employed along the way? Even a casual glance at the two melodies shows that they share not only cadence points but also whole melodic phrases. This is a very important feature of several categories of melismatic chant.

Both responds begin with a phrase which rises to *d*, like the antiphons we have seen in Examples 1.7–8. Tonally it sounds more like the start of Example 1.8 than Example 1.7, because the ascent favours the notes G–a–c–d rather than G–b–d. Before the three-syllable figure through which *d* is reached there are several repetitions of the first note G (including that two-note figure on accented syllables). Musically they are treated like a prolonged upbeat, however important the Latin words are. We can see that a convention is in operation whereby the rise to *d* is delayed until the last three syllables, and everything before that is declaimed on G. This is a common opening in responds in mode 7, and in the analysis of responsories by W. H. Frere it is labelled O^a. Frere's labels are added to other phrases in the example, and it is easy to see that *Ecce ego mitto vos* and *Facta autem hac voce* share a lot of melodic material. This technique of sharing material is a crucial feature of other genres of chant as well, principally the gradual and tract of Mass, and will come up again in the historical survey in Chapter 2. As far as our two responds are concerned, the sharing appears even more consistent when it is realized that *G1* and *G2* are largely identical, but approach the second half which they have in common from different directions; the same goes for *g1* and *g2*.

The way in which common phrases are used again and again in different responsories is clearest at the cadences. The differing numbers of syllables to be accommodated means that the first part of the phrase will be handled more flexibly. And some phrases are individuals which are unique to a single responsory, or used only very rarely.

As one might expect, some standard melodic phrases were very popular, others less so. And two complete melodies, one in mode 2 and one in mode 8, were used for many texts. Here all the melodic phrases are standard, so to speak, and are reproduced in the same order, making allowances, of course, for the length of the text. (The 'alleluia' phrases at the end of *Facta autem* are an addition for Whitsuntide, and stand outside the set of standard phrases.)

Obviously these chants are far more ornate than the antiphons in Examples 1.7 and 1.8. Those elaborate cadence figures are the most obvious difference, but most phrases have a few syllables with five notes or more. Yet beneath the surface the same sort of tonal strategies as in the antiphons can be discerned. The opening phrase in both the responsories and the antiphons, despite the different surface manner, rises from G to *d*. The phrases labelled *G1*, *g1* and *g2* have the same aim at first, then fall back to G. There is nothing in the antiphons which traces the same path as *F3* (but we could find it in other antiphons). Having come down to *F* at the end of phrase *F3*, the phrase *G2* for 'et mente' and 'magnalia' takes us through the familiar *F–a–c* chain of thirds. As with the antiphons, some phrases oscillate around a central tone. *F3* starts like this (there is a resemblance to the first half of the responsory verse in Ex. 1.6), *g1* and *g2* briefly treat *c* like a reciting note (again like the first half of Ex. 1.6), and the non-standard phrases 'sicut serpentes' and 'unusquisque linguam suam' treat *d* in something of the same way.

Responsory melodies have the same sort of mobility as the antiphons, but their manner of expression is much more impressive. Their weight is equal to that of the lessons which precede them, whereas antiphons remain simple framing chants for the psalms. Even after singing through just these two examples, the constant recourse to the same or similar cadences makes itself strongly felt. It may seem a rather ponderous way of bringing a phrase to a close, after just two words in some cases. But 'ceremonious' would be a better word than 'ponderous', because the main point is not to deliver the text as if spoken. One can pronounce the text of *Ecce ego* in about fifteen seconds, but to sing it at a moderate tempo takes at least three times as long. This is ritual music, on which the thoughts of the worshippers are carried up to contemplation of the sublime. The ceremonious style of delivery, the repetitions, the echoes from pole to pole across the whole cycle of responsories through the year, are all part and parcel of the ritual character of the music, the way one must sing in the divine presence.

We turn now to those chants at Mass which by their ceremonious manner and their use of standard melodic phrases most resemble the Office responsories. These are the graduals.

The graduals of the Mass

The gradual is the chant sung after the Epistle at Mass (see Table 1.1 above). The chants of Mass are much less numerous than those of the Divine Office. In most Masses only one introit, one gradual, and so on, will be sung. (There are a few exceptions, for example on the Saturdays of the Ember Days, when there are four graduals, matching the extra lessons.) To cover the Sundays and main feast days of the church year, roughly 100 to 150 of each category of chant is required. In general, the style of Mass chants is more ornate, more ceremonious, more solemn and splendid than that of comparable Office chants. For there are antiphons at Mass – the introit and communion – as well as in the Office; and the gradual at Mass is comparable with the responsory of the Night Office.

Graduals, like responsories, consist of a first section, the respond, and a verse, with a repeat of the respond. (The repeat fell out of use after the Middle Ages.)

Example 1.10 is a gradual in mode 3, *Benedicite Dominum V. Benedic anima mea*. Several things are immediately noticeable. The text is shorter than that of the responsories above, but the music is yet more florid and the chant is altogether longer than the responds. The main cadence figures are longer than in the responsories, and there are several melismas in the middle of a phrase; the longest is on 'nomen'. 'Nomen' has its own internal form; the first group of ten notes is repeated and then enlarged: *ccccaccaG* – *ccccaccaG* – *cc[daccdcde]cccaccaG*; then a fourth phrase unlike the others. The surface detail of the melody includes a lot of note-repetition (*repercussio* is the technical term for this), most of it on c but also a bit on *F* at the start. This is not syllabic declamation as in an Office psalm, but a sort of fluttering on a single syllable. Finally, although the *finalis* of the responsory is *E*, that note is not particularly emphasized in the course of the piece. In fact it seems rather to be avoided, and the *E*-cadences at the ends of the two sections come as a surprise. From what has gone before we would expect a final cadence on *D*. In fact the cadence at 'virtute' comes in *D*-mode graduals as well. Another unexpected feature of the melody is the appearance of *b♭*s. (These are not notated in all manuscripts; the Worcester manuscript leaves them out; some sources choose *c* instead.) This seems to be because of the importance of *F*: phrases moving in the tonal area immediately above *F* and then down to *F* need *b♭* rather than the uncomfortable *b♮*. But there are no cadences on *F* itself (nor in any other graduals in this mode).

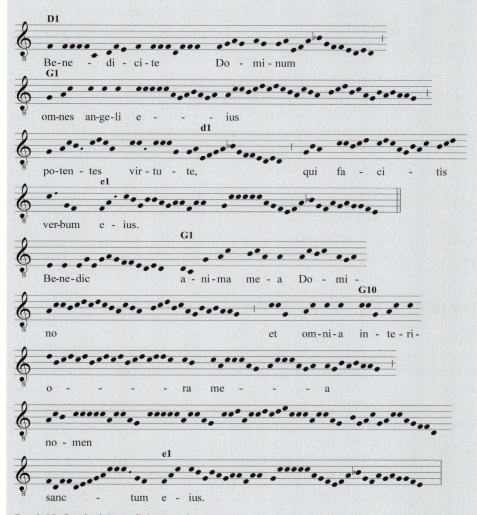

Ex. 1.10 Gradual *Benedicite Dominum*

Gr. Benedicite Dominum

O praise the Lord, ye angels of his, ye that excel in strength: ye that fulfil his commandment. V. Praise the Lord, O my soul: and all that is within me praise his holy Name. (Ps. 102:20 and 1)

Faced with as ornate a chant as this, one is tempted to try and identify a tonal framework underneath the surface detail. That is the way we often analyse later music. Can we get a sense of the tonal structure of the chant, for example by mapping out the important tones? It seems clear enough that 'Benedicite' is sung to an ornamented *F*, 'omnes angeli' moves up to a reciting note *c* before that *c* dissolves in a shower of repetitions and turns which will eventually descend on *G*. We could imagine that the singer-composer had an arsenal of such flourishes at his disposal, while being guided at a structural level by some of the simpler types of phrase clearly seen in antiphons, somewhat less clearly in responsories.

As with the responsories, standard phrases are commonly used from gradual to gradual, a certain number of phrases being proper to each mode. One or two constellations of such phrases were popular enough to constitute a complete melody, that is, the same standard phrases are sung more or less complete in the same order. The verses of a large group of graduals in mode 5 can almost be regarded as having a common 'tone' in this sense. Most homogenous is a group which includes the gradual *Iustus ut palma*, and that is what the group is usually called. The *Iustus ut palma* graduals are usually notated ending on *a* but assigned to mode 2. If they were notated in *D* they would frequently need an *E♭* as well as *E♮*, not available in the notation of the time, whereas when notated a fifth higher both *b♭* and *b♮* can be used.

The tracts of the Mass

The tract is the chant sung after the gradual and before the Gospel at Mass in Lent (see Table 1.1 above). A lot of attention has been paid to tracts, despite their small number. They have several verses and are sung straight through, without the repetitions made in responsories and graduals. They are sung in one of only two modes, modes 2 and 8. There are not many mode-2 tracts, but those in mode 8 are more numerous than the graduals in modes 7 and 8 combined. (See the numbers on p. 223 below.) And since they have several verses each, the total amount of singing is considerable.

Many of their surface features are comparable to those in graduals. Tracts are prevailingly melismatic, although they do not display melismas with an internal repeat structure. As in the graduals, the ends of text units are marked by lengthy vocalizations. If several verses are to be sung in direct succession, it seems only natural that the singer should declaim them in a similar way, and this is indeed what we find. Within their respective modes, they tend to follow the same tonal route and use the same musical phrases. Some very interesting conventions are evident here. If there were more space, I would line up a group of tract verses synoptically one above the other and plot their course and the phrases they share. (This is an instructive exercise in copying, cutting and pasting.) Instead, I shall have to attempt a description in words.

The tracts in mode 8 are the more numerous. Most have three verses, some just two, half a dozen have four verses and two have five. Nearly every verse begins and ends with a phrase ending on G. The phrases are not all the same, however. There is a set of standard G-phrases to start the very first verse, a different set for starting subsequent verses. There is just one phrase which always ends the last verse, and another set of G-phrases for ending previous verses. Some of the verses are only two phrases long, which means they will both be G-phrases. For longer verses one of the G-phrases for internal verse-endings is used, but there is also a set of phrases ending on F. Even within these fairly narrow conventions, not many verses follow an identical course, that is, there is usually some difference not only in the number of phrases, but also in the choice of G- or F-phrase. Almost no phrases are unique to one tract. Here are a couple of examples, adapted from the tabulation of mode-8 tracts by Apel (p. 319):

	verse 1	verse 2	verse 3	verse 4
Beatus vir	Ga F2 G2 G3	G1 G2 G3	G1 G2 Gn	
Iubilate	Ga F2 G4 G3	G1 G2	G4 G3	. . .f2 G2 Gn

Most of the tracts in mode 2 have more verses that those in mode 8, *Deus, Deus meus* having as many as fourteen. Again there is a tonal pattern, the same sequence of cadence points being followed time and time again: *D–C–F–D*. And a limited number of stock phrases are available to conduct the singer along that course.

The introit of the Mass

Having seen something of the wide range of styles in different categories of chant, from simple antiphons to elaborate, even ecstatic graduals, we need to fit three other chants of the Mass into the stylistic picture.

The introit, as its name indicates, is the chant sung at the start of Mass (see Table 1.1 above). It is an antiphon to frame the singing of a psalm, therefore comparable with the Office antiphons. In fact, even the earliest medieval books with full texts for singing (from the late eighth and ninth centuries) give only one verse and the doxology in the great majority of instances; in a few cases there are just two psalm verses. The earlier practice – of singing as much of the psalm as was needed to accompany the solemn entrance of the minister and his assistants – appears to have died out by the time we can see the melodies with notation.

Stylistically, introits occupy a very interesting middle ground. On the one hand we have seen the simpler Office antiphons, often mobile and lyrical, with relatively little

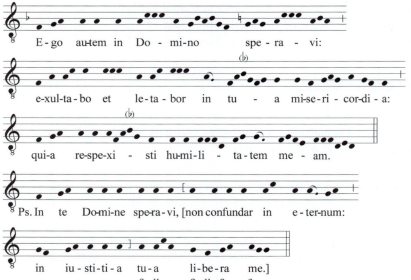

Ex. 1.11 Introits *Gaudete in Domino semper* and *Ego autem in Domino speravi*

surface ornament. On the other hand are graduals where the melismas occupy the foreground and, at least at a first hearing, the underlying structure is not easy to grasp. Introits have longer texts than the average Office antiphon and perhaps for this reason a number of words are usually delivered in recitation or embellished recitation. The degree of ornamental embellishment employed throughout the introit is generally higher than that in Office antiphons. The longer texts and more solemn delivery are appropriate for the greater importance of Mass in comparison with the Office hours. In the latter, antiphons are part of the static, contemplative psalm-dominated cycle. The Mass is much more dynamic, and the introit stands alone, announcing the beginning of the mystery.

Two examples in mode 1 will serve to illustrate some typical features of the introit (see Ex. 1.11).

Gaudete in Domino semper concentrates on the lower part of the range in this mode, touching c only once at 'Nichil' (no doubt to highlight the important word). *Ego autem in Domino speravi* uses c first as an adjunct to the reciting note a and then as a reciting note in its own right. We have seen a lot of those repeated cs in the previous example, the gradual *Benedicite Dominum* (Ex. 1.10), and they recur in offertories (with the same intensity as graduals) and communions (where their use is more like that in introits). *Ego autem* has two sets of repeated fs in the last line, and that, too, is found in the other Mass chants.

Very many syllables are set to note-groups of three to six notes. Some recur again and again. Take for example the three-note group which takes one step up and returns to the first note. The graphic sign used to notate this was known as the 'torculus', while the three-note group with one step down and return was written with a 'porrectus'. (On notation see section 4.iii.) These terms are useful for avoiding such phrases as 'the three-note group which takes one step up and returns to the first note'. There are no less than seven examples of the torculus in *Gaudete in Domino*. It seems that, like the repeated cs and fs in *Ego autem*, this figure belongs to the basic way of singing an introit. Several lines undulate constantly. At the same time, the phrases usually have a clear direction, or just as clearly undulate around one dominant note.

Ex. 1.11 (*cont.*)

Intr. Gaudete in Domino semper

Rejoice in the Lord alway: and again I say, Rejoice. Let your moderation be known unto all men. The Lord is at hand. Be careful for nothing; but in every thing by prayer and supplication with thanksgiving let your requests be made known unto God. (Philipp. 4:4–6)

Intr. Ego autem in Domino speravi

My trust hath been in the Lord: I will be glad and rejoice in thy mercy: for thou hast considered my trouble. (Ps. 30:8–9)

Ex. 1.12 Communions *Servite Domino, Quis dabit ex Sion* and *Adversum me exercebantur*

Com. Servite Domino

Serve the Lord with fear, and rejoice with trembling: embrace discipline, lest ye perish from the just way. (Ps. 2:11)

The communion of the Mass

It is fairly easy to get a sense of how an introit 'works', musically. The structural tones are clear, the degree of solemnity which separates them from simple Office antiphons is also easy to appreciate. Its nearest relative in the Mass, the communion, is not as easy to grasp. The communion is the chant sung at Mass when the bread and wine are consumed (see Table 1.1 above). Communions are usually shorter than introits. They were apparently also sung as framing chants for a psalm, but little trace of this remains, even in the earliest notated books. So it is not as if the distribution of the consecrated elements to the faithful in the Eucharist is accompanied by any climactic musical item.

The communions (there is a core repertory of about 140 in medieval sources) are surprisingly heterogeneous. There are more non-psalmic texts among the communions, more than half of the total, than among any of the other Mass chants (except alleluias, because so many alleluias are high medieval additions to the oldest layer of chant). Ten of them also turn up as Office antiphons, and no fewer than thirty as Office responsories (with a verse, when sung in the Office). There are traces of the solemn way of singing Mass chants which we have just seen in the introits, but also a number of very simple, syllabic passages. Some of the communions which draw upon the gospel reading earlier in the Mass have a narrative character which is unusual among Mass chants. All this has proved fascinating material for chant historians.

Three examples, all in the same mode 5, give an idea of the range of style and the individuality of many communions (Ex. 1.12).

Servite Domino in timore is short, *Quis dabit ex Syon* middling, and *Adversum me exercebantur* is long. The ceremonious cadences can be seen even in the short *Servite Domino* ('ei', 'iusta'), and even more so in the other two pieces. In *Adversum me*, both at 'te Domine' and 'misericordie tue' there is a slow and gradual descent to the final F. An Office antiphon would have done this more quickly. On the other hand, there is a syllabic

---

Ex. 1.12 (*cont.*)

Com. Quis dabit ex Sion

Oh that the salvation of Israel were come out of Zion! when the Lord bringeth back the captivity of his people, Jacob shall rejoice, and Israel shall be glad. (Ps. 13:11)

Com. Adversum me exercebantur

They that sit in the gate speak against me; and I was the song of the drunkards. But as for me, my prayer is unto thee, O Lord, in an acceptable time, O God, in the multitude of thy mercy. (Ps. 68:14)

phrase in *Servite Domino* at 'apprehendite disciplinam', and a short recitation on *c* in *Quis dabit ex Syon* at 'cum averterit'. That matches the way in which this communion frequently hovers around the note *c*, something often found in introits and especially graduals, as we have seen in Example 1.10 above. *Adversum me* is so long that it contains musical repetitions, as if to give the piece an individual, memorable musical shape. There is an unusual use of the neume known as the 'pes', in pairs *a–b♭* at '[exerce]-bantur', '[se]-debant' and again at '[psal]-lebant', and yet again (modified for the intermediate cadence) at 'qui bibebant vinum'. Perhaps this can be understood as a decorated recitation on *a*.

Servite Domino and *Adversum me exercebantur* both stay within the range of a sixth *F–d*. *Adversum me* is notated with *b♭*s and, despite its length, stays firmly anchored to *F*. The first phrase, going quickly up through *F–a–c* and descending slowly again to *F*, stays in the mind as an element of tonal reference, so that we hear the cadences on *G* and *a* as 'imperfect' or secondary. *Servite Domino* has *b♮* throughout, and the piece wavers between phrases which stress the scale-segment *Gac* and those where the segment *FGa* is predominant. The last phrase opts for the latter, but an ending on *G* would not be unthinkable.

Quis dabit sounds quite different, with its hovering on *c* and especially the exultant rise to high *f*, certainly appropriate for the word 'exultabit'. Only the phrase in the middle uses *b♭* and makes a clear cadence on *F* for the first time in the piece.

Communions, even if in the same mode, are therefore very individual creations. There are historical reasons for this, an important one being that more than about a quarter were borrowed from antiphons and responsories of the Office, as already mentioned. In fact, we have already seen an example of this. That slow and gradual descent to the final *F* in *Adversum me*, at 'te Domine' and 'misericordie tue' can be seen in Example 1.9, a pair of responsories, the cadence of the phrases marked 'G' and 'G2'. There it was in the G-mode. But it is common in responsories in F mode as well, ending on *F*. So close attention to musical detail can uncover interesting clues about the history of a chant.

The offertory of the Mass

The offertory is sung when the bread and wine are brought to the altar at Mass (see Table 1.1 above). Like the communions, offertories are very individual chants. But their dimensions are far greater. Like the Office responsory and the gradual, the offertory consists of a first main section (I call it the respond, though it is also often referred to as an antiphon) and from one to four verses. After each verse the last part of the respond is repeated. The part to be repeated is referred to as the 'repetendum' ('that which is to be repeated'). Here are the three categories of chant:

Great Responsory of the Office:	Respond – Verse – Repetendum
Gradual of the Mass:	Respond – Verse – Respond
Offertory of the Mass:	Respond – Verse 1 – Repetendum – Verse 2 – Repetendum (etc. for other verses)

The offertory respond is usually extended and ornate, with frequent use of the hovering effect on *c* that we have seen in the gradual (and to a lesser extent in the introit and communion). Even more impressive are the verses, some of the longest creations in the chant repertory. Descriptive expressions such as 'ecstatic' and 'virtuoso' come easily to mind. It is true that we know very little about the medieval style of delivery of these (or any other) chants, but clearly the singer (a soloist) sustained long arcs of melody in a way demanding considerable gifts and training. The word 'ecstatic' is suggested by the way the melody floats freely, without obvious internal structural devices such as repetitions and sequences. This is very far removed from the virtuoso singing of a Baroque opera aria, for example, where the phrases match and complement each other in a very obvious way. In several offertories the effect is heightened when words are repeated, something unique to this category of chant. And in many verses there is a long melisma, thirty or more notes on a single syllable.

Iusticie Domini recte (Ex. 1.13) is an offertory from the Lenten season, but there is nothing penitential about the melody, if we equate musical splendour with joyful praise. But we should not expect such a general matching of mood in a modern sense. The words of the offertory are selected from Psalm 18 and speak of the sweetness of God's statutes and how they rejoice the heart. That would seem to be justification for the soaring rapture of the melody. Yet other offertories are just as splendid, musically, and have a much less optimistic text. *Eripe me*, for example, has the following text, given here with the letter 'M' to show where the longest melismas fall. (* marks the start of the repetendum after the verses.)

Eripe me de inimicis meis, Deus meus: et ab insurgen[M]*tibus in me* * *libera me, Domine.*

V.1 *Quia ecce captave*[M]*runt animam meam animam meam et irruerunt for*[M]*tes in me.*

V.2 *Quia factus es adiutor me*[M]*us et refugium me*[M]*um in die tribulationis me*[M]*ae.*

[Deliver me from mine enemies, O God : defend me from them that rise up against me.

For lo, they lie waiting for my soul : the mighty men are gathered against me.

For thou art my help and my refuge in the day of my tribulation.]

Ex. 1.13 Offertory *Iusticie Domini recte*

It might be said that by placing the melismas in the last verse three times on 'my', the composer wished to emphasize the personal interest of God in the singer, or his people generally. Yet that explanation seems too sophisticated. It seems more likely – and this is what a more systematic study of text and music throughout the repertory has to demonstrate – that the musical style is the one thought fitting for the offertory as a category of chant, and is not meant to illustrate or express any particular words of the text like the word-painting in a sixteenth-century madrigal.

To return to *Iusticie Domini recte*, Example 1.13. It is one of many chants in mode 4, that is the lower (plagal) E-mode, which hovers on the note *F* so much that the cadences on *E* sound inconclusive, 'imperfect' to use a later musical terminology. The respond has the range *C–a*. In the first verse there is shift into a slightly higher range, and there are almost as many repeated *cs* as *fs*. The range of verse 1 is *C–c*. Because it is a verse it ends not on the final of the mode, *E*, but on *F*, which to modern ears sounds almost more natural than *E*. But the range continues to shift upwards, and the splendid final verse, with melismas on 'compla[M]ceant' and 'sem[M]per', frequently reaches *e* and once touches top *f*.

(For this transcription we must abandon the Worcester manuscript. Like most sources after the eleventh century it has no offertory verses. The eleventh-century manuscript Montpellier H159, from Dijon, is used instead. This is a good source not least because *b♮* and *b♭* are clearly distinguished from each other, especially important in E-mode chants.)

One could spend a lot of time trying to catch in words the essence of this freely unfolding melody. The first words, all the way to 'dulciora', are like an ornamented recitation on *F*, or between *F* and *a*. There is a brief descent to *C*, but the fixation on *F* is soon resumed, and indeed is prominent in the first verse as well. This is static, hovering, floating music to a high degree. The melody has a 'timelessness' – to use another cliché which nevertheless seems appropriate – which is suggested by the lack of clear periodic structure. The two melismas in the second verse, on 'complaceant' and 'semper', are characteristic: 'complaceant' starts with two identical strings and a reiteration or echo of the three-note group *caG*, and can be heard relatively clearly as a self-contained, 'composed' structure. But the grand final melisma on 'semper' has

←⎯⎯⎯

Ex. 1.13 (*cont.*)

Off. Iusticie Domini recte

The statutes of the Lord are right, and rejoice the heart, sweeter also than honey, and the honeycomb: by them is thy servant taught. V.1. The commandment of the Lord is pure, and giveth light unto the eyes: the fear of the Lord is clean, and endureth for ever: the judgements of the Lord are true. V.2. Let the words of my mouth, and the meditations of my heart: be alway acceptable in thy sight. (Ps. 18, phrases from vv. 9–12 and 15)

Ex. 1.14 *Alleluia Oportebat pati Christum*

Alleluia. Oportebat pati Christum
It behoved Christ to suffer these things, and so to enter into his glory. (Luke 24:26)

practically no internal repetitions. There is a lot of reiteration of *c*, often followed by a drop onto *a*, but nothing else that one can grasp easily.

The alleluia

If we now turn to an alleluia (Ex. 1.14), we can see something quite different. Firstly, the verse *Oportebat pati Christum* uses music from the *Alleluia*-section. Secondly, the melisma of the *Alleluia*-section (and therefore those parts of the verse which use the same music) has a clear repeat-structure, indicated by the letters above the staff. (The transcription is made from the Worcester manuscript, as usual, which omits the repeat of phrase 'd' found in other sources. It was customary not to write out in full the melisma-repeat at the end of the verse. Both these omissions are enclosed in square brackets.)

Interestingly, these internal repeats are a relatively late musical development. There is a small corpus of old alleluias dating back to the Carolingian period, whose musical style tends to be rather restrained and does not include the obvious repetitions of Example 1.14. But in the course of the ninth century, and indeed in subsequent centuries as well, many more were composed, often new melodies for old texts, and these later compositions very often display internal repeats.

The hymns of the Office hours

The texts of all the examples in this section so far have been prose, very often psalmic, nearly all biblical. One category of chant, however, has a verse text in strophes. This is the hymn, sung at the various hours of the Divine Office, at least outside Rome, which did not welcome poetic texts in the liturgy. Three melodies are given in Example 1.15, all transcribed from the Worcester manuscript. In each case only the first strophe of text is given.

Christe, qui lux es et dies is a very old text, mentioned in the monastic rule of Cesarius of Arles in the sixth century. Like very many hymn texts, it has four-line strophes in iambic metre, adopted for hymns at an even earlier date by St Ambrose of Milan (*c*.340–397). In the Rule of St Benedict (*c*.530) hymns are referred to as 'ambrosiani'. Whether the melody is as old as this cannot be proved. Certainly it sounds very simple, syllabic, within a range of only four notes, the last line repeating the first. It was sung at Compline, when no very special music was required.

A solis ortus cardine has a text by Sedulius, who lived in Italy in the first half of the fifth century. It is actually the start of a long poem recounting the life of Christ from his birth to his ascension into heaven, in which each strophe begins with a new letter of the alphabet, first strophe 'A', second strophe 'B', and so on (hence the term 'abecedarian' hymn). Sedulius did not write the hymn for liturgical use, but parts of it were excerpted for the Office. (Another part, beginning *Hostis Herodes impie*, was used at Epiphany.) This widely known melody ranges far more freely than the previous one. Like so many E-mode melodies it emphasizes the chain of notes *D–F–a–c*, touching on *d* as well, to which the final *E* (first and last lines) sounds like a foil. The hymn was sung at Lauds, appropriately for the text.

Sanctorum meritis is a Frankish text, sometimes attributed to Hrabanus Maurus (Abbot of Fulda, Archbishop of Mainz, *c*.780–856) but probably not by him. The classical metre here is more complicated, three asclepiads, each with twelve syllables, then a glyconic verse with only eight. One might hear the words in groups of three syllables, accented on the first, with a break in the pattern for the last line. In classical

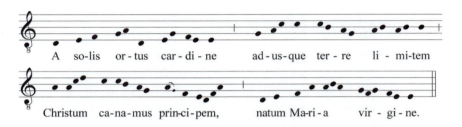

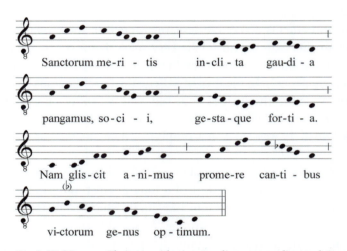

Ex. 1.15 Hymns *Christe, qui lux es, A solis ortus cardine* and *Sanctorum meritis*

Christe, qui lux es et dies
Christ, who art the light and day,
you drive away the shadows of night,
bringer of light, bearing it before you,
proclaiming the blessed light.

A solis ortus cardine
From the pole where the sun rises
to the bounds of the earth,
let us sing of Christ the Prince,
born of the Virgin Mary. (Sedulius)

metre, however, reckoning in long and short syllables, the last line is just a shorter form of the first three.

—   — | — ˘   ˘   —   — ˘   ˘   — | ˘   —
San- cto-   rum me- ri- tis in- cli- ta gau- di- a

—   — | — ˘   ˘   — | ˘   —
vi-   cto-   rum ge- nus op-   ti- mum

If the hymn were sung with notes of equal length, neither the accentual nor the classical metre would be apparent. The melody is not known except from the Worcester manuscript, and may well have been composed there. The clarity of the form, A–A–B–C, is matched by the clearly defined tonal range of each phrase. The first line uses the upper and lower segments, respectively, of the D-authentic scale, that is, *d–a*, *a–D*). The third line uses the lower and upper segments, respectively, of the F-plagal scale, that is, *C–F*, *F–c*.

The hymns of St Ambrose (at least four known hymns are usually agreed to be authentic) were intended for singing by the faithful laity, and something of this character survives in many of the thousands of hymns (and hundreds of melodies) in medieval chant books. However, they were the only such chants in the early medieval Latin liturgy.

Chants for the Ordinary of Mass (*Ordinarium missae*): Kyrie, Gloria, Credo, Sanctus and Agnus Dei

The place during Mass where these chants were sung can be seen in Table 1.1 above. They are linked by the fact that their texts remained the same from one Mass to another, but they have no common history and are musically heterogeneous. For all of them many different melodies were composed in the Middle Ages. Over fifty Gloria melodies are known from medieval manuscripts, and well over 200 melodies each for Kyrie, Sanctus and Agnus Dei. The Credo was sung to one principal melody during the Middle Ages, occasionally to others, but from the fifteenth century onward many more were composed. The musical history of the chants for the Ordinary of Mass therefore extends well into the late Middle Ages, not least because they were

←

Ex. 1.15 (*cont.*)

Sanctorum meritis

For the merits of the saints let us make a joyful noise audible to all,
O brethren, and comport ourselves with spirit,
for the heart swells with the desire to show forth in song
the best sort of victor.

frequently enhanced with trope verses. So as well as the introductory sketch given here, they will be mentioned briefly in Chapter 3 below, alongside such new types of chant as sequences and tropes.

By way of examples, the first chant in each category in the Worcester manuscript has been transcribed.

The Kyrie

The Kyrie has a symmetrical form, Kyrie × 3, Christe × 3, Kyrie × 3, which invited melodic symmetries. Example 1.16 is a good example of these patterns.

The trope verses *Clemens rector* (T1–T9) are found with this melody in many manuscripts, which was sung both with and without the extra Latin verses. If we put the trope verses on one side for the moment, we see that, within the first three Kyrie acclamations, K1= K3. The same happens in the Christe acclamations, C1 = C3. But the middle Christe has the same melody as the middle Kyrie, K2 = C2. There is some nice balancing of registers here, since K1/K3 occupies the middle range centred on *D–a*, K2/C2 is in the lower range *A–D*, while C1/C3 is in the higher range *a–d*. Every verse ends with the cadence *CCD–D*.

K1/K3 has its own internal repeat-structure, form a–a–b. There is an echo of this in K7 in a double sense, that is, there is an echo of K1/K3 and a partial repeat. This is made more pointed in K9, where an extra internal repeat is added. We could represent the form as:

K7 $a - a' - b$
K9 $a - a' - a' - b$

The trope verses use the same melody as the Kyrie, and precede each invocation. More repeats. In K7 and K9, a, a′ and b are separated from one another, to be preceded by the respective trope verse as usual. Trope verses were usually sung by a pair of soloists, the rest by the choir. The total effect is an almost hypnotic series of repeats and echoes, ringing the changes on register, but always returning to the same cadence. It sounds like some modern form of litany, and that reflects the origins of the Kyrie, as a litany chant where the invocations were followed by a long series of saints' names, all to the same simple melody. In the litany in ancient times, and still today, it was and is the people who respond. The Kyrie in Example 1.16 is obviously a sophisticated composition for soloists and choir.

The Gloria

The Gloria is a hymn of praise, not in the sense of the hymns described above but a freely assembled constellation of verses of different lengths. Some very simple Gloria

Ex. 1.16 *Kyrie Clemens rector*

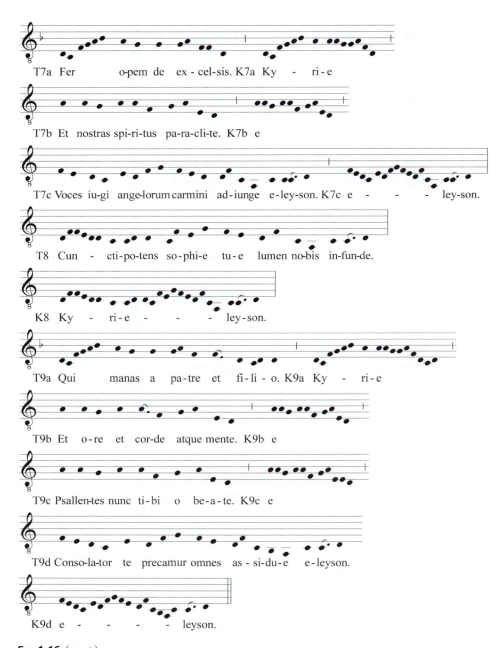

Ex. 1.16 (*cont.*)

Kyrie Clemens rector

Kyrie text: Lord, have mercy. Christ, have mercy. Lord, have mercy.

T1 Merciful and eternal ruler, immeasurable father, have mercy.

T2 And hearken unto our voices, blessed Lord.

melodies repeat the same melodic shape for each verse or pair of verses, adjusting the melody to the number of syllables required. That sounds like the technique of chanting psalms, and one of them, Gloria XV in the standard Vatican edition, is not far removed from psalm-singing. It is almost entirely syllabic. Each phrase begins *E–G–a*, the cadence at the half verse is *G–a–b–a*, and the final cadence is *G–a–G–E*. That is more or less identical to the fourth psalm tone (see above, Ex. 1.5). In the Gloria some verses use only part of the tone.

One of the shorter verses:	Quoniam tu solus sanctus	*E G a a G a G E*
One of the longer verses:	Gratis agimus tibi / propter	*E G a a G a b a*
	magnam gloriam tuam	*a a a a a G a G E*

The Gloria given in Example 1.17 is a good deal more complicated than this. The surface of the melody is moderately melismatic, sometimes with eight or more notes to a syllable. The first half of the piece concentrates on the range *D–a*, with frequent cadences *CDD* (as in the Kyrie above, Ex. 1.16). But from 'suscipe deprecationem nostram' there is a shift up to the range *a–d(e)*, with cadences correspondingly a fifth higher, *Gaa*. The most obvious melodic repetitions are indicated by superscript letters. (Note that 'b' is usually preceded by 'c', but not the first time it is used.) The higher-lying verse in the second half 'Tu solus altissimus' uses 'a' a fifth higher; this is the only obvious instance of sharing between the two halves, except for the ubiquitous cadence.

The Sanctus

The Sanctus is the choral chant between the Preface and the Canon at the Eucharist. That is, it interrupts the priest's prayers, or rather, the Preface leads directly into it, with a formula such as:

Ex. 1.16 (*cont.*)

T3 Our starry heaven, benign toward us, have mercy.

T4 Reign for ever over your people, king of the host of angels, Christ, have mercy.

T5 Equal with the Father, hear our diligent prayers, O King,

T6 Increasing our faith, do thou hasten to help these who believe in thee, have mercy.

T7 Bring help from above [O Lord], and add our voices, O Holy Spirit [E], to the continual song of the angels [have mercy].

T8 Almighty, pour the light of thy wisdom upon us.

T9 Thou who remainest with the Father and the Son [O Lord], with voice, heart and mind [E], now singing to Thee, O blessed one [E], consoler, we all pray constantly to Thee, have mercy.

Ex. 1.17 Gloria in excelsis Deo

(Priest) ... Et ideo cum Angelis et Archangelis, cum Thronis et Dominationibus, cumque omni militia caelestis exercitus, hymnum gloriae tuae canimus, sine fine dicentes:	... Therefore with Angels and Archangels, with Thrones and Dominations, and with all the army of the heavenly host, we sing the hymn of thy glory, evermore saying:
(Choir) Sanctus, sanctus, sanctus Dominus Deus Sabaoth. ...	Holy, holy, holy, Lord God of hosts. ...

(This hymn of the angels, from the vision of Isaiah [Isaiah 6:3], and comparable with the vision of John [Revelation 4:8], is also quoted in the Te Deum.)

Although not as obviously symmetrical as the Kyrie and Agnus Dei, there are possibilities for melodic correspondences between the four sections (five, counting the repeat of the Hosanna): Sanctus – Pleni – Hosanna – Benedictus – Hosanna. Example 1.18 shows an example of this. The obvious correspondences are marked with superscript letters. The melody swings gently down from *c* to *F* and back up again. So we could say that 'Pleni sunt celi et terra' and 'gloria tua' is an extended version of the opening 'Sanctus, sanctus'. The Benedictus is made up of the phrase at 'gloria tua', that is, the extended form of 'b', twice over. 'Hosanna' contains something like a melodic sequence, the five notes *c–d–e–d–c* being repeated immediately a third lower *a–b♭–c–b♭–a*.

The Agnus Dei

The Agnus Dei given in Example 1.19 is the oldest of the four melodies from the Ordinary of Mass quoted here, judging by its wide distribution in the earliest preserved manuscripts and its restricted melodic range. As given here, transcribed from the Worcester manuscript, it is enlarged by trope verses, also among the oldest

---

Ex. 1.17 (*cont.*)

Gloria in excelsis Deo

Glory be to God on high, and in earth peace, good will towards men. We praise thee, we bless thee, we worship thee, we glorify thee, we give thanks to thee for thy great glory, O Lord God, heavenly King, God the Father Almighty. O Lord, the only begotten Son Jesu Christ; O Lord God, Lamb of God, Son of the Father, that takest away the sins of the world, have mercy upon us. Thou that takest away the sins of the world, have mercy upon us. Thou that takest away the sins of the world, receive our prayer. Thou that sittest at the right hand of God the Father, have mercy upon us. For thou only art holy; thou only art the Lord; thou only, O Christ, with the Holy Ghost, art most high in the glory of God the Father. Amen.

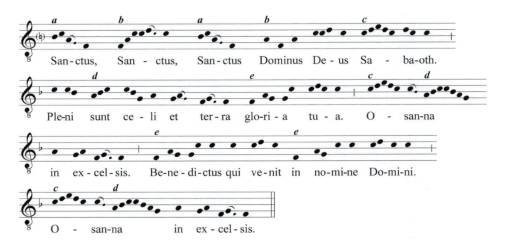

Ex. 1.18 Sanctus

Sanctus

Holy, holy, holy, Lord God of hosts, heaven and earth are full of thy glory. Hosanna in the highest. Blessed is he that cometh in the name of the Lord. Hosanna in the highest.

such verses known, though not as old as the base melody. There is one trope verse to introduce the first invocation Agnus Dei. Three more trope verses are placed in the middle of the Agnus invocations. The Agnus is sung three times, always to the same melody. (The third time, the ending changes from 'miserere nobis' to 'dona nobis pacem', though this is something first found in manuscripts from the end of the millennium onwards. The number of three invocations was also not stable in earlier times.)

   The Agnus Dei takes up the words from the latter part of the first chapter of John's gospel, which tells of John the Baptist: 'The next day John seeth Jesus coming unto him, and saith, Behold the Lamb of God, which taketh away the sin of the world' (John 1:29) This is alluded to in the introductory trope verse, *Quem Iohannes*. The

→

Ex. 1.19 (*cont.*)
HAVE MERCY UPON US.
O LAMB OF GOD: THAT TAKEST AWAY THE SINS OF THE WORLD,
T2 King of kings, joy of the angels, Christ,
HAVE MERCY UPON US.
O LAMB OF GOD: THAT TAKEST AWAY THE SINS OF THE WORLD,
T3 Light never failing, peace never ending, and mankind's redemption, O glory!
GRANT US THY PEACE.

Ex. 1.19 Trope *Quem Iohannes in deserto. Agnus Dei*

Quem Iohannes in deserto. Agnus Dei

Int. He whom John in the desert foretold, rejoicing and saying, Behold:
O LAMB OF GOD: THAT TAKEST AWAY THE SINS OF THE WORLD,
T1 Thou that sittest at the right hand of the Father, the only, the invisible King,

introduction is the only verse to touch (briefly) on the upper bb. Its cadence on E is, as it were, an imperfect one, contrasting with D in the Agnus Dei. Trope verses T1 and T3 also cadence on E, while T2 turns down to D at the last moment. Otherwise the melodic character of the trope verses matches that of the Agnus Dei closely.

At the end of Mass, the versicle *Ite missa est* is intoned by the priest to which the choir responds *Deo gratias*. Nearly 200 different melodies have been traced for this seemingly insignificant item. Even more are known for the closing versicle and response of the Office hours, V. *Benedicamus Domino*, R. *Deo gratias*. Some are shared between the two, many are borrowed from other chants, such as the Kyrie, or the melismas of Office responsories.

Further reading

Four books discuss the principal forms and styles of Gregorian chant in greater or lesser detail.

Wagner, *Gregorianische Formenlehre*, is the third and final part of his *Einführung in die gregorianischen Melodien*. The principal reference work in English for many years was Apel, *Gregorian Chant*. After thirty years this was joined by the second volume in the revised New Oxford History of Music, *The Early Middle Ages to 1300*, ed. Crocker and Hiley. The fourth reference work is Hiley, *Western Plainchant*.

There are good articles on all chant categories in both editions of *NG* and *MGG*. For all topics the on-line bibliography at www-musikwissenschaft.uni-regensburg.de/cantus may be searched by keyword.

Chapter 2

The beginnings of Gregorian chant; other rites and other sorts of chant

Gregorian chant was established as the chant repertory of the Carolingian Empire, the dominant political power in the late eighth and ninth centuries, and this ensured its survival through the rest of the Middle Ages and, in various transformations, down to the present. Which is how Gregorian chant comes to occupy a central position in this book. But it was not the only sort of medieval chant. In the Latin West other chant repertories were sung for Latin rites independent of Rome. And in the Eastern Roman Empire yet others – the chant of the rites of Jerusalem, Antioch and Constantinople, the Georgian and Armenian rites, and various types of Slavonic chant – achieved a greater or lesser degree of fixity, enabling us to study them today. Even if they cannot be described in detail in this short book, their existence should be borne in mind as a parallel to the Gregorian chant repertory dominant in the West.

2.i The Christian church in the late Roman Empire; Rome and the Franks

The early centuries

Gregorian chant is the musical element in a rich ritual, a ritual developed and performed by a stable religious community. Instability threatens or destroys the tradition, if things cannot be remembered and repeated year after year. The stable conditions in which chant could flourish were achieved in principle (if not every-where in practice) after Christianity was recognized as one of the official religions of the Roman Empire under Constantine the Great (324–37). We cannot trace particular pieces of chant back to the fourth century, but the progressive elaboration of religious ritual can clearly be observed in documents from that time onwards.

The earliest Christians were Jews, and it has often been speculated that musical elements of Jewish ritual were perpetuated in early Christian worship. While this may indeed have been the case, it is very difficult to demonstrate with concrete examples. If one could point to a particular melody or melodic pattern, used for a similar text (allowing for the difference of language) in a parallel ritual situation in the two religious traditions, all with a reasonable claim to date back to the first three or four centuries AD, one would feel to be on firm ground. But such examples are practically non-existent.

The threat to, and partial collapse of, social order in the last phase of the Roman Empire is the main reason why the record of Christian worship in the early centuries is incomplete. Under Constantine's successor, Constantius II (337–61), the heretical form of Christianity called Arianism was declared official. The next emperor, Julian the Apostate, actually favoured non-Christian cults, whereas Theodosius the Great (379–95) declared Christianity to be the official state religion in 391 and banned heathen cults. After Theodosius the unity of the empire ended. In 404 the capital in the West was moved from Rome, under threat from the Goths, to Ravenna, while Constantinople/Byzantium, refounded by Constantine in 324, maintained itself as the great capital of the Eastern Roman Empire after the end of the Western Empire in 476.

Conditions were therefore more favourable in the East, where not only Constantinople but also Antioch, Jerusalem and Alexandria were centres of great importance and developed their own forms of worship. While the Roman church was recognized as pre-eminent, its authority in matters of worship was inevitably limited. In the West, where political and social instability during the centuries of migration by Germanic tribes was greater than in the East, some essential elements of worship remained common. But there are considerable differences, in their Latin texts and their melodies, between the liturgies for which we have concrete evidence: on the one hand Rome, and on the other Milan, Benevento, the Spanish peninsula, and Gaul.

We cannot describe chanting in early Christian worship with any precision. New songs seem to have been just as important as psalms from the Old Testament. The seemingly obvious connection with Jewish worship is not straightforward. Although psalms were sung in the temple of Jerusalem before its destruction by the Romans in 70, temple worship was a very special, indeed unique, ritual, not imitated by Christians or anyone else. Meetings in the Jewish synagogue were primarily for reading, instruction and prayer, but not psalm-singing or other community singing. (Psalm-singing in the synagogue is not actually documented before the eighth century.) Christians met privately, often for a common meal at the house of a prominent member of their community, and here the eucharistic service might also be performed. So, while it would be foolish to deny the possibility that singing in Christian worship drew upon tones and patterns sung by the Jews, one cannot speak of a simple transfer of ritual practices.

The Eucharist had become separated from the evening meal by the second century, and was preceded by readings, prayers and instruction. A description of it by Justin Martyr (d. *c.*165) does not specify chanting, whereas singing still accompanied the evening gatherings. There is some evidence that psalms were beginning to be preferred to non-biblical songs by the third century, psalms being safer in a time of controversy with heretical sects. A great stimulus to psalm-singing came in the fourth century, when many Christians joined groups of ascetics in the deserts of Egypt. The chief occupation of the monks and hermits was prayer, achieved effectively by the continuous chanting of the Psalter. Those who lived in communities would not sing the Psalter in unison together. One monk would sing a psalm while the others listened, sometimes adding a refrain. This practice remained constant when monasticism spread to Europe. For example, the Rule of the Master (written near Rome *c.*520) and the Rule of St Benedict (about a decade later) organize monastic life around set times of prayer, and specify the content of each service, including a considerable number of psalms. For both, solo singing of the psalms, by single monks in order of seniority, is the norm. The community would frame the recitation by singing antiphons.

St Benedict

Most of what is known about St Benedict (*c.*480–*c.*550) is found in the second book of the *Dialogues* of St Gregory (*PL* 77, 149–430). He was born at Nursia (modern Nórcia, near Spoleto). About 500 he withdrew to a life of seclusion in a cave at Subiaco. Disciples gradually joined him and he eventually founded twelve monasteries, each with twelve monks. Internal disputes caused him to move with a small band to Montecassino in about 525, where he died. His sister Scholastica was buried with him. The Rule which he composed about 530 or 540 to direct the way of life of his monks was partly influenced by the slightly earlier anonymous 'Rule of the Master', and by other monastic rules, and it also draws upon the practice of Roman urban monasteries of the time.

The most important task of the monks is the celebration of the Divine Office, referred to as the 'Opus Dei', the work of God. (Passages from the Rule are given in text box 1.2 above.) The Rule of St Benedict was adopted by more and more communities across Europe over the next three centuries. It was brought to England *c.*690 by St Wilfrid, and established in Germany by St Boniface in the early eighth century. By the time of Charlemagne later in the century it was known everywhere. St Benedict's life, as recounted by St Gregory, became the pattern for many monastic saints, or at least their biographies.

Worship in towns and cities differed from the meditative practices of monasticism. In the fourth century a morning and an evening service became established, whose chief character was one of praise. The psalms to be sung (148–150 in the morning, 140 in the evening) did not change – quite different from the way monastic communities would repeatedly sing their way through the whole Psalter. Of great interest are the descriptions of services in Jerusalem in the early fifth century by the pilgrim Aetheria (or Egeria). Here the morning and evening services are preceded by sessions of psalm-singing by monks. (The services take place at sites connected with Christ's death and resurrection.) On the other hand, the holding of a popular nightly vigil service became common in the same period, where people sang hymns and psalms. A famous description of this practice in St Ambrose's church in Milan in 386 by St Augustine speaks of it as something recently introduced from the East. St Ambrose (d. 397) is the author of hymns in a simple style very suitable for congregational singing. (At least, their strophic texts are in iambic tetrameter, and have an attractive swing; we do not know their original melodies.) Such hymns were also taken into the monastic Office by St Benedict, though not into the Roman Office.

Mass chants

Up to the eighth century, documentary evidence gradually accumulates for the introduction of particular items in the Mass. From at least from the fourth century a psalm was sung between the two lessons, the ancestor of the gradual. Some references to it mention a congregational response. At this time in the West there is no evidence that an alleluia chant was sung after the gradual, although in the East that was often the case. Another psalm was sung at the communion.

The other chants of the Roman Mass appear later. In many cases we are uncertain of the facts because of the lack of specific references in writings of the fifth to seventh centuries, after which things become clearer. The principal witness is a detailed description from around the year 700 of how Mass was performed in Rome in the presence of the pope. This is a document known as *Ordo Romanus I*, because it is the first one presented (with fifty other such documents) in the standard modern edition by Andrieu. Each chant is mentioned in its proper place, and who sings it.

Of the introit it can only be said that it had become established by the late seventh century. The phrase 'Kyrie eleison' was certainly sung as a popular refrain in litanies at least since the fourth century (Etheria/Egeria heard it thus). Then, like the introit, it turns up at the beginning of mass in the late seventh century, but we do not know exactly how it got there. And it is sung by the choir, not by the people. It is possible that it is a relic of a procession preceding mass, a procession in which a litany had its usual place. During the introit chant, the priest and ministers would proceed to the altar, then the (remnant of) the litany would be sung.

According to the *Liber pontificalis*, the Gloria was introduced into the mass by Pope Symmachus (498–514) on Sundays and saints' days; before this (and for some time after) it was sung in the morning office.

The Alleluia, sung after the gradual as the second chant between Epistle and Gospel, seems to have attained this position at a relatively late time in the West, though this was the custom at Jerusalem by the fifth century, followed by other Eastern liturgies. The later seventh century appears to be the period of its introduction into the Roman mass. The case of the Tract is difficult. Again, the *Ordo romanus I* of around 700 has it in place after the gradual in Lent, but how long it had been sung there is unclear. It has often been viewed as very ancient, on the grounds that (i) it is sung by a soloist without any choral sections, thus preserving the character of archaic solo psalmody, and (ii) its musical style makes copious use of standard melodic phrases, regarded as a symptom of oral transmission reaching far back into the depths of time. However, there seems no clear way of deciding the question one way or the other. Finally, the offertory, too, is clearly mentioned for the first time in *Ordo Romanus I*, and we have very little idea how it reached its later medieval state, a long, ornate chant with up to four verses. To read an explanation of the complicated ceremonial surrounding the offertory is an object lesson in old Roman ritual, and a clear reason for the great length of the chants. According to *Ordo Romanus I*, the singing of the introit, offertory and communion alike continued (presumably with as many psalm verses as was required) until the pope gave a sign to terminate the performance.

The Sanctus is part of the prayers at the Eucharist coming after the preface and before the canon. The priest leads into the Sanctus by referring to the praises of the angels, whereupon the choir takes up the chant. This can be traced back to the end of the fourth century. The Agnus Dei, on the other hand, is much later. The *Liber pontificalis*, once again, is the authority for this: it says that Sergius I (687–701) introduced it into the Mass, to be sung by clergy and choir while the bread was being broken.

At Rome the Credo was not sung at Mass. The Synod of Aachen in 798, however, ordained that it be sung between Gospel and offertory throughout the Frankish realm, and this was indeed done. When the German Emperor Henry II was in Rome for his coronation he demanded that Benedict VIII include it in the Mass.

Text box 2.1 *Ordo Romanus I*

Ordo Romanus primus, as it has long been called, dating back to around 700, is the oldest of a series of documents setting out the order of Roman services, mostly made by Frankish precentors for guidance in their own services. The following extract is taken from Andrieu's edition, the translation is based on that of Atchley. It shows the pope arrived at the church where Mass is to be celebrated and the final preparations before the introit is sung. Note the strict regulations about which subdeacon is to read the Epistle and which singer is to sing the gradual. There are references to all four of the leaders of the *schola*. The introit will be sung during the solemn procession from the sacristy, where these preparations are being made, to the altar.

Then a district-subdeacon, holding the pontiff's napkin on his left arm over his unrolled planeta, goes out to the gate of the sacristy, and says, *The choir*. They answer,

I am present. Then he asks, *Who is going to sing the psalm?* and they answer, *So-and-so, and so-and-so.*

Then the subdeacon returns to the pontiff, offers him the napkin, bowing himself as low as his knees, and saying, *My lord's servants, so-and-so the district-subdeacon will read the epistle, and so-and-so of the choir will sing.*

And then no change may be made in either reader or singer: but if this should be done, the ruler of the choir (i.e. the fourth of the choir who always informs the pontiff on matters that relate to the singers) shall be excommunicated by the pontiff.

When this has been announced, the subdeacon attendant stands before the pontiff until such time as the latter shall sign to him that they may sing the psalm. As soon as the signal is given, he immediately goes out before the doors of the sacristy, and says, *Light up!*

And as soon as they have lit their candles the subdeacon attendant takes the golden censer and puts incense in it in front of the sacristy doors, so that he may walk before the pontiff.

And the ruler of the choir passes through the presbytery to the precentor or the succentor or vicesuccentor, and bowing his head to him says, *Sir, command!*

Then they rise up and pass in order before the altar, and the two rows arrange themselves in this manner: the men-singers on either side outside the doors [of the presbytery], and the children on each side within.

Immediately the precentor begins the anthem for the entry.

Cf. E. G. C. F. Atchley, *Ordo Romanus primus* (London, 1905), p. 127. Original text edn Michel Andrieu, *Les Ordines Romani du haut moyen âge*, Spicilegium sacrum Lovaniense 11, 23–4, 28–9 (Louvain, 1931–61). . . . .

Office chants

The singing of groups of psalms with antiphons, and responsories after lessons, is already organized in a clear fashion in the Rule of St Benedict (*c.*530–540) and hymns also have a regular place. The information in the Rule about the form of the Office hours is quite detailed and had been modified and enlarged only slightly by the time the first preserved manuscripts with Office chants were written. In Benedict's time the psalms would have been sung by a single monk, the rest singing their antiphon in unison. When we see the cycles of antiphons and responsories in writing, from the ninth century onward, the difference between the two is clear: the antiphon is a short chant framing the singing of a psalm, the psalms themselves being sung in sets of three to six depending on the type of institution and the Office hour in question. A responsory, on the other hand, stands by itself after a lesson.

In medieval books the responsories of the Night Office are long, elaborate melodies, whereas at the other hours a single short responsory was sung after the short reading, the *capitulum* (chapter). But were the 'great' responsories of the Night Office sung in St Benedict's time in the way we know them from medieval chant books? It is possible that the short responsory (*responsorium breve*), rather than the Great Responsory (*responsorium prolixum*) preserves something of the character of responsories in Benedict's time. A solo singer would have begun with a verse taken from, or otherwise related to, the lesson just read. The choir would repeat it. The lead singer would then sing another verse or verses of the same sort, the choir responding each time with the same verse as they had sung first time. So the idea is not to recite a complete psalm (solo), with choral antiphon. The choir 'responds' to the soloist's specially chosen verses.

Example 2.1 is a short responsory for Lauds on the First Sunday in Advent, sung to one of the popular melodies for such responsories. It would be sung after a chapter, really just a sentence, such as this: 'Hora est iam nos de somno surgere: nunc enim propior est nostra salus quam cum credidimus' (Now it is high time to awake out of sleep: for now is our salvation nearer than when we believed; Romans 13:11). The responsory takes phrases out of Psalm 79 which are appropriate for Advent, looking forward to the Lord's coming: 'Veni ad liberandum nos, Domine Deus virtutem' (Come to set us free, O Lord God of hosts; cf. v. 3 and 5) 'Ostende faciem tuam, et salvi erimus' (Shew the light of thy countenance, and we shall be whole; from v. 8.)

Ex. 2.1 Short responsory *Veni ad liberandum nos*

Short R. *Veni ad liberandum*
Come to set us free, O Lord God of hosts. Shew the light of thy countenance, and we shall be whole. (Ps. 79, cf. 3, 5, 8)

The example shows how the short responsory was sung in the later Middle Ages. But it is easy to imagine that something similar was done much earlier. The second half of the verse has the same melody as the first half of the respond. That is a cue for the choir to come in with the second half of the respond. The cantor could continue with more verses in the same vein, until he takes up the different melodic phrase at the start of the *Gloria patri*. But he gives the same cue to the choir as before, so that they can round off the whole responsory.

So far there has been mention only of the solo singing of psalms, punctuated by choral refrains. In the late eighth and early ninth centuries, however, a change in favour of the choral singing of psalms can be seen in the Carolingian church. This is when the performance of psalms by two sides of a choir, singing verses alternately, becomes the rule.

The date of the chants for Mass and Office: a caveat

As repeatedly said in the previous paragraphs, *Ordo Romanus I* of about 700 is the first firm evidence for the presence of several chants at Mass, and how they were performed (soloists, choir or whatever). Books containing cycles of chant texts are preserved from about a century later, apart from fragments whose significance is often difficult to assess. Notated books are still later. How far back into the history of the chants before 700 is it possible to see? Even if we can push back the history of the texts to, say, the sixth century (which some believe to be possible), what about their melodies? The difficulties are certainly great, and will continue to occupy experts for years to come. And yet: if it was possible for singers to remember melodies by heart from one year to the next – something beyond the experience of most of us, but obviously managed without undue difficulty in the Middle Ages – why not from one decade to the next, or one century to the next?

One more difficulty has to be faced. When the melodies become visible in musical notation at the end of the ninth century (for Mass chants, the end of the tenth century for Office chants), they appear to have come a long way from whatever simple beginnings there may have been. What we see are sophisticated melodies for a trained choir and soloists. When did they replace the simple responses which the people sang in the morning and evening services and at Mass in the early centuries? The answer is tied up with the formation of choirs such as the Roman *schola cantorum*, to which we shall turn in a moment.

Gregory I 'the Great' (590–604)

Many of the items in Mass whose history was sketched above postdate the papacy of St Gregory (Pope Gregory I, 'Gregory the Great', 590–604). Gregory was certainly a

figure of great importance in European history, an exceptional leader and adminis-
trator at a troubled period in Italy's history, and a great theologian. As any pope must
have had to do, he regulated aspects of liturgical practice. But there is no definite
evidence that he was responsible for the day-to-day singing of chant in Rome, let
alone that he could have decided exactly how each melody should be sung, or even
composed a greater or lesser number of them. Legends about his activity as a composer of chant are datable no earlier than the late eighth and ninth centuries. Their
purpose is to provide a stamp of authority and authenticity to the chant established
in the Frankish Empire, to assert its pedigree, so to speak.

Gregory was born *c.*540 of a senatorial family and as early as 573 had been made
prefect of the city. Several of the old offices of state survived, at least in name, even
though the imperial Roman power had long been replaced. Rome had been sacked
twice in the fifth century, and suffered greatly during the war between the Goths and
the Byzantines (535–53), as the Eastern emperor Justinian tried to win back Western
Europe. Then came the next invasion of another Germanic tribe, the Lombards,
who reached Italy from Scandinavia in 563 and established a number of more or less
independent duchies in north Italy, but also Spoleto and Benevento in the south,
while the Byzantines held on to the Exarchate of Ravenna, the duchies of Rome and
Naples, the southern extremes of Italy, and Sicily. Through all this the papacy persisted as a rallying point for political and social order as well as religion, in the case
of religion complicated by the fact that both the Goths and the Lombards supported
the Arian heresy. Since Byzantine power was insecure, the papacy had to take the
lead politically. The Lombard invasion had effectively destroyed most of monastic life in Italy outside Rome. Gregory founded his own monastery of St Andrew
on the Celian Hill, and here monks from the monastery at Montecassino, which
St Benedict had founded, found refuge. He founded six others in Sicily. He entered
his own monastery as a monk *c.*573, but was called back into public life to be, first, one
of the seven deacons of Rome (the group from which future popes were commonly
elected), then representative at the Byzantine court. About 585 he returned to Rome
and his monastery, where he was abbot. Five years later he became pope himself.

Gregory's political and administrative work was crucial to the survival of the
church in general, and the papacy and monasticism in particular. Gregory was also
the last of the great 'doctors' of the church. The extent to which he was concerned with
liturgical matters, including chant, is much more difficult to assess. He laid down
that deacons should be appointed not for their singing voices but for the ability to
preach and care for souls. He regulated the use of the acclamation 'Alleluia' as a suffix
to chants in the Easter season, and countenanced the singing of the Kyrie with Latin
verses on festal days, while on weekdays the Greek petitions alone should be sung.

In none of Gregory's writings is there a reference to a special choir for the singing
of chant. Later tradition would credit him with the founding of a *schola cantorum*
(song-school), but there is no evidence of such an institution until later in the

seventh century, when Sergius I (pope 687–701) is said to have been educated there. A document of the late seventh century about the activities of a number of popes and abbots in Rome credits Gregory with the 'edition' of chants for the church year ('cantum anni circoli nobili edidit'). Unfortunately the same is said of several other figures as well, and Gregory is not singled out as particularly important in this respect. On the other hand, a number of proper prayers for Mass are reckoned to be by him, and his homilies were drawn upon regularly for the Nocturns of the Night Office.

The *schola cantorum*

At the beginning of this chapter the importance of a stable environment for the learning, performance and transmission of chant was stressed. Monasteries, Benedictine or otherwise, provided such an environment. In fact they were essential not only for the maintenance of religious worship but also for the preservation of literacy in the West. Very few other stable communities existed which had an interest in preserving knowledge in written form, religious knowledge first and foremost, of course, but also texts from classical antiquity. Another institution which played a leading role as far as chant was concerned was the Roman *schola cantorum*, to which ecclesiastical authorities elsewhere might look for guidance. What do we know of this institution?

As mentioned above, the earliest definite news that a *schola cantorum* existed to serve the papal liturgy refers to the education of the future pope Sergius I (687–701). It seems possible that it was the result of new organizational measures in many branches of the papal administration taken after the middle of the seventh century. *Ordo Romanus I* and later Roman ordinals refer to four leading members of the *schola*, of whom the *primus* or *primicerius* is the administrative head, the *quartus* something like the musical director. There seem to have been just seven adults, all subdeacons, and an uncertain number of children. The *schola* was in fact not just a choir but an institution where gifted children from the lower classes, often orphans, would receive an education fitting them for the service of the church, either in the papal entourage at the Lateran or in the city. (Children from aristocratic families would go straight into the papal entourage.) The extent of their musical gifts can hardly be assessed, but from contemporary documents it is clear that they would have to master the Psalter, enough to distinguish those of quick intelligence. Today musical ability and above-average intelligence are not necessarily regarded as going hand in hand. In the Middle Ages, however, schools attached to cathedrals and collegiate churches always had a double function: performance of the liturgy and an education for service in church or state. Monasteries were much less important for the education of children, whose numbers were usually very restricted, or there were none at all. The Roman *schola cantorum* was something of a special case, but schools with a similar function and organization were of great importance for the cultivation of sacred music. In Rome, both Sergius I, as already related, and Sergius II (844–7) rose through the *schola cantorum* to the highest office of all.

The pope celebrated Mass in different churches week by week, instead of staying in the Lateran. As many as fifty churches were involved in the course of the year. The *schola*, too, was naturally involved in this 'stational liturgy', whereby each church was a 'statio'. At a practical level, the system helped hold together very many churches of the enormous city under the wing of the papacy out on the east side. When Roman service books were copied in Francia, the names of the stational churches were preserved in the subheadings for each Mass, although as an instruction to be followed literally they no longer had any significance.

Ireland and England

When in 596 St Gregory sent missionaries to England, to re-establish Christianity in lands overrun by the pagan Angles and Saxons, he chose as their leader Augustine, prior of his own monastery of St Andrew. Among those who followed later in the eighth century was John, archcantor of St Peter's and abbot of the monastery of St Martin, who came to Northumbria in 680. The winning of England for Christianity proceeded along more than one path, however. In the interval between the Roman withdrawal from Britain around 400 and the arrival of the Jutes, Angles and Saxons in the middle of the fifth century, Palladius from Gaul and especially the Briton St Patrick had worked as missionaries in Ireland. Here Christianity flourished while in England it was obliterated. Irish Christianity then spread to south-west Scotland. Its most influential centre there was the monastery on the island of Iona, founded in 563 by St Columba (Colum Cille).

Such was the strength of Irish monasticism that a host of heroic missionaries travelled across Europe in the later sixth and seventh centuries, still famous in the cities where they ended their days, for example Kilian in Würzburg and Virgil in Salzburg. Most famous of all was Columban (*c*.543–615), who came from Bangor with twelve companions to France in 591 or 592 and travelled across to Germany and down into Italy, founding monasteries as he went: Annegray, Luxeuil, Fontaines – he composed a 'Rule' to regulate life in them – leaving Gallus at a place south of Lake Constance where another famous monastery was later to rise, and Bobbio in the Appennines, where he died.

Not long after this, Oswald Prince of Northumbria was converted to Christianity while in exile on Iona. On winning his kingdom in battle he invited St Aidan to Northumbria, giving him the island of Lindisfarne for a monastery. Christianity in Northumbria flourished in a remarkable way, especially in the twin monasteries at the mouth of the Tyne and the Wear, founded by Benedict Biscop, St Peter at Wearmouth in 674 and St Paul at Jarrow in 682. The eventual 'victory' of the

Christianity which had come from Rome over that from Ireland had happened at the Synod of Whitby in 664, when the Roman way of calculating the date of Easter was settled upon. Despite the distances and difficulties of travel across Europe, the English church maintained close relations with Rome. Bishop Wilfrid of York (634–709), educated at Lindisfarne, travelled three times to Rome, Benedict Biscop six times, bringing back from his fifth journey 'innumerabilem librorum omnis generis copiam' (an innumerable quantity of books of all sorts). Those are the words of Bede (*c.*673–735), Jarrow's most famous scholar.

There is a possibility that the English way of performing the liturgy, learned from Rome, may have had influence in Carolingian France, for soon it was the turn of the English church to send missionaries to the mainland of Europe, such as Willibrord of Northumbria (658–739), 'apostle of the Frisians', founder of the church of Utrecht and the monastery of Echternach; and Boniface (Wynfrith) of Crediton (680–754), 'apostle of Germany', who worked at first with Willibrord. Boniface was called to Rome in 722, where Gregory II (715–31) approved his mission. He established the faith in Bavaria, Thuringia and Hesse, and became Archbishop of Mainz before suffering a martyr's death in his old age back in Frisia. Even more interestingly, it was to an English scholar, Alcuin (*c.*735–804), master of the cathedral school in York, that Charlemagne turned for his chief advisor in religious and educational matters. The two had met in Parma in 781. At the same time it should be recollected that the English monasteries probably did not follow the Benedictine form of the Office hours. The specifically Benedictine form of monasticism made its way rather slowly across Europe, until the Carolingian preference for it made its universal adoption certain.

The Franks

And so to the Frankish dynasty of the Carolingians. The eighth century was an unhappy one for the papacy. Relations with Byzantium were often poor. Martin I (649–55) was deposed in 653 and died a prisoner in Todi. Gregory II opposed the iconoclastic party of Emperor Leo III ('the Isaurian'). When Byzantium became too weak to protect Rome against the Lombards, Stephen III (752–7) turned to the new power in Gaul, the Franks, for aid.

The Franks were important allies. Their leader Clovis (482–511) had been baptized a Catholic Christian in Rheims on Christmas Day in 497 or 498. Their power expanded throughout the next two centuries, driving the Visigoths out of south-west France and conquering what is now south-west Germany. In 732 Charles Martel beat the invading Arabs and stopped their northward expansion out of Spain. In 759 Pepin drove them out of their stronghold in Narbonne. Charlemagne would eventually subdue the Saxons in north-west Germany as well.

Pepin became first Frankish king of the new Carolingian dynasty (751–68) after Pope Zacharias (741–52) had given his permission for the deposition of the last Merovingian king. Pepin was crowned in Soissons by Boniface, acting as papal legate. A second coronation followed in St Denis, when Pope Stephen came to France in 754 and performed the ceremony himself. Pepin invaded Italy, destroyed Lombard power, re-established the Duchy of Rome and the Exarchate of Ravenna, now placed under papal, not Byzantine, authority.

Pope Hadrian I (772–95) followed the example of Stephen by calling upon the help of Pepin's son Charlemagne. Charlemagne campaigned twice as far as Rome in the 780s, and was finally crowned Emperor by Leo III (795–816) on Christmas Day 800.

These struggles for power in Europe are significant for the subject of this book to the extent that they affected the stability of the church and the performance of the liturgy. It was crucially important that both Pepin and Charlemagne earnestly desired the establishment of correct liturgical practice in the Roman way. We know of specific contacts which would have furthered their purpose. Stephen stayed more than half a year in Francia in 753–4, though apparently the Roman *schola* did not accompany him. Pepin's brother, Bishop Remigius (or Remedius) of Rouen, went to Rome in 760 to ask for a teacher of chant, and the *secundus scholae* Simeon was sent north, with an 'antiphonale' and a 'responsale', while Rouen monks learned in Rome under the *primus scholae* George. Bishop Chrodegang of Metz (d. 766) is said to have introduced the 'cantilena Romana' in his church.

The overall situation in the early ninth century

Taking stock of the situation in the early ninth century, when the first surviving books with the texts of chants for Mass were written, we can see the following.

In Rome, liturgical practice has been established from the later seventh century on the firm footing of a *schola cantorum*. But Roman practice is not universally followed in Italy, as we know from the different texts and melodies preserved, respectively, in books from Milan in the north and Benevento in the south. Much less would we expect to find it elsewhere in Europe. The church which stabilized in England in the seventh and eighth centuries was concerned to follow Roman use, proud of its Roman heritage. English missionaries were influential in Germany, and Alcuin of York became Charlemagne's liturgical advisor. Alas, the plundering of Lindisfarne by the Northmen in 793 marked the start of a disastrous period for the English church. Benedictine monasticism may have been almost completely wiped out. It was not until the later tenth century that a full revival was accomplished, as witness the production of liturgical books, including chant manuscripts.

The outlines of the church services in Gaul before the time of Pepin are reasonably well known, and it is clear that Roman practice was not followed here either. When the Roman liturgy displaced the Gallican, the old chant, whatever it was, appears to have been lost, for the displacement happened before the advent of musical notation. And yet, it has been speculated that the Franks left their imprint on the Roman chants, that is, the musical language of the melodies they eventually notated in the ninth century was like a strong Frankish dialect of the Roman language of chant. This matter will have to be taken up in a moment, in section 2.ii.

The establishment of Roman or Frankish-Roman liturgy and chant in Germany, still partly pagan in the eighth century, is one of the great success stories of the ninth century. One of the oldest of all manuscripts with chant notation, written *c.*830, comes from Regensburg in Bavaria. The manuscripts from St Gall (south of Lake Constance) from the end of the ninth century onwards are some of the most valuable of all sources preserved.

Spain has hardly been mentioned. During the Visigothic period in the sixth and seventh centuries, a Latin liturgy distinct from the Roman (and Gallican) developed and survived intact under the Arab domination of the ninth to eleventh centuries. It was a liturgy related to other Latin liturgies such as the Roman, but different in several formal respects, with different texts and different melodies. The melodies reached the stage of being notated with neumes, but not on the staff. By one of the great ironies of music history, staff notation reached Spain in the wake of the Christian reconquest, but was used, not for the old Spanish (or Mozarabic) chant, but for the Roman chant which the conquerors brought with them. Practically all the hundreds of melodies of old Spanish chant which we can see in neumes remain untranscribable.

One other Latin liturgy was lost long before this. After the Vandal conquest of North Africa in the fifth century, the African coast and southern Spain were regained by the Byzantines in 535. But the spread of Islam at the end of the seventh century took North Africa definitively out of the Christian orbit.

Questions about what the Franks learned

All this time we have been talking about liturgies and liturgical practice whose melodies were not yet notated. There is still, chronologically speaking, a large gap, between the early ninth century just reached and the date of the earliest surviving notated books with chant for the whole year. At this point, therefore, some very interesting questions arise:

- Is the chant in the earliest notated books of about 900 the same as what the Franks learned in the period of close contact with Rome, that is, the late eighth and early ninth centuries?
- Did the Franks learn exactly what was sung in Rome, or did they (consciously or unconsciously) adapt it to their previous way of singing, perhaps some sort of old 'Gallican' chant?

- Even if the Gregorian chant in the books from around 900 really is Roman, and therefore what the Franks learned around 800, how much earlier can it be assumed to have been sung this way? At the time of *Ordo Romanus I* about 700? In the time of Gregory the Great about 600?

Chronological coordinates suggest some possible answers. One is the date of the Latin text being sung, for different versions of the Latin can to some extent be dated. Another is the introduction of particular feast days into the calendar, or the rearranging of the annual cycle in some other way (like the introduction by Gregory II, 715–31, of Masses on the Thursdays in Lent).

Ultimately, however, a great deal depends on the practical considerations mentioned above: in the absence of musical notation, everything depends on the ability of singers and a well-functioning institutional environment which will enable the chant to be learned and performed year after year. It is therefore time to think about how the chant was learned and what features of an orally transmitted repertory it shows.

The whole matter is made much more complicated (and interesting!) by the existence of a complete year's cycle of chants for both Mass and Office in a quite different chant dialect in a small number of Roman manuscripts. This is usually called 'Old Roman chant', though it is debatable how old it actually is. It is the *only* chant recorded in manuscripts written in Rome itself, starting in the eleventh and ending in the thirteenth century. After that, Roman manuscripts have only 'Gregorian' chant. In the next section, therefore, the relationship between the Gregorian and Old Roman chant has to be assessed, with a side look at possible Gallican elements in Gregorian chant.

Gregory again

A final curiosity which should be mentioned is the legend that St Gregory 'composed' or 'codified' the chant which is named after him (also providing a title for this book). This seems to have gathered strength in the eighth century. The English were proud of the fact that their liturgical practices had come directly from St Gregory, through the missionary he had sent, Augustine. But they did not go as far as to claim that Gregory had composed the chant. Bede's *Historia ecclesiastica gentis Anglorum* (History of the English Church and People), completed in 731, does not refer to Gregory in this way, nor does a biography written between 704 and 714 by a monk of Whitby. The monk recounts the story of a dove, symbol of divine inspiration, perched on Gregory's shoulder as he composes his commentary on Ezekiel. The Ezekiel commentary would later be transformed into a chant book with neumes, most clearly visible in the frontispiece in the antiphoner of Hartker of St Gall, written around the year 1000.

Yet Egbert, Bishop of York from 732, after journeying to Rome to obtain the *pallium*, the cloak of office, reported seeing 'blessed' Gregory's antiphoner and missal. And late eighth-century fragments of an antiphoner now in Lucca are prefaced by a long verse prologue which attributes the contents of the chant book to Gregory. The first lines turn up in two other manuscripts with the chant texts for Mass, from the early ninth century, and one more from the end of the eighth century has a brief attribution. Manuscript M in the edition by Hesbert:

> *Gregorius praesul   meritis et nomine dignus*
> *unde genus ducit   summum conscendit honorem*
> *qui renovans monumenta patrumque priorum*
> *tum conposuit hunc libellum musicae artis*
> *scholae cantorum.*

> [Gregory, in deeds and in name a worthy leader,
> who has ascended to the highest honour at the place where his ancestors lived,
> who, renewing the monuments (memorials) of the fathers of old,
> then composed this book of musical art
> of/for the *schola cantorum*.]

Manuscript B:

> *In Dei nomen incipit antefonarius ordinatus a sancto Gregorio per circulum anni.*
> [In the name of God here begins the antiphoner for the year's cycle ordered by St
>   Gregory.]

At about the same time as the *Gregorius praesul* prologue, Paul Warnefrid (d.799), who taught at Charlemagne's court, composed a life of St Gregory which does not say anything about his liturgical, let alone musical activity. The biography by John Hymmonides written in 872–3, however, has a great deal to say about these things. 'The most studious Gregory very usefully compiled an antiphoner-cento of chants.' He founded a song school with two dwellings, one by the Lateran palace and one by St Peter's. Visitors to the Lateran can still see the antiphoner, his couch and his *flagellum* (which might be a whip to impress his teaching on pupils, but might also be his *ferula*, his staff of office). Gregory was often ill, and once wrote to the patriarch of Alexandria saying that he sometimes scarcely had strength to rise from his bed to celebrate a Mass lasting three hours on high festivals.

John goes on to tell of the reception of Gregorian chant in other lands, in Germany and Gaul (where the singers cannot perform it properly), and in England. Other writers relate what a close personal interest Charlemagne took in singing chant, and John confirms this, and that Metz was established as a chant centre. One detail is particularly intriguing. The Roman singers are accused by the Franks of singing incorrectly. In response, the Romans 'probably showed the authentic antiphoner' – 'authenticum antiphonarium probabiliter ostentarent'. That is an odd way of putting it. It almost sounds as if the book had musical notation, which would certainly have decided the matter. But it is more likely that it was a question of which version of the Latin text, or even which piece to sing (which verse for a gradual or responsory, perhaps). The story is at least indicative of the difficulties which the Frankish singers must have faced in learning the Roman chant, of 'getting back to the source' as Charlemagne put it: 'ad perennis fontis necesse est fluenta principalia recurramus'.

The Franks saw things differently. Notker of St Gall – strictly speaking, an Alemannian, writing in East Francia after the division of the empire – wrote a biography of Charlemagne, at the request of Emperor Charles III 'the Fat' after the latter had visited St Gall in 883. In it he says that twelve Roman singers were sent to teach the Franks but deliberately tried to sow confusion. The embarrassed pope then suggested that Frankish singers come to Rome to listen secretly to the singing of the papal choir. Which they did, and were later able to teach chant at the royal palace at Aachen and at Metz. Notker does not, incidentally, refer to the chant as 'Gregorian'.

Further reading

On the earliest period, the article by McKinnon, 'Christian Church, Music of the Early' in *NG2* is a standard guide, supported by the same author's collection of texts in translation, *Music in Early Christian Literature*. There is a handy introduction to the early development of the liturgy by Bradshaw, *Early Christian Worship*. Jeffery, 'Jerusalem and Rome', points out parallels and divergences in the early establishment of liturgical practices. Dyer has written several excellent articles on psalm-singing in the early period, including 'Monastic Psalmody of the Middle Ages', 'The Singing of Psalms in the Early-Medieval Office', and 'The Desert, the City and Psalmody in the Later Fourth Century'. Bailey's book *Antiphon and Psalm in the Ambrosian Office*, although concerned especially with the Ambrosian chant of Milan, contains a thorough discussion of early psalmody.

The situation in Rome is again elucidated by Dyer in two articles, 'The Schola Cantorum and its Roman Milieu in the Early Middle Ages', and 'Prolegomena to a History of Music and Liturgy at Rome in the Middle Ages'. See also Dyer's description of the Roman offertory ceremony in 'The Roman Offertory'. Dyer's articles 'Gregor I.' and 'Schola cantorum' in the German encyclopaedia *Die Musik in Geschichte und Gegenwart*, are also valuable.

The contrasting accounts of John the Deacon and Notker about the learning of Roman chant by the Franks are translated in Strunk, *Source Readings*, revised edn 1998, pp. 178 and 181.

Rankin, 'Carolingian Music', is a particularly illuminating summary of the Carolingian achievement.

See also Hiley, *Western Plainchant*, chs. VI–VII.

2.ii Learning chant in an oral culture, establishing models for performance, centres of excellence; Old Roman and Gregorian chant

The Roman *schola cantorum* and comparable institutions in Milan and Toledo, and then in the Frankish empire and elsewhere, were 'centres of excellence' (to coin the fashionable term), where models for performance were established. There is a lot of controversy about exactly when musical notation was first used to support the teaching and transmission of chant. Some of the arguments are rehearsed in section 4.iii below. Were there notated books when Roman singers were teaching the Franks? The balance of the available evidence seems to argue against this possibility. The books with the texts of chants for Mass which have survived from the late eighth and early ninth centuries do not have any notation. It is true that we must have lost many, but not only are those notated books which have survived later in date, they also have different sorts of music script, as if there were no authoritative central source for them to copy. Furthermore, early notations are 'adiastematic', that is, they do not indicate the pitches of notes. The signs used, known as neumes, give precise information about the number of notes to be sung to a syllable, the rise and fall of the melody, and, at least in some manuscripts, some indications of rhythm and stress. But the exact pitches still had to be learned by heart. Pitch-notation was used only from the eleventh century (in a few places) or twelfth century onward. And even then, with a chant book with staff notation to hand, a cantor would still be teaching his choir to sing from memory, something which they continued to do for several centuries to come. So the question which has to be discussed now is not when or where notation was first used but how chant might be learned and performed from memory. How did the system work? Can we see features of chant which are especially well adapted to making it work?

In section 1.v I have stated the numbers of chants sung during the year in their various categories, and on p. 223 below there are more statistics. Whatever one's attitude to statistics, it is clear that a great deal of music was involved. Some environmental factors, as we could call them, would have made it easier to learn than we might at first imagine. Life in an ecclesiastical institution proceeded with a well-regulated rhythm free of many of the distractions which plague modern life and disturb concentration of the mind. Our modern experience of music is also far more variegated, not to say chaotic, than that of the singer in a medieval choir. As to the melodies themselves, very many follow well-established patterns which make them easy to remember as individuals. The examples in section 1.v above showed this in several different cases. For instance, there were antiphons in melodic families (Ex. 1.7). We can imagine the lead singer chanting the initial phrase, and the rest of the melody coming easily to the minds of the choir, for there were so many other antiphons which 'went like that', so to speak. Then there were more complicated, even virtuosic, melodies (Exx. 1.9–10). Many of their florid cadences, and quite often whole phrases, turn up repeatedly in different pieces. Singing the 600 or 800 responsories during the year does not therefore involve learning so many completely different pieces. The goal, the path to be followed, and many of the steps along the way, are established by convention. If the conventions are properly learned, they make it possible to sing a large number of pieces going the same way.

However, it has to be said that very many chants do not fall so conveniently into melodic families, or do not use standard melodic phrases following a conventional path. Frere's analysis of responsories managed to assign over 450 items to melodic groups. Sometimes the affiliations between the melodies were very loose, but still, at least a few phrases would recur. But this still left over 300 melodies unaccounted for. Many of them are not, of course, totally dissimilar from those in the groups, but for the medieval singer there was less here which might be drawn from ingrained knowledge of how responsories of a particular type normally went. Many introits, communions and especially offertories, must have been learned as individual melodies. It is true that these pieces, too, have a stock of short turns of phrase, melodic cells (but hardly more than that), which turn up in more than one chant. Their melodic contours will be partly determined by their tonality, the mode they are in. It is clear that some phrases in F-mode, for example, would sound out of place in G-mode: not all, but enough to narrow the field of possibilities as the singer's memory, working unconsciously, guides him through the chant.

How often did the choirboy have to hear a piece before he could repeat it faultlessly, in the service shortly afterwards, or next day, next week, next year? What about the trained adult singer? Once? three times? a dozen times? We should like to know more about this, beyond the obvious fact that it worked.

Although the amount of music was enormous, we should not exaggerate it. The duties of singing the more difficult pieces were shared. The evidence for this at least from secular churches is fairly extensive. The ordinals (instruction books about how to perform the liturgy) for the church of Salisbury give detailed information about the compilation of the *tabula*, a table drawn up each week where the duties of individual singers were specified. Not everyone sang everything.

There is unfortunately no space here to rehearse theories of how memory functions. In the performance of chant two principal processes were at work, sometimes more of the one, sometimes more of the other. Many pieces would be learned as distinct tunes with little connection to other chants. Many others would be more like a string of well-known phrases. 'String' is the operative word, rather than 'conglomeration' or 'jumble', since the phrases would not combine in any old order but had to make musical sense, reflecting the structure of the text being sung. In many instances, one phrase would act as a cue for the next.

The last few decades have witnessed much discussion about the capabilities of oral tradition and the point at which musical writing began to play an essential role in ensuring that chants were learned and passed on in a uniform state. When chant books with the year's cycle of chants for the Proper of Mass appear at the end of the ninth century, they (and their successors) show great uniformity. Yet differences there are. How did they arise? One argument would be that chant was transmitted orally right up into the ninth century, notated more and more often from the late ninth century onward, but not necessarily from written exemplars, more likely from the cantor's memory. He would be notating what he had learned, not copying from a book. The differences between manuscripts would then come from the slight divergencies of memory, or deliberate preferences of the cantor in question, acting in good faith, of course, believing he knew what St Gregory would have wanted. The other view is that the uniformity can only be explained by the existence of written exemplars. At the time when the Franks made a special effort to learn Roman chant in the late eighth and ninth centuries, they would have invented a musical notation to help the process and ensure uniformity across the realm. The success of the project is then seen in the books that have survived from a century later.

Since we cannot reproduce the conditions of learning and performing chant 1,200 years ago, parallels have been drawn with other orally transmitted literatures or bodies of chant. One of the catalysts of the debate was the parallel drawn by Leo Treitler between chant and Homeric poetry and a modern counterpart, Serbian epic poetry passed on orally from singer to singer. This forced chant historians to confront questions about the age and condition of the chants notated in the oldest books, the legend of Gregory, and the role of musical notation, and to take cognizance of modern writing on the way memory functions in preserving and helping a performer re-create texts or music. The age of oral transmission of Gregorian chant is long past, but other types of chants still preserve this method. The following passage comes at the start of an article about one of these types of chant, and (as the authors no doubt intended) paints a picture very like what we may imagine to have been the situation in Carolingian song schools:

> Of all the musical traditions in the world among which fruitful comparisons with medieval European chant might be made, the chant tradition of the Ethiopian Orthodox Church promises to be especially informative. In Ethiopia one can

actually witness many of the same processes of oral and written transmission as were or may have been active in medieval Europe. Music and literacy are taught in a single curriculum in ecclesiastical schools. Future singers begin to acquire the repertory by memorising chants that serve both as models for whole melodies and as the sources of the melodic phrases linked to individual notational signs. At a later stage of training each one copies out a complete notated manuscript on parchment using medieval scribal techniques. But these manuscripts are used primarily for study purposes; during liturgical celebrations the chants are performed from memory without books, as seems originally to have been the case also with Gregorian and Byzantine chant. Finally, singers learn to improvise sung liturgical poetry according to a structured system of rules. (Shelemay, Jeffery and Monson, p. 55).

It is worth pointing out that the Ethiopian repertory of standard phrases used for multiple texts is just as large as the Gregorian.

Two ways of singing a responsory: Old Roman and Gregorian

To give some point to the theoretical discussion, a set of examples now follows. In Example 2.2 there are transcriptions of two responds (not the verses), *Magi veniunt ab oriente* and *Omnes de Saba*, both for Epiphany. They stand close together in chant books and it would be fairly natural for them to use the same mode and the same standard phrases. This is what we find in the transcriptions A and B. Both responsories have the same opening phrase, here labelled 'O'. The next line in both responsories ends on *G* but the approaches are different. However, the third line is the same ('g3') apart from a few notes at the start. The first respond *Magi veniunt* then has two lines ('cuius stellam' and 'et venimus') which do not correspond to anything in the shorter *Omnes de Saba*. But both responds end with the same line, 'G4', the fourth phrase to end on *G*. These responds are good examples of a melodic group in mode 8 which has a common stock of phrases adaptable for different texts. We can easily imagine the singer learning the model to which these responds correspond and the appropriate melodic phrases.

Perhaps it will have been noticed how smooth the melodic contours are. There are very few leaps and a great deal of wavy motion within a narrow range. This is typical of what is known as Old Roman chant. The transcriptions are made from one of only two antiphoners to survive which contain Old Roman Office chants, written in Rome in the twelfth century. *We do not have any Gregorian chant manuscripts from Rome itself before the late thirteenth century.*

After that come the Gregorian versions of these two responds, transcriptions C and D. Transcription C is also in mode 8, and uses standard Gregorian phrases appropriate for that mode. The labels given to the phrases here are borrowed from the analysis by Frere (compare Ex. 1.9 and the discussion above). There are some general similarities between the Old Roman and Gregorian versions, although the surface detail is different. The range of the individual phrases is similar, for example when both versions go up to *cd* at 'ubi est' and down into the lower tessitura before the final phrase. Note that the texts are not quite the same: 'inquirentes' Roman, 'querentes' Gregorian; and the magi arrive 'cum muneribus' in the Roman version but not in the Gregorian.

But transcription D shows something different. The Gregorian melody is in the higher G mode, mode 7. It uses very little standard melodic material. There is no similarity between the Roman and Gregorian melodies.

What has happened? Here we have a Roman version of the twelfth century, and a Gregorian one of the tenth (transcribed from a manuscript of the thirteenth, it is true, but comparison with early sources shows no changes). One explanation might be that the Frankish singers learned the Roman melodies. They made a fair shot at A, transforming it into their own dialect in the process. For some reason they failed to learn B and invented their own melody, not using much standard melodic material at all. But there is another way of seeing it. The Gregorian version, with the older manuscript tradition, might be what the Franks heard in the eighth–ninth centuries. Two centuries later, the Roman way of singing had become less sharply contoured, with more passing notes to fill in leaps, more undulation around the structural tones, so that these are in fact less audible. And instead of maintaining the rather unusual mode 7 melody of *Omnes de Saba* (D) they fell back on standard mode-8 phrases.

A lot of work in analysing and comparing the two versions has still to be done, but some important points should have become clear. Both Gregorian and Old Roman chants make use of standard melodies and typical phrases. They operate in the same way, and differ not in basic principles and procedures but in their surface detail. For example, both use a number of standard antiphon melodies. In many cases these are more or less the same melodies, since in these simple tunes there is no room for the florid surface detail where Old Roman and Gregorian diverge so markedly. There are several areas where the Old Roman melodies rely more on common melodic formulae than the Gregorian. Some introits, for example, have the same melody in the Old Roman manuscripts, but diverge in the Gregorian. Is this a case of the Gregorian (Frankish) singers varying what had been a uniform original, or the Roman singers falling back onto the common coin of introit melody? Another more striking case is that of the verses of the Old Roman offertories. The Gregorian pieces are wonderful and unique, the Old Roman ones use a very restricted set of formulae. (The verses are sung in one of only two ways: either a two-phrase musical formula is sung as many times as necessary to accommodate the text; or a decorated recitation using the figure *bca–bca–bca* . . . etc. is used.) Did the Frankish singers take

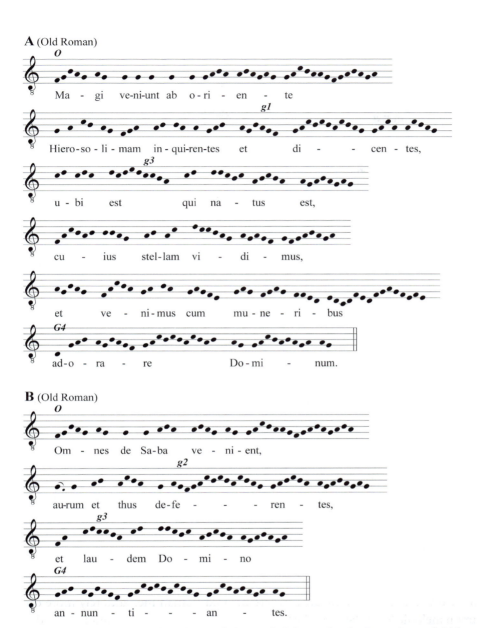

Ex. 2.2 Responsories *Magi veniunt* and *Omnes de Saba venient* in Gregorian and Old Roman versions

R. *Magi veniunt ab oriente*

There came wise men from the east to Jerusalem, inquiring and saying, Where is he that is born? whose star we have seen, and we are come [with gifts] to worship the Lord. (cf. Matt. 2:1–2)

R. *Omnes de Saba venient*

All they from Sheba shall come: they shall bring gold and incense; and they shall shew forth the praises of the Lord. (Isaiah 60:6)

C (Gregorian)

Oa

Ma - gi   ve - ni-unt ab   o - ri - en-te

G5

Ie-ro-so - limamque-ren - tes et di - cen - tes,

F5

u - bi   est   qui   na - tus   est,   cu - ius stellam vi - di - mus,

G5

et   ve-ni - mus ad - o - ra-re   Do-mi - num.

D (Gregorian)

(cf. D2)

Om - nes   de Sa-ba   ve - ni - ent,

(cf. F5)

au - rum   et thus   de - fe - ren - tes,

Ft

et   laudem Do - mi - no   an-nun - ti - an - tes.

Ex. 2.2 (*cont.*)

flight on their own at this point, leaving the 'original' Roman melody far below. Or did the Roman tradition somehow decay and resort to simpler ways of dealing with the multiple verses?

Perhaps my choice of epithets implies a preference for the idea that the Gregorian version best represents the chant learned by the Franks from the Romans in the eighth–ninth centuries, and that the Old Roman melodies are the result of two more centuries of oral transmission. But other factors may also have to be taken into consideration. There are other Italian chant repertories with a florid surface comparable with that of Old Roman chant: the Ambrosian chant of Milan and the Beneventan chant of south Italy. We know far too little of Mozarabic (old Spanish) chant and even less of Gallican. But as far as we can tell, they are both less florid than the Italian repertories. Is it possible that the Franks 'translated' the Roman melodies into their own more rugged dialect?

Text box 2.2 Singing from memory and singing from books

Singing from memory was the norm for the performance of the liturgy. The *cantatorium* borne by the cantor when he sungs the gradual, in the description of *Ordo Romanus I*, is not a score from which he reads the notes but a demonstration that he sings texts approved by authority.

The change to singing from books came at different times in different churches. Harrison (102–3) cites instances where they were first used in choir in England in the fourteenth century. The arrangement at the collegiate church of Ottery St Mary (refounded in 1337) was as follows:

Three was to be the usual number to sing from one book, and the statutes provided for three Antiphonals, three Psalters and three Graduals on each side of the choir, a book at the choir-step with the music to be sung there, and one in mid-choir for the rulers at Mass. Every canon and vicar was to have a Processional, so that they should not be inconvenienced by having to share a book when singing in procession. At Matins there were to be three candles on each side (the canons beng obliged to provide their own), but on simple feasts and ferias the boys and secondaries were to sing the Invitatory and the *Venite* and the boys were to sing the beginning of the respond and its verse 'without book or light'.

Frank L. Harrison, *Music in Medieval Britain*, 2nd edn (London 1963), pp. 102–3.

A clear answer to these questions cannot be given, but they give us a cue to proceed to the next section, where the other types of Latin chant are briefly discussed.

Further reading

On memory, Carruthers, *A Book of Memory*, has become a standard text; many of Treitler's key articles were reprinted in *With Voice and Pen*. So too were those of Kenneth Levy, who argues for a notated archetype of the Mass chant repertory in Charlemagne's time, in *Gregorian Chant and the Carolingians*. Several essays by Karp in *Aspects of Orality and Formularity in Gregorian Chant* contribute substantially to the debate.

Ethiopian chant is singled out here because of the stimulating results of recent research. The article quoted above is Shelemay, Jeffery and Monson, 'Oral and Written Transmission in Ethiopian Christian Chant'. Transcriptions were published in *Ethiopian Christian Liturgical Chant: An Anthology*, edited by Shelemay and Jeffery.

The debate about the relationship between Old Roman and Gregorian chant continues to fill volumes. McKinnon, *The Advent Project*, gave priority to the Gregorian. Nowacki, 'The Gregorian Office Antiphons', brings matters to a point as far as the antiphons are concerned. For other specialist studies of individual categories of chant, see Hornby, *Gregorian and Old Roman Eighth-Mode Tracts*, and Maloy, *Inside the Offertory*.

2.iii Chant in the Latin West outside the Roman tradition

Given the unsettled state of Western Europe in the fifth to eighth centuries, briefly described in section 2.i above, it is hardly to be expected that a single form of the liturgy and its chant would have been performed. Rome, which alone had the spiritual authority for a hypothetical uniformity of that sort, had no practical means of ensuring that its customs were followed elsewhere. Nor does it seem to have wanted to do so. The attitude of Gregory the Great seems characteristic. He had sent Augustine to convert the pagan English in 597, and Augustine, having encountered diverse customs on his way through Gaul, wrote to Gregory for advice about the customs he should present to the English. Gregory replied that he should make use of anything he knew that seemed right and proper for the English. 'Quae pia, quae religiosa, quae recta sunt, elige' (Those things which are pious, religious and right, choose them). This section is about the sorts of Latin chant other than the Roman which have survived from the early Middle Ages.

As just related, Gregorian chant was established in the Frankish realm in the late eighth and ninth centuries. Gregorian chant may well be what was sung in Rome at that time, whereas Old Roman chant may be its descendant, the result of two centuries more of oral transmission, eventually becoming visible in chant books from Rome in the later eleventh century, before being superseded by Gregorian chant in the later thirteenth century. Whatever the relationship between the two, they are Roman in the sense that their texts are undoubtedly those sung in Rome since at least the seventh century, and many are probably older even than that. But there are or were other repertories of Latin chant outside Rome: the chant of the Ambrosian, Beneventan, Mozarabic (old Hispanic) and Gallican liturgies.

The Ambrosian rite of Milan survived throughout the Middle Ages and is still sung today. The rite of Benevento in south Italy was superseded by the Roman rite during the eleventh and twelfth centuries, but a fair number of chants survive in transcribable manuscripts. The Mozarabic rite of Spain survived the Moorish occupation of most of the peninsula but not the Christian reconquest of the eleventh century, which brought with it the Roman liturgy and its chant. Mozarabic chant had actually been fully codified before this, but in neumes which we cannot transcribe into pitch notation. The survivals of the Gallican rite – the liturgy celebrated in Gaul before the Carolingian move closer to the Roman model – are sparse and heterogeneous, and some scholars prefer the idea of several Gallican rites rather than one which united the whole area. The south-west seems to have shared some practices with Spain, the south-east with Milan. Tours in the north-west had other traditions, and when we mix in the influence of Syrian colonies in the south, passing Irish missionaries, and knowledge of Roman practice brought back by visitors to the Eternal City, it is clear that uniformity of practice is out of the question. (This was probably also true of most other areas. The impression of greater uniformity is chiefly based on liturgical books of a later period.)

Of the chant of the Celtic church we know next to nothing, and, regretfully, in a book of this scope it has to be left aside. The same could be said of Gallican chant were it not for the possibility that some traces of it may be found in Gregorian chant.

Gallican chant

Of the above-mentioned sorts of chant, Gallican chant is the most difficult to pin down. By 'Gallican' we mean the chant of the liturgy or liturgies which developed in Gaul up until the eighth century, when Gregorian chant was adopted by the Franks. It may include elements preserved from the last century of Roman rule, which survived the Visigothic period and the gradual conquest by the Franks. We have descriptions of how the liturgy was performed, what form it took, including what sort of chants were sung. Quite a lot of information about it can be gleaned from the historical writings of Bishop Gregory of Tours (*c.*538–*c.*594) and there is a description of it in the so-called *Expositio antiquae liturgiae gallicanae*, once attributed to St Germanus of Paris but now thought to have been written in Burgundy in the early eighth century. But we have very little in the way of actual texts, and no music – obviously, since musical notation did not arrive until Gregorian chant was well established. The *Antiphona ad praelegendum* was a chant like the Roman introit, there was a *Responsorium* after the Epistle (sung by boys) and an *Antiphona ante evangelium* before the Gospel. The *Sonus* was sung during the offertory procession, and the *Trecanum* at the communion. For some other chants there is a less obvious Roman counterpart or none at all, while correspondences with Spanish or Milanese practice are frequent.

We might be tempted to leave Gallican chant at that. But in recent years a number of scholars have argued that when the Franks adopted the Roman liturgy they amalgamated their old Gallican chant with the imported Roman chant. They point to the reports about the difficulties the Franks had in learning Roman chant, and the obvious differences between Gregorian and Old Roman chant. Could Gregorian chant be a Frankish-Roman, or Gallican-Roman amalgam, a hybrid? It is clear that the Franks reorganized the liturgy after the Roman model, and took over all the

Roman texts. We know from the existence of prayer books for the Mass from the eighth century that quite a lot of Roman liturgical material was already known in Gaul, but this may not mean that Roman singing was known very well. The Franks may already have been familiar with the techniques of adapting typical melodies and standard melodic formulae, or they may have had to learn them from scratch. But – and it is a big 'but' – is it possible that they sang Gallican melodic formulae in place of the Roman ones, or a mixture of the two?

Careful searching through medieval chant books has revealed among the Gregorian pieces a number which have very probably survived from the old Gallican liturgy. The texts would have had no place in Roman use, and their melodies may well have remained more or less intact. Several of these have a distinctly colourful literary character which contrasts with the generally concise and sober Roman texts. As Walahfrid Strabo remarked *c.*840: 'The Gallican church was also provided with men who were no less skilled [than the Italians], and had a great deal of material for the Offices. Some of the Roman Offices are said to have been mixed with theirs; many people claim that they can distinguish between Roman and other chants by both words and melody' (Harting-Corrêa, p. 167). If the texts have a recognizable character, what about the melodies?

A rough distinction can be made between two sorts of evidence. On the one hand are the pieces of Gallican origin, whose melodies, as recorded in books of the eleventh century and later (!) in staff notation, may well retain old Gallican turns of phrase. The difficulty here is that there are not enough of them, and they are too heterogeneous in type: we have some antiphons (including *antiphonae ante evangelium*), a group of litany-type pieces called 'preces', a Gloria melody, the psalm tone known as the 'tonus peregrinus', and a few other items. That is not enough of a basis against which to test the whole 'Gregorian' repertory for possible Gallican elements.

However, a number of scholars, taking their lead from Dom Jean Claire of Solesmes, have proposed that a large group of pieces in *D*-tonality have Gallican roots, on the grounds that this tonality was avoided in the Roman tradition (as found in the Old Roman manuscripts, which, it will be recalled, date from the eleventh to thirteenth centuries). According to this theory, Gallican melodic characteristics may be discerned in, for example, tracts in mode 2 and graduals in transposed mode 2 (a group known as the 'Iustus ut palma' type). Claire believed that the tonal preferences could be discerned among an old layer of short responsories and antiphons for the ferial Office. Given the late date of the sources, however, it is very difficult to assess the reliability of such evidence, and extrapolating from it such wide-ranging theories about the relationship between Gallican and Roman chant and the nature of the Gregorian melodies seems risky indeed. If we are satisfied that the Old Roman is a later version of the Gregorian chant, then we shall not be so concerned to look for

Gallican elements in Gregorian. Nevertheless, the last word has not yet been said on the matter.

The Ambrosian chant of Milan

With Ambrosian chant we are on much firmer ground, since a number of manuscripts with staff notation have survived from the twelfth century onward. Ambrosian chant was originally sung in a large area of north Italy, and there are traces of it in south Italy as well. Of all the old chant repertories of Italy, either proven (Gregorian, Old Roman, Ambrosian, Beneventan) or hypothesized (Aquileian, Ravennan) it is the only one apart from Gregorian to have survived more or less intact to the present day. It is a good illustration of the general situation whereby the Roman liturgy and its chant way was for centuries only *primus inter pares*, 'first among equals', with neither the ambition nor the means to become the only approved model. The eventual 'triumph' of Gregorian chant, even in Rome in the late thirteenth century, was not repeated in Milan.

The Ambrosian liturgy has many of the same forms of worship as the Roman, but even when there is an exact correspondence in liturgical form, the Latin texts are usually different. In the Mass, the Ambrosian introit is the *Ingressa*. There are three readings, prophecy, Epistle and Gospel, and in between them come the *Psalmellus* and *Alleluia* or *Cantus* respectively (the *Cantus* is the equivalent of the Roman tract, sung in Lent). Immediately before and after the Gospel at Christmas, Epiphany and Easter, the *Antiphona ante evangelium* and *Antiphona post evangelium*, respectively, were sung. The *Offerenda* accompanied the offertory procession. At the fraction in the communion ritual the *Confractorium* (not the *Agnus Dei*) was sung – this was the equivalent of the Roman communion – and the *Transitorium* after the Paternoster. Gloria, Credo and Sanctus were the only chants for the Ordinary of Mass. Most of the Office hours were the same as in Roman use. (No sources for monastic forms of the Milanese liturgy survive.) The most important hours musically were Matins and Vespers. Matins was something like a combination of the Roman Night Office and Lauds. On saints' feast days an extra service called Vigils was sung after Vespers, most of its chants being shared with Vespers. The categories of Office chant – antiphon, responsory and hymn – are also the same as in Roman use, but there are many sub-categories of antiphon, particularly those sung during the highly developed processional rituals. Most of these seem to have been 'free-standing' chants and did not frame a psalm. (At least, the manuscripts do not specify one.) The Ambrosian name for a procession was 'psallentium' and the processional chants are known as *Psallendae*.

The 'surface' of many of the Ambrosian Mass chants and the more solemn Office chants is highly elaborate, often proceeding in stepwise motion in long waves of melody, where a sense of phrase-structure is easily lost. In view of what has been said above about the relationship between Gregorian and Old Roman chant, it is worth quoting the leading authority on Ambrosian chant, Terence Bailey, on this melodic style:

> It would be unreasonable to suggest that all ecclesiastical chants were originally simpler, but progressive elaboration does seem to have been a general phenomenon. Gregorian melodies – the first to be codified – are for the most part freer of extravagant melismas than the repertories recorded later. The suggestion is that the versions of the Roman melodies fixed by notation represent the general level of elaboration in eighth- or ninth-century ecclesiastical chant. The Old Roman repertory, first notated two or three centuries later, is considerably more elaborate than the Gregorian; and the Ambrosian, codified later still, is the most elaborated of the three . . .

Bailey sees here the results of 'a stylistic change that was unimpeded in an oral tradition but constrained (as in Gregorian regions) where the melodies had been fixed forever by notation' (*NG2* vol. 1, p. 453).

Perhaps because of concern to preserve ancient tradition in the face of Roman power, the number of chants remained somewhat smaller than the Gregorian, and newer types of chant such as sequences and tropes were not adopted. (The extremely long alleluia melismas, however, may be the counterpart of the *longissimae melodiae*, the sequence melodies to which Notker of St Gall set texts.)

Example 2.3 is a *transitorium* in D-mode, and thus belongs to one of only two melody types for this liturgical category, one in D and one in G. The text is of Byzantine origin, translated from the Greek, and is also found in the Bangor antiphoner (late seventh century, possibly from Bobbio, founded by St Columbanus). Apart from the wavy melodic surface and small number of leaps (the leap *E–a* is noticeable precisely because there are so few others), the chant is made up of varied repetitions of a single melodic idea. As Bailey has repeatedly shown, this is characteristic of *transitoria* and many other Ambrosian melodies. (It is similar to the way many Old Roman offertory verses were sung – see the previous section 2.ii.) The phrases are set out vertically above one another to make the repeat-structure clear.

The Beneventan chant of south Italy

In south Italy, the area roughly corresponding to the Lombard duchy of Benevento had its own liturgy and chant, dating back to the seventh and eighth centuries.

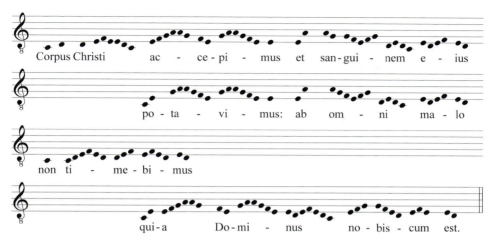

Ex. 2.3 Transitorium *Corpus Christi accepimus*

Transitorium *Corpus Christi accepimus*
We partook of the body of Christ and drank of his blood against all evil: we shall not fear, for the Lord is with us. (cf. Matt. 26:26; John 6:55; Ps. 120:7)

Montecassino was an important monastic centre in the region. Similarities and concordances with Ambrosian chant have prompted the speculation that both are the descendants of Lombard liturgical practice, originally linked but driven apart by the Frankish conquest of the Lombards in the north.

As in Milan in the north, the order of services in the Beneventan liturgy was similar but not identical to the Roman. The Latin texts are different from those sung in Rome, and those melodies that have survived are also different. There are some similarities in general melodic style between Old Roman, Ambrosian and Beneventan chant which set them apart from Gregorian. Beneventan chant, like the other two non-Gregorian repertories, favours a rather ornate surface style, with much stepwise, undulating motion. This may simply be how Italians generally liked to sing chant, as opposed to the more clear-cut Frankish way of singing, which they recorded for all to learn and perform as 'Gregorian' chant. Or it may be that here again we have an example of what happens during long centuries of oral transmission.

What survives of Beneventan chant is found in books of the eleventh and twelfth centuries. But these books are not purely, or even principally, Beneventan. Their principal contents are Gregorian, and the Beneventan items are included as additional items, alongside the Gregorian, presumably by musical scribes who did not wish all trace of the old ways of singing to be lost. By the time these books were made – and they are the oldest from the region – Beneventan chant had already been largely superseded by Gregorian. It has actually survived by the skin of its teeth, and could easily have shared the fate of Gallican chant. And it was remembered long enough to be recorded in staff notation, which Spanish chant did not achieve. We can see a much greater quantity of old Spanish chant in manuscripts up to the eleventh century, but, alas, only in staffless neumes. So of all the non-Roman chant repertories, only Ambrosian survives more or less complete in staff notation. However, enough Beneventan chant is transcribable to make safe generalizations about it. Over 160 pieces are preserved, for both Mass and Office. Some of the texts are shared by the Roman and (rather more) by the Ambrosian liturgies, so it is possible to compare settings of the same text in the different chant traditions. (Lack of space prevents our doing so here: the reader is referred to Kelly's excellent study.)

Some interesting historical data suggest a chronology for the decline of Beneventan chant. Among the chief saints of Benevento are the Twelve Brothers, venerated since 760, when Arichis II, Duke of Benevento, had their mortal remains interred in the palace church of Santa Sofia. The chants for Mass on their feast day are Beneventan. Eight years later, the relics of St Mercurius were brought to Benevento, but no chants for his day are known. Was strength already ebbing away from the old chant tradition? Less than a century later, in 838, even more prestigious relics arrived, those of the apostle St Bartholomew. But the chants for his Mass are in Gregorian style. Certainly the days of the chant were numbered when in 1058 Pope Stephen IX forbade singing the old melodies (which were interestingly referred to as 'Ambrosian'): 'Tunc etiam et Ambrosianum cantum in ecclesia ista penitus interdixit' (And then he completely banned the Ambrosian chant in this church). So it is indeed fortunate that a small proportion of the repertory has survived in transcribable notation.

Hispanic chant

After the reconquest of most of Spain except the south by Christian forces in the eleventh century, the Roman liturgy and its chant, transmitted mostly in manuscripts with Aquitainian notation, was introduced. The chant sung by Christians before then, living under Muslim domination, fell into disuse. It had by this time been notated, but in adiastematic neumes. The contours of the melodies and their musical forms are easily recognizable, but their pitches are not. This is one of the great tragedies of chant history.

This untranscribable chant has gone under several different names. 'Mozarabic' is the term for the Christians living under Muslim rule, hence 'Mozarabic chant'. In fact some of the chant dates from before the Muslim invasion of the Iberian peninsula in 711. 'Visigothic' refers to the rulers before that date. 'Old Hispanic' or simply 'Hispanic' is general enough to cover the whole period from the seventh to the eleventh centuries, which is the period under consideration.

Although we have no notated manuscripts from the seventh century, the so-called Orationale of Verona from the end of the century has text incipits for many chants and these match up well with the books of the tenth and eleventh centuries which survive. The many liturgical references and descriptions in the writings of Isidore, Archbishop of Seville (d. 636), show that the form of the services remained basically constant over five centuries.

The number of chants contained in the notated manuscripts (more than a dozen) is enormous, the loss correspondingly great. There are approximately 3,000 Office antiphons and 500 responsories, and the chants for the Mass are also numerically comparable with those of Gregorian chant. Of the long melismatic chants there over 120 *Psalmi* (equivalent to the Gregorian gradual), about 100 *Laudes* (equivalent to the Gregorian alleluia), about a dozen *Threni*, sung in Lent (like the Gregorian tract, but instead of the *Psalmo*, not the *Laudes*), and over 100 *Sacrificia* (equivalent to the Gregorian offertory). There are, however, fewer of the *Praelegenda* (equivalent to the Gregorian introit), between fifty and sixty, and only a dozen *Ad accedentes* (equivalent to the Gregorian communion). There are also several categories which do not have a Roman counterpart. (There are different liturgical traditions within the Hispanic family, which make exact figures misleading.)

Musical analysis of the melodies is perfectly feasible, up to a point, and reveals structures just like those of Gregorian antiphons, responsories, alleluias (with repetitive melismas), and so on.

The Fourth Council of Toledo in 633, under Isidore's leadership, decreed 'one order of prayer and singing in all Spain and Gaul', and it has been surmised that Hispanic and Gallican chant must have had much in common. In the absence of Gallican documents, and because the melodic idioms of Hispanic chant are unknown to us, the relationship cannot be pursued very far.

Two styles of neumatic notation are found in the surviving manuscripts. The one was used in northern churches, in León and Castile and favours vertical forms (cf. French neumes). The other is found in sources from Toledo and has a pronounced tilt to the right, sometimes verging on the horizontal.

Curiously, even before the revision of Roman chant after the Council of Trent in the sixteenth century, a different form of Hispanic chant was restored or newly promulgated. Manuscripts from around 1500 containing this chant have survived, but no medieval predecessors have been found. The chants were published in a new missal and breviary by Cardinal Jiménez de Cisneros in 1500 and 1502, respectively. They do not match the melodies of the early medieval manuscripts, and their origin remains a puzzle.

Further reading

The most thorough-going attempt to summarize what it known of Gallican chant, including the evidence for its partial survival within Gregorian chant, is the article 'Gallikanischer Gesang' by Michel Huglo and Olivier Cullin in *Die Musik in Geschichte und Gegenwart,* new revised edition. In the matter of the relationship with Gregorian it goes much further than Huglo's article 'Gallican Chant' in *The New Grove Dictionary,* 2nd edition. By far the most work on Ambrosian chant has been accomplished by Bailey; apart from survey articles in *The New Grove Dictionary* and *Die Musik in Geschichte und Gegenwart,* he has so far published no fewer than seven studies and editions of particular chant categories. Kelly has covered the old Beneventan area in *The Beneventan Chant.* On Hispanic chant, see the article 'Mozarabic Chant' by Randel and Nadeau in *NG2.* Randel made a combined index of all surviving sources. See also Hiley, *Western Plainchant,* ch. VIII. For all topics the on-line bibliography at www-musikwissenschaft.uni-regensburg.de/cantus may be searched by keyword.

2.iv Chant in the East: the Byzantine and other traditions

While the Western Roman Empire collapsed as a result of external pressure and internal decay, a contributory factor in the proliferation of different liturgical practices in the Latin language, the Eastern Roman Empire, with its capital in Constantinople (Byzantium), was able to maintain itself as a great power until well after the end of the millennium. Other great Christian centres – Jerusalem, Antioch and Alexandria – were in those areas of the Eastern Empire which were overrun by Islam in the seventh century. Since religious customs often need the support of the secular power to maintain the authority a dominant position, this meant that Byzantine liturgical practice is much better documented in manuscript form than any other of the Eastern liturgies. Nevertheless, a good deal has survived or can be reconstructed. This is of great interest to scholars of the early liturgies in the West as well, since what has been lost in one area can sometimes be deduced by analogy with parallel developments in another area. In the present book there is unfortunately no space to describe the chant of the Eastern churches – the subject needs a book of its own – so that only the barest outlines are sketched here.

There are no records of the chant of the church in Jerusalem. The destruction of the city by the Romans in the year 70 lessened the influence of the Christian community. It regained importance after Helena, mother of the Emperor Constantine, began a fashion to visit the places associated with Christ's ministry, crucifixion and resurrection, so that in 451 the patriarchate of Jerusalem was created. After the Islamic conquest the patriarch usually resided in Constantinople. Its liturgy is not completely lost, however, because the Armenian church adopted it in the fifth century, and Armenian documents survive where those from Jerusalem itself do not. More relics of Jerusalem practice can be found in the Georgian liturgy, which was formed under the influence of Georgian monasteries at St Sabas near Jerusalem and on Mount Sinai. Moreover, there is evidence that the Greek-speaking monasteries of Palestine were among the earliest to arrange their chants in eight weekly sets, the set for each week being in one of the eight modes. And the musical notation used there is the ancestor of the dominant type of Byzantine musical notation.

Both the Armenian and the Georgian liturgies were and are sung in the vernacular, and this is generally the case with all Eastern liturgies. In the West, by contrast, Latin was the universal language of the church, even if the form of the liturgy and the pieces performed were by no means uniform across Western and Central Europe.

The church in Alexandria was most important in the early centuries, second only to Rome in rank. After the Islamic conquest it became isolated. The language of the liturgy is Coptic, a descendant of ancient Egyptian, and the church is usually known as the Coptic Church. Practically everything we know about its chant depends on what can be heard today, recorded, transcribed, analysed from oral tradition, for it was never systematically written down.

Third in rank of the early patriarchal sees was Antioch. It became divided on doctrinal matters concerning the true nature of Christ. The 'Nestorian' or 'East Syrian' church sent missionaries as far as India and China. The 'Jacobite' or 'West Syrian' church adopted the Syriac language. A third party, the 'Melkite' church, had a Greek liturgy, as did the 'Maronite' church of Lebanon. Few early manuscripts survive to tell us what chant was sung, and, as for Coptic chant, modern research depends on melodies passed down through the centuries orally.

Another church whose chant has been studied on the basis of oral tradition is the Ethiopian church, whose customs derive partly from the Jacobite and Coptic traditions. But it had its own liturgical language, *Ge'ez*, from an early date, and the liturgy and music developed largely independently. Research into the orally transmitted chant has enabled scholars to understand the significance of a system of notational signs used from the late sixteenth century onwards. There are over 650 of these signs. They do not function like Western neumes or staff notation, but more as a sort of shorthand, each one standing for a short melodic phrase. (The signs, called *melekket*, are actually text abbreviations, derived from the phrase of text most commonly associated with the musical phrase.)

Both the Armenian and Georgian churches had notated chant books, thought by some scholars to date as far back as the tenth century. This would make them roughly as early as the oldest Byzantine chant books with notation, and not much later than the oldest Western notated books. Now, it has been argued that certain features which the earliest Byzantine systems have in common must derive from an earlier 'ancestor', which suggests that the beginnings of notation in both the Carolingian realm and in Byzantium date back to the same period, roughly the late eighth to early ninth centuries.

In fact, we must distinguish between two systems of notation in Byzantine books. The earlier one, seen in manuscripts from the ninth century onward, is known as 'ekphonetic' notation. It is used to mark up lessons. Each phrase of the text to be intoned has a sign at the beginning and another one at the end, and these indicate the pitch to be chosen for recitation and which of the several melodic formulae are to be sung. Then about a century later there appear manuscripts with much more fully notated melodies for the hymns, antiphons and all the other chants of the Byzantine liturgy. Scholars distinguish several types and chronological stages. In the earliest books, from the tenth century, notation signs do not appear above every syllable but remind the singer of key points in the melody. In the eleventh century it became usual to notate each syllable. The signs used up to the mid-eleventh century are usually referred to as 'palaeo-Byzantine' and divided into three families. 'Theta' notation is dominated by sign like a Greek *theta*, which appears to have been used to mark the occurrence of brief melismatic formulae in predominantly syllabic chants. 'Chartres' notation was used in early manuscripts from Constantinople and Mount Athos, whereas 'Coislin' notation appears to have originated in Palestine. It was the latter which was eventually developed further so that each note was represented by its own sign. That is also the principle on which Western neumatic notation worked, but the two systems took divergent courses. In order to specify exact pitches, Western neumes were placed on a staff, and the vertical height of the signs is an analogue of their musical pitch. Each Byzantine sign, on the other hand, specified the interval from the previous note, sometimes called a 'digital' notational system. 'Coislin' notation became interval specific about the middle of the eleventh century. (Hermannus Contractus, 1013–54, monk of the Reichenau, invented a similar system, apparently without knowledge of Byzantine notation. Indeed, he wrote about it at the same time or slightly earlier than the earliest preserved Byzantine examples: see section 4.iii below.)

Byzantine chant, like Gregorian chant, had an eight-mode tonal system. It is usually referred to as the 'oktēōchos', meaning 'eightfold sound'. (This term is sometimes used now to designate the Western set of modes as well, one word presumably felt to be more convenient than a phrase like 'eight-mode system'.) This is another element of chant practice which seems to have originated in the Jerusalem liturgy and the Greek-speaking monasteries of Palestine. The best-known hymn writer at this time was John Damascene (d. *c.*749), monk at St Sabas near Jerusalem, whose name acquired legendary status. The *oktōēchos* had a particularly important role in

Byzantine hymnography, however, for the chants of a whole week would be sung in one mode, those for the next week in the next mode, and so on. Modal sets of chants of this sort are also known from the Georgian, Armenian and some of the Syrian liturgies.

Some chants of the Byzantine liturgy are roughly equivalent in function to several of the Gregorian categories, such as the gradual, alleluia and communion, all in florid musical style. The numerous *stichēra* are roughly equivalent to Latin antiphons. But Latin chant has nothing to compare with the tens of thousands of Byzantine hymns. These are mostly strophic, in accentual verse and with syllabic musical settings. They include the grand sets which make up the *kanōn*, which constitutes a poetic trope on the nine biblical canticles of the Orthros (morning Office). Each of the nine canticles has its own *ōdē*, the nine odes thus making up the *kanōn*. The *ōdē* in its turn is a hymn with three of four strophes. The first strophe, called the *heirmos*, serves as model for the others, called *troparia*.

In contrast to the anonymity of most early Latin chant, the authors of Byzantine hymns (at least their texts) are often known. *Kanōn* composition flourished just as Roman chant was being established in the Frankish realm. Among the greatest authors are reckoned John Damascene (d. *c*.749) and Kosmas of Jerusalem (*fl*. first half of eighth century) in Palestine, then Abbot Theodore (d. 826) of the Stoudios monastery in Constantinople, his brother Joseph, and two hymn writers who had come from Sicily, Methodius and John the Hymnographer (d. 846 and 883, respectively).

Byzantine chant provided the foundation for the liturgical chant of lands evangelized from Constantinople. Sts Cyril and Methodius brought it as missionaries to the South Slavs in the mid-ninth century, the liturgical texts being translated into what is now called Old Church Slavonic, possibly sung in at least some cases to their original melodies. This process continued systematically over the next centuries, as the Orthodox liturgy, as it is usually called, was established in the principality of Kiev as well. By one of those common accidents of history, the earliest-preserved notated Slavonic manuscripts can sometimes be used to help fill gaps in our knowledge of early Byzantine practice. Very many manuscript sources, particularly in Russian libraries, have still to be investigated thoroughly. Indeed, many details of the transfer of Byzantine liturgy and its chant to what are now Serbia, Bulgaria, Romania and the Ukraine are not yet fully known.

Further reading

There is no convenient survey of the chant of the Eastern churches in all its aspects – liturgy, chant, notation – and the most reliable guides are the articles in *NG2*: Aram

Kerovpyan, 'Armenia, II. Church Music'; Kenneth Levy and Christian Troelsgård, 'Byzantine Rite, Music of the', and 'Divine Liturgy (Byzantine)'; Marian Robertson-Wilson, 'Coptic Church Music'; Kay Kaufman Shelemay, 'Ethiopia, II. Orthodox Church Music'; Christian Hannick and Dali Dolidze, 'Georgia, II. Orthodox Church Music'; Christian Troelsgård, 'Psalm, III. Byzantine Psalmody'; Miloš Velimirovié and Leonora DeCarlo, 'Russian and Slavonic Church Music'

Peter Jeffery, 'Oktoechos'; Gudrun Engberg, 'Ekphonetic Notation'.

Chapter 3

Tradition and innovation in medieval chant: from the ninth to the sixteenth century

This chapter explains how church musicians built upon the Roman-Frankish foundation, responding to the changing and expanding needs of the church in the high Middle Ages, and how the newly composed chant often reflected different stylistic concepts. Most writers on chant would prefer not to think of the new music as 'Gregorian' at all. Of the types of chant discussed below, the new Office music might be called 'neo-Gregorian', because at least the forms of antiphon and responsory are traditional, even if the melodies become increasingly untraditional. But sequences, tropes, the new Latin songs and the representational ceremonies ('liturgical dramas') are categorically un-Gregorian.

3.i Adapting the model to suit present needs: local enhancement of the repertory, new types of chant

However successful the Franks may have been in adopting Roman liturgical practice and its chant, they still had to supplement it with a considerable amount of new material. They venerated a number of saints unknown to the Romans, and needed to find chants to sing on the corresponding holy days. Other new festival days came into the calendar, such as All Saints' Day (1 November) and Trinity Sunday (a week after Whitsunday). Then there were a number of special ceremonies, which the Franks had used of old and which they wanted to retain. The chants for these occasions, if by good fortune they have been preserved in readable notation, sometimes look different in style from 'classical' Gregorian. The suspicion is that they may be relics of what is loosely known as 'Gallican' chant, the chant sung in Francia before the great Roman-Frankish transfer. (See Chapter 2.iii above.)

One chant in particular brings all these issues together: the sequence. This is a long melody sung directly after the alleluia at Mass, in fact connected to the alleluia without a break in performance. It was only sung on the most important feast days of the year. Musically it has a very individual structure and style, quite different from anything in the 'classical Gregorian' repertory. It is a prime example of a powerful new creative surge in ninth- and tenth-century chant, since, wherever their beginnings are placed (there is controversy about this), sequences were composed in considerable numbers when most of the older genres had achieved stability.

The various types of new chant commonly designated as tropes constitute another fascinating set of additions to the core repertory. A few are purely melodic extensions to phrases of a traditional melody, many are new phrases of text and music which gloss the old chant, and in yet other cases extra Latin text is grafted onto an older melody. Not the least interesting aspect of both the trope and sequence repertories is their regional distribution. Some pieces became widely known, but many never travelled outside the area or even beyond the church where they were composed.

The reason for this is clear enough, if the chant was composed for a local patron saint, a saint venerated in only one diocese or in the church where his or her relics were preserved. Further striking examples of pieces for local saints are to be found in the cycles of chants for the Office on feast days of many local saints. These cycles, known as *historiae*, appear in modest numbers in the ninth century, when the Franks wanted to provide special chants for non-Roman saints. A high point was reached in the eleventh and twelfth centuries, partly because many churches wanted to affirm their individual identity and traditions in the age of controversy between church and state and between monastic and diocesan authority. Frequently a new biography (*vita*) of the saint in question would be commissioned, which would provide the starting point for the texts of chants to be sung in the Office.

The cycles of chants in a *historiae* frequently display 'non-Gregorian' stylistic features. What is more, their authors are often known. In both respects they seem to belong to a different age, compared with the anonymous Gregorian melodies.

While in the *historiae* new chants were being composed in the traditional genres of antiphon and responsory, other new pieces strike out on different paths. These are the new songs performed above all in the Christmas season, especially on New Year's Day, the 'Feast of Fools'. They often display virtuosic strophic form and adventurous melodic contours.

Yet another new musical form is to be found in the 'dramatic' or representational ceremonies performed from the ninth century onwards. The earliest is a dialogue between the Marys visiting Jesus's tomb and the angel(s) they find there. Its purpose is to underline the mystery of Christ's resurrection from the dead. From the eleventh century onward, this simple scene was enlarged and complemented with others from Eastertide, and other seasons of the year (for example Christmas and Epiphany) were treated in a comparable way.

The next sections discuss each of these new sorts of chant in turn: *historiae*, sequences, tropes, songs for Christmas and other festivals, and representational ceremonies.

3.ii *Historiae*, sequences, tropes, new Latin songs, 'dramatic' ceremonies

Historiae

While the sequences, tropes and songs for Christmas are new categories of chant, *historiae* are cycles of chants in the traditional categories of antiphon and responsory, for the Office hours. New wine in old skins, so to speak. Composing such a cycle was no small undertaking, since it might consist of a dozen great responsories and more than twenty antiphons. The cycle is often called an 'Office'; I have generally used the medieval term 'historia'. It formed the counterpart to the saint's biography, the 'vita' (the life, death and miracles) or 'passio' (concentrating on the martyrdom of one who died for the faith). It would have been possible to take chants from the Common of Saints for the saint's day: chants for a martyr if the saint had been put to death for the faith, chants for a confessor if the saint in question were a bishop or king who had ended his days peacefully, chants for a virgin if so she were, and so on. This was certainly often done, not least where the saint was only of secondary rank in the church observing the feast day. But if the saint were the main patron of the church in question, new chants were often composed.

We can already see this happening soon after the establishment of Roman practice in the Frankish realm (and Benedictine practice for the monasteries there). The oldest surviving manuscript which records the full cycles of chants for the Office hours is Paris 17436, written about 870 probably at St-Médard at Soissons for the Emperor Charles the Bald and his palace chapel at Compiègne. Only the Latin texts are given, the time not yet having arrived when it was customary to notate books completely. And here, side by side with saints universally venerated, such as John the Baptist, Peter and Paul, Laurence and Michael, Agatha and Cecilia and many others, we find newly composed cycles of chants for north French saints such as Germanus of Auxerre, Medardus of Soissons, Vedast of Arras, Denis of Paris, Crispin and Crispinian (known from Shakespeare's *Henry V*), and Quentin. The Office for Denis goes back to the activity of Abbot Hilduin of Saint-Denis (814–40).

More and more new *historiae* can then be found from this time onward. At the beginning of the ninth century Stephen, Archbishop of Liège, born about 850, educated at Metz and in the palace school, archbishop from 901 to 920, composed new Offices for the Holy Trinity, for Lambert and for the Invention of Stephen. About the same time Hucbald of Saint-Amand composed a new set of antiphons (beginning with *In plateis*) for St Peter. The *historia* for Gallus may have been composed by the monk Ratpert (d. 900). The Office of Cuthbert was probably written in England around 930. And so the story goes on, throughout the Middle

Ages, eventually reaching all parts of Europe. The veneration of local saints was of course of considerable importance on both a religious and a political level. When the Emperor Frederick Barbarossa had Charlemagne canonized on 29 December 1165 his intention was to emphasize the god-given nature of royalty, naturally reflected in his own person. A new cycle of chants was composed for the occasion or soon after, but their author is not known by name. Other royal saints for whom cycles were composed include two Canutes of Denmark, Erik of Sweden, the German emperor Henry II and his wife Kunigunda, Louis IX of France, Ludmila of Bohemia, Olaf of Norway, Oswald of Northumbria, Stephen of Hungary and Wenceslas of Bohemia. Chant cycles for other saints of great importance to a particular nation include those for Adalbert (Wojciech) of Poland, David of Wales, Henry of Finland and Patrick of Ireland. The Dominicans had cycles for Dominic and Peter the Martyr, the Franciscans for Francis, Clare and Antony of Padua. Hardly less distinguished are some of those who composed *historiae*. They include Pope Leo IX (1049–54), Abbot Peter the Venerable of Cluny (1122–56) and several other prominent abbots. The music theorist, mathematician and astronomer Hermannus Contractus of the Reichenau (1013–54) wrote *historiae* for Afra the martyr of Augsburg, Wolfgang Bishop of Regensburg, Magnus the martyr of Füssen and several others. Even the great composer of polyphonic music Guillaume Du Fay (1397–1474) composed a plainchant Office of the 'Recollectio Festorum Beatae Mariae Virginis'. The repertory as a whole is vast indeed. Sadly, practically none of these chants are sung today because of the gradual establishment of conformity with Roman use after the Middle Ages.

The chants for Thomas of Canterbury, composed soon after his murder in 1170 by an eye-witness, Benedict, who became Abbot of Peterborough, are among the earliest in regular rhyming, accentual verse. As in other branches of chant, this type of text rapidly became the norm. Indeed, saints' Offices as a whole are often referred to as 'rhymed Offices'. But that definition, if applied strictly, would rule out most of the *historiae* composed before the late twelfth century, and many later ones as well, and these are arguably even more interesting musically than the rhymed sort.

Not everything sung on the day of the saint in question was newly composed. The usual psalms remained in place. Sometimes, but not often, a new antiphon for the psalms at Compline and the Little Hours might be composed. The composer's chief task was to compose new antiphons for First and Second Vespers (at least the antiphon for the Magnificat, sometimes one or more antiphons for the psalms), antiphons and responsories for the Night Office, and antiphons for the psalms and Benedictus at Lauds. An interesting feature of most Offices from the tenth century onwards is that the sets of antiphons and responsories follow the numerical order of the modes: first responsory in the first mode, second responsory in the second mode and so on. The Latin chant texts commonly follow a logical sequence as well. The readings in the Night Office will naturally be taken from the saint's *vita*, arranged chronologically, and the antiphons and responsories also have a 'story line' (though they usually form independent series in this respect).

Example 3.1 gives the responsory *Celestium minister donorum* from the Office for St Cuthbert of Lindisfarne, composed for the court chapel of King Athelstan of England (924–39) or his father Edward the Elder (899–924), transcribed here from the manuscript Worcester F.160. It is taken from the Second Nocturn of the Night Office. The readings for this Office are taken from Bede's Life of St Cuthbert, and in this Nocturn there have been three readings from Chapter 11 of Bede, about a sea voyage which would have ended in disaster but for Cuthbert's prayers. But the responsories have texts about other deeds of the saint. *Celestium minister donorum* refers to five miracles related in each of Chapters 29 to 33 of Bede, respectively. Cuthbert restores five different persons to health: the wife of one of the royal bodyguard, by sprinkling her with water he has blessed and giving her some to drink; a young girl, by anointing her with holy oil; the husband of the wife previously healed is made well by a morsel of bread which Cuthbert has blessed; a young man is healed by Cuthbert's prayers; and finally Cuthbert visits a plague-stricken village and by kissing a sick boy brings him back from death's door.

The melody has some vestiges of 'classical' Gregorian responsories. The verse uses the traditional tone for mode 8. But the endings of 'Celestium', 'perunctam' and 'reddidit' come up from the tone below the *finalis G*, a non-Gregorian feature, and the usual cadences for mode-8 responsories are hardly to be found at all: 'benedicta' has one, and another rare one is used at 'comitis' and 'crismate'. The phrase for 'pane a se benedicto' is used as an opening in several post-classical responsories. The melismas on 'perunctam' and 'sanitati' have an internal repeat form: a–a–b–a and a–a–b, respectively.

Over the next century more and more new *historiae* were composed, and many of them continue the trend away from classical Gregorian idioms. Some of the most 'progressive' were composed in south Germany, the most radical of all being those by Hermannus Contractus (1013–52), monk of the Reichenau, writer on music theory, astronomer, mathematician and other things besides. It is noteworthy that they are still settings of prose texts. Musical style, one might say, galloped ahead of literary style by half a century, at least in some places.

The example chosen here to illustrate the newest style, Example 3.2, is not by Hermannus, however, but is taken from the Office for St Thomas of Canterbury, composed soon after the murder of the archbishop in 1170 by an eye-witness, Benedict, subsequently Abbot of Peterborough. The responsory *Mundi florem* is the totally dominated by the notes most consonant with the *finalis G*: *d* and *g*. The text is cast into the common mould of 4+6 syllables, usually accented ´ - ´ - / ´ - - ´ - -. All but two of the twelve verses end on *G* or *d*. What is more, nearly all *words* aim for *G*, *d* or *g*. There are sub-tonal endings at 'funeri', 'veteri', 'cerebri' and 'veteri'. Needless to say, the traditional verse tone of mode 7 is not used for V. *Vox cruoris*. All traces of the classical Gregorian style are effaced in the interests of the new 'pan-consonant' melodic style.

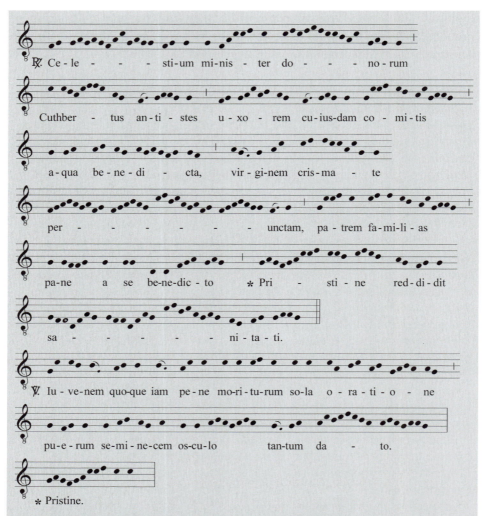

Ex. 3.1 Responsory *Celestium minister donorum* (St Cuthbert)

R. *Celestium minister donorum* (Cuthbert)

R. Bishop Cuthbert, minister of heavenly gifts, restored to her original health the wife of a certain count by means of blessed water, a girl anointed with holy oil, and a father, by bread which he had blessed. V. Also a youth on the point of death, by prayer alone, and a half-dead boy, by giving him a kiss.

Two antiphons from the Thomas Office (transcribed from the Peterborough antiphoner Cambridge, Magdalene College, F.4.10), show how shorter texts in regular, rhymed verse were set to music (Ex. 3.3). *Granum cadit* is the first of the antiphons for the psalms at Lauds, *Opem nobis* is the antiphon for the canticle Benedictus. The texts are again in two of the commonest verse-patterns used in rhymed Offices. *Granum cadit* has lines of 7,

Ex. 3.2 Responsory *Mundi florem* (St Thomas of Canterbury)

R. *Mundi florem* (Thomas)

R. Weeping Rachel, cease now lamenting the flower of the world, to be crushed under foot by the world. When the murdered Thomas is given over to be buried, a new Abel succeeds the old one.

6, 7 and 6 syllables, respectively, the so-called 'Goliardic verse' because often used in the verses of the wandering scholars or 'Goliards'. *Opem nobis* has lines made of 4+6 syllables. (These patterns are found in many sequences as well.) The melodic phrases are neatly placed in one or other of the scale segments proper to the mode. In *Granum cadit*, mode 1, these are *D–a, a–D, a–d* and *a–D*. In *Opem nobis* the phrases likewise aim for the main tones of the mode, *c* or *g*, and there is hardly a hint of alternative tonal areas (perhaps *f–d–b♭* at 'O Thoma porrige' and 'nos viam dirige').

Sequences

Sequences were sung after the alleluia of Mass on important feast days of the church year from at least the late eighth century in Francia. They were in fact a florid extension of the alleluia after the alleluia verse had been sung. As far as we can tell, the procedure for singing them was:

Ex. 3.3 Antiphons *Granum cadit* and *Opem nobis* (St Thomas of Canterbury)

A. *Granum cadit* (**Thomas**)

The grain falls to the ground, it brings forth an abundance of wheat; the alabaster bottle is broken, the power of the ointment is fragrant.

A. *Opem nobis* (**Thomas**)

Thy power, O Thomas, exert for us, govern the upright, raise up the fallen; amend our ways, our deeds and our life, and lead us in the way of peace.

- Alleluia, with a melisma on the syllable '-a';
- Verse, sometimes with the same melisma on the final syllable of the verse;
- Alleluia, with the sequence melody in place of the melisma.

(Several Old Roman and Milanese alleluias have extended melismas for the repeat after the verse. A Carolingian book of chant texts from the end of the eighth century indicates that a 'sequentia' is sung with some alleluias, and the writer Amalar of Metz also speaks of the 'sequentia' after the alleluia.)

It is not easy to sort out the early history of the sequence, however, because they are effectively invisible until they appear in neumatic notation at the end of the ninth century. And by this time they are usually written down in a section of their own, not joined to the alleluias which they embellish. This has led some scholars to argue that the sequence melodies, or at least the majority of them, are independent musical creations, joined on to the alleluia in practical performance but not growing out of the alleluia musically. Many of the sequences that have come down to us do indeed sound different from alleluias in melodic style.

Most medieval collections of sequences present them as melodies with texts. The relationship between music and text is peculiar, seen from the 'classical Gregorian' point of view, for the texted sequences are uniformly syllabic: that is, each single note of melody has its own syllable of text.

There is a famous description by the monk Notker of St Gall of composing Latin sequence texts, as a preface to a collection he had written. He says that he found the sequence melodies difficult to remember. A priest came to St Gall fleeing from the Northmen, from 'Gimedia' (usually reckoned to be Jumièges on the Seine), with a chant book where words had been set to melodies on the principle of one syllable per note. Notker applauded the principle but did not think much of the Latin texts, and therefore began to write his own, eventually creating a 'hymn book' of some forty texts, completed by 884. He showed his work to his teachers (who included Irish monks), who appear to have known the method already.

Notker's texts were then taken up very widely in East Francia. But many others were composed in other centres. Comparing Notker's texts with others to the same melodies is a fascinating exercise for Latin philologists. New melodies were also continually being composed, so that the medieval sequence repertory as a whole consists of hundreds of melodies and thousands of texts. The sequence is a very happy hunting ground indeed for those tracing the passage of particular melodies and texts across Europe, the formation of different cycles for the church year in different places, and lines of influence between various centres.

The melodies themselves fully deserve all the attention they have received. Most are lengthy (some very lengthy) compositions. Another peculiarity of the melodies is that each melodic verse is repeated, while the text continues. (A small group of early melodies are short, without the repeat structure. Notker texted eight of them, as opposed to thirty-two of the longer repeating type. Most dropped out of use after the end of the millennium.) Quite a number deliberately move into a higher register, usually a fifth higher, at some point, and end up cadencing on a higher note than in the first verses.

Example 3.4 is one of the grandest of sequence melodies, already widely known in the ninth century, texted by Notker (*Congaudent angelorum chori* for the Assumption of the Blessed Virgin Mary) and by many other authors (often for Christmas; anonymous, alas). It is given here from the Worcester collection London Cal.A.xiv, where it has the popular Christmas text *Celica resonent*.

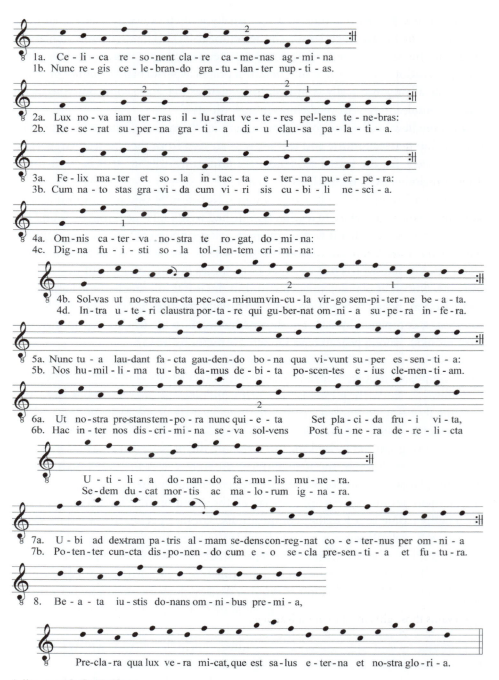

1 liquescent in first half-verse
2 liquescent in second half-verse

Ex. 3.4 Sequence *Celica resonent* (Christmas)

The melody has an almost hypnotic character in the way the verses come back again and again to the same cadence formulae. Not only the final three notes, coming to the key note from below (the so-called 'Gallican cadence'), but the lead-in is repeated: in verses 1–2, then another one in verses 4–7 (with an intermediate ending for 4a). The melody pushes up and up: in verse 4 up to *e*, then *f*, and then, after the restart at 4b ('reculer pour mieux sauter') up to *g*. From now on the endings are a fifth higher than for the first three verses. High *aa* is touched once in verse 5, then ever more insistently in verse 6 and 7.

The double-versicle structure of most sequences was no doubt exploited for *alternatim* performance. Some early manuscripts indicate that another form of alternation was employed, between texted and untexted renderings of each verse. We cannot gauge the effect of a medieval performance, but the soaring melodic lines, coupled with the syllabic text-music manner, seem to endow these compositions with unique energy and rhetorical power.

Sequences of this type, both great and small, were sung throughout the whole Middle Ages. However, as part of a general move towards rhythmic, rhyming texts from the later eleventh century onward, more and more sequence texts of the twelfth century onward were composed in accentual verse. Some of these new

←───

Ex. 3.4 (*cont.*)

Seq. *Celica resonent*

1a Let the heavenly hosts repeat aloud their hymns

1b to celebrate joyfully, now, the nuptials of the King!

2a A new light, shining forth upon the earth, dispelling the ancient gloom,

2b opens wide, already, with grace from on high, the long-closed heavenly courts.

3a O joyful Mother, alone in giving birth while yet remaining for ever a Virgin,

3b knowing not the marriage-bed, thou yet remainest fruitful on account of thy Son.

4a Lady, our whole choir prays to thee; 4b. loose all the bonds of sin, Virgin, ever-blessed.

4c Thou alone wast worthy to blot out our sins 4d. through the One, imprisoned within thy womb, who governs all things in heaven and on earth.

5a Now they praise him rejoicing for the blessings he has bestowed, by which they live the life of heaven:

5b we repay him with our humblest song, earnestly begging his mercy.

6a So that, giving us peaceful times, grant that we may enjoy a quiet life, bestowing on thy servants those gifts most to our advantage,

6b Saving us, when in mortal peril, by his unction, may he lead us after death to that abode that knows neither death nor evil.

7a Where seated at the benevolent right hand of the Father, he reigns coeternal with Him,

7b mightily ordering all things throughout all the ages, present and future.

 8 Granting holy rewards to all the righteous, by which, in truth, a brilliant light shines forth, which is eternal salvation and our glory.

texts retain something of the variety of the older pieces, with verse-pairs of different length and construction. Others are very regular, maintaining the same verse-pattern through all verse-pairs, sometimes with melodic correspondences between the verses (which is not difficult to accomplish where the text units are of uniform length).

Example 3.5 is an example of a sequence in rhyming, accentual verse. It was written for St Victor, patron of the famous Augustinian abbey of the same name in Paris, which was an important centre of learning in the twelfth century (famous for the great theologians and philosophers Hugh, d. 1141, and Richard of St Victor, d. 1173). The sequence dates from this period and may have been composed by Adam of St Victor or a later musician of the abbey. The exact date and extent of Adam's activity is not clear, but later generations attributed many sequence texts to him. The year of his death has been set variously at 1192, 1177 and most recently 1145, making him a contemporary of Hugh and also of Peter Abelard in Paris. Adam was precentor of Notre-Dame but left for St Victor in 1133.

Ecce dies triumphalis is one of the more expansive Parisian sequences of the twelfth century, and exploits different verse-patterns. The different verse-lengths and the musical endings from below (the so-called Gallican cadence) are reminiscent of the old sequence. The regularity of the verse-structures and the frequent note-groups (as opposed to single notes) are new. It is fascinating to trace the various metre- and rhyme-schemes, and the shape of the melody as well, rising steadily up to *d, f, g* and *aa*, with internal repetitions (see verses 7, 12 and 13). The artful phrase-structure of these pieces resembles nothing so much as that in the contemporary Parisian polyphony.

Sequence composition continued throughout the Middle Ages. Some verse-patterns (like the one at the start of *Ecce dies triumphalis*) were so common that it was possible to substitute one popular melody for another. Conversely, many different texts would be sung to the same popular melody. This technique is known as making a *contrafactum*. (A database covering these concordances of text and melody would be a most useful research tool.) After the renewal in the twelfth and thirteenth centuries, when the new rhymed sequences made their way into the repertory of practically every church (in some places more than others, of course), two themes in particular inspired new compositions. The veneration of the Blessed Virgin Mary brought with it great numbers of new sequences. Sequences were also composed at a more local level for the Mass on the feast day of an important saint. Whereas most of the Mass Proper chants were selected from the *Commune Sanctorum*, a new alleluia and sequence were often composed.

Some religious reform movements of the fifteenth and sixteenth centuries set their face against sequences, principally because of their non-biblical texts. The same attitude was taken during the deliberations of the Council of Trent (1543–63),

Ex. 3.5 Sequence *Ecce dies triumphalis* (St Victor)

Seq. *Ecce dies triumphalis* (Victor)

1a Behold the triumphal day! Rejoice, O spiritual host, with spiritual joy;

1b May you be devoted with your whole heart and let the heart's exultation express itself in song.

2a The heart can never be joyful unless it first be cleansed of the world's contagion.

2b If you wish for life, avoid the world, let delight in this world fall fast asleep within you.

3a Victor, in the first flower of youth, nay, Christ within Victor conquered by his grace;

1 liquescent in first half-verse
2 liquescent in second half-verse

Ex. 3.5 (*cont.*)

3b He conquered the flesh, he conquered the world, he conquered the furious enemy, overcoming all through faith.

4a The wondrous victory of the invincible martyr wondrously inspires us to joyful admiration:

4b Bring forth songs of gladness, mother church, praising the king of glory in his soldier.

5a Untiring soldier of Christ, bearing Christian witness, he refuses any wage:

5b He strives with all his being for the crown, he wishes none of the usual pay to support his existence.

6a Realizing this, cruel Maximianus, bent on evil deeds, lost his senses:

6b His visage paled, his voice roared, in dreadful rage he becomes like a beast.

7a The judge Asterius with his most impious henchman Euticius, thirst after cruelty, equal in malice.

so that Roman service books thereafter contained only four: *Victime paschali laudes* for Easter (eleventh century, by Wipo of Burgundy), *Veni sancte spiritus* for Whitsuntide (late twelfth century, possibly by Innocent III, d. 1216, or Stephen Langton, Archbishop of Canterbury, d. 1228), *Laude sion salvatorem* for Corpus Christi (thirteenth century) (a *contrafactum* of the twelfth-century sequence *Laudes crucis attollamus* for the Holy Cross), and *Dies irae dies illa* (thirteenth century, possibly by Thomas of Celano, d. *c.*1250) for the Mass of the Dead. *Stabat mater dolorosa*, a Latin religious song probably by a Franciscan author, was formerly attributed to Jacopone da Todi (d. at the beginning of the fourteenth century). It was adopted in some places in the Mass, rejected after the Council of Trent, but reinstated for the feasts of the Seven Sorrows of the Blessed Virgin Mary. Of these, *Victime paschali laudes* is rhymed and most verses are in regular rhythm; the others are fully regular. This means that the fine sequences with texts by Notker and his contemporaries fell into disuse and have not been revived in the modern liturgy. To a medieval churchman the modern situation, whereby no sequences are sung on

---

Ex. 3.5 (*cont.*)

7b He is dragged through the city, he is hung on the rack, tortured as he hangs, but no injury breaks the martyr.

8a With joyful spirit God's athlete stands, despising the body, overcoming the extraordinary pains.

8b In his torment his spirit wavers not, nor is the strength of his soul troubled.

9a O how wonderful, O how laudable is God's mercy!

9b Through whom such constancy is given to the martyrs in mortal conflict.

10a Because he stood firm his foot was cut off, but still the stump never strayed from the path that Christ trod:

10b Fearlessly he gives his foot for Christ, he who is give his head, a sacrifice for Him.

11a He rejoices at the loss of his foot, his faith suffers no fracture, like a mustard seed his strength increases, the greater the torture.

11b The torturer rages at Victor, but his fury turns to amazement, for Christ's presence gives Victor strength.

12a He is crushed by a miller's grindstone, then beheading ends his life, so that through death he enjoys the reward of immortality.

12b Sing Victor's praises, rejoice O spiritual host, praise with heart, hand and voice, and end the day of triumph with praise in the highest.

13a O how happy is this day, upon which the warrior triumphs! I how joyful, how solemn, the day on which Victor enters into the eternal courts:

13b Where there is no yesterday or tomorrow, but only the same today, where there is health and life and infinite peace, where God is all.

Amen.

such high feast days as Christmas, Epiphany, Ascension and Trinity Sunday or the main feasts of the Blessed Virgin Mary, would have been unthinkable.

Tropes

The term trope has been used (and misused) to cover a multitude of additions to the 'standard' chant repertory. The word comes from Greek *tropos*, meaning a turn of phrase. It is still occasionally used thus in modern English, particularly in the art of rhetoric, to mean a figure of speech such as metaphor. While it is true that the medieval use of the term is not consistent, it is most often used for extra phrases of chant added to the introit of Mass, and less often to the offertory and communion. Usually a verse of trope will be sung first, introducing the start of the introit. Further verses will be interpolated between the phrases of the introit. As far as the Latin text goes, the trope verses introduce or enlarge upon the introit text. The melody is usually in the same semi-florid musical style of the introit, and is so pitched as to fit smoothly into the parent chant. On the other hand, it lacks some of the characteristic melodic idioms of the introit and often displays 'non-Gregorian' features such as phrase-endings from below.

Tropes of this sort were composed from the ninth to the eleventh centuries but fell out of use thereafter. A few tropes achieved wide currency, but most remained restricted to a particular geographical area (south Germany, north France, Aquitaine, England, north Italy, south Italy, etc.) and some to a particular institution (St Gall, the Reichenau, Benevento, Winchester, etc.). Many are known only from manuscripts with neumes and did not survive into the age of staff notation, so that they cannot be transcribed today.

It seems to have been the practice for two solo singers to perform the trope verses, leading into introit phrases chanted by the choir. This alternation no doubt enhanced greatly the solemnity of the opening chant of Mass, for the full performance of the introit itself involves repetitions: introit – psalm verse – introit – *Gloria Patri* – introit. The introit is commonly split into five phrases, each introduced by a trope verse. New trope verses are often provided for the introit repetitions, and also to introduce the psalm verse and the doxology (*Gloria Patri*). That makes seventeen trope verses in all. The whole performance can last ten or fifteen minutes.

There is space here only for a modest example, for the feast day of the Holy Innocents (28 December), commemorating the slaying of the children at Herod's command (see Ex. 3.6). The eleventh-century manuscript probably made at Winchester for Worcester, London A.xiv has what was once a large collection of tropes. (Unfortunately, many leaves are now lost. One of its illustrations appears on the cover of this book.) For Holy Innocents it has two verses to introduce the Mass, and four sets of trope verses for the introit. (Presumably the cantor decided which should be sung in any one year.) The introit is a rather short one, *Ex ore infantium*, so for the purpose of troping it is divided into only two phrases, each one being prefaced by a trope verse. The first set of trope verses in London A.xiv has two verses for the first run through the introit and two more trope verses for the final repeat of the introit. The next is a single verse to introduce the introit. The third set of trope verses has two verses for the introit and one for the *Gloria Patri*. The fourth set is another pair for the introit. It is entirely typical of trope collections that many different sets of different shapes and sizes may be found. Tropes have proved to be another happy hunting-ground for those who like to trace interrelationships between manuscripts, varieties of musical style, and different sorts of Latin text.

Example 3.6 transcribes the first trope sets, each consisting of two verses. (To 'translate' the neumes of manuscript London A.xiv, manuscripts from Chartres and Utrecht with staff notation were consulted.)

Many introits have texts from the book of psalms. If a feast day commemorates an event of the New Testament (such as the slaughter of the Innocents) the psalm verses will have to be understood as presaging the event in some way, often rather indirectly. *Ex ore infantium* is a verse from Psalm 8: 'Out of the mouth of very babes and sucklings hast thou ordained strength, because of thine enemies'. The trope verses, on the other hand, can make a much more direct reference to the children, to say the least. A translation is given here with indications as to who is supposed to be singing (trope verses in italics, introit in small capitals).

[Invitation to the boys to sing]
> *Sing now, O boys, chanting songs to Christ, eia!*

[The boys sing]
> 'OUT OF THE MOUTH OF VERY BABES AND SUCKLINGS HAST THOU PERFECTED PRAISE.'

[Commentary]
> *For they pour forth their blood in thy name,*
> BECAUSE OF THINE ENEMIES.

[Invocation to Christ]
> *O thou clement one born of God, receive the praise of the children:*

[The praise of the children]
> 'OUT OF THE MOUTH OF VERY BABES AND SUCKLINGS HAST THOU PERFECTED PRAISE.'

[Commentary]
> *They who fight for thee, the newborn, pouring out their blood,*
> BECAUSE OF THINE ENEMIES.

Di-ci-te nunc pu-e-ri psal-len-tes   car-mi-na Chri-sto,

EX   O - RE   IN-FANTI-UM   DE-US

ET LACTEN-TI - UM   PER-FE - CI - STI   LAU-DEM:

Sanguinem nam-que su - um fu-de-re   no-mi-ni tu-o.

PROPTER IN-I - MI - COS   TU - OS.

Na - te De - i   cle - mens par - vo - rum su - sci-pe   laudes.
EX ORE INFANTIUM and ET LACTENTIUM as above

Qui ti - bi   iam na - to   cer - ta - runt san - gui-ne   fu-so.
PROPTER INIMICOS as above

Ex. 3.6 Trope *Dicite nunc pueri*, introit *Ex ore infantium* (Holy Innocents)

We find trope verses of this sort not only for chants of the Proper of Mass (introit, offertory and communion) but also for some Ordinary of Mass chants: Kyrie, Gloria, Sanctus and Agnus. The case of the Kyries is particularly interesting because the added verses are not the only sort of troping to embellish them. Here we also find new Latin texts apparently added to the melodies according to the principle of one syllable per note. A performance would go something like this:

> Latin texted version of Kyrie 1 sung by soloists
> Normal version with text 'Kyrie eleison', first invocation, sung by the choir
> Latin texted version of Kyrie 2 sung by soloists
> Normal version with text 'Kyrie eleison', second invocation, sung by the choir
> – and so on for all nine invocations.

It has nevertheless been pointed out that the earliest sources we have for some Kyries already give them with the Latin texts. It is therefore possible that they were so conceived from the outset, and that plain performance of the melodies without the Latin words was done only on less important occasions.

Some of the Latin texts (whether added or original) were particularly well known in the Middle Ages and were used in later centuries as nicknames for the melodies, even when the Latin texts were no longer sung. So in the *Graduale Romanum* published in 1908 (see section 5.ii below for this epoch-making publication) the first Kyrie is called 'Lux et origo', the next one 'Kyrie fons bonitatis', and so on. An example was used earlier, in section 1.v (see Ex. 1.16; see also the troped Agnus Dei, Ex. 1.19).

A text for wordless melodies or phrases was usually called a 'prosa' or 'prosula' in the Middle Ages. Such prosulas were composed for alleluias, offertories and for the melismas which often form a melodic climax to the great responsories of the Night Office. Very often the original words are worked into the new ones, rather like luxuriant exegetical flowers upon the stem of the old text.

New songs for Christmas and other festivals

A great deal of Gregorian chant is made up of phrases of irregular length. Its texts are mostly in prose, the words and syllables are delivered with very variable numbers of notes. There is no obvious, regular rhythmic pulse and the relationship of one part of the melody to another often seems rather vague. In these respects it contrasts strongly with polyphonic music from the thirteenth century onward, where the different voices are held together rhythmically in regular measures. There is some evidence that sequences such as *Ecce dies triumphalis* (Ex. 3.5 above) might be sung with a regular beat, for example in triple time, with a long note for accented syllables, a shorter one for unaccented syllables. However, a distinction was often made from the thirteenth century onward between 'cantus planus' and 'cantus mensurabilis', meaning 'unmeasured' and 'measured' music respectively, implying that plainchant melodies did not usually fall into regular metrical units. The seeming lack of regular internal melodic structure in older chant, its formal diffuseness, is also made good in *Ecce dies triumphalis* and in the antiphons and responsories in rhymed Offices (for example, the antiphons from the Thomas Office cited in Ex. 3.3). The regular text units are obviously reflected in the melodies. As already remarked, the texts often resemble the strophes of a hymn.

Just when some chant texts were taking on the regularity of hymns, new strophic songs were composed which extend the poetic and musical techniques of hymn-writing in very imaginative ways. These new songs are not usually called hymns (which retained their usual place and style in the Office hours unchanged), but 'conductus', 'versus' or 'cantio'. The word 'conductus', favoured in north France, implies that the songs might be sung in procession. 'Versus', often found in sources from south France, seems intended to point to the difference from prose ('prosa'). 'Cantio' (found in later sources from Central Europe) is simply a word for 'song'.

The first substantial collections of these new songs appear in the twelfth century, in manuscripts from southern France (three of them in Aquitainian notation passed through the hands of Bernard Itier, the librarian of the abbey of St Martial in Limoges), from Norman Sicily, and in the famous 'Liber Sancti Jacobi' or 'Codex Calixtinus', made in central France (perhaps Vézelay) for Santiago de Compostela. The latter manuscript, and especially the sources for the liturgy on New Year's Day, the Feast of the Circumcision or 'Feast of Fools', from Beauvais and Sens in the early thirteenth century, show how the songs were used in the liturgy. Among their functions was as a substitute for the Benedicamus Domino at the end of the Office hours, or as a processional song while the reader of a lesson approached the pulpit, and when he returned. Some refer to the singer who was to wield the 'baculum' on the 'Feast of Fools' as a sign of office, in charge of the conduct of the services on that day.

Many of the songs have refrains (like some old processional hymns, though their poetic technique is quite different). Most striking is their imaginative handling of rhyme and rhythm. Within a strophe, the length of the lines is often varied, and rhyme is used to mark both longer and shorter text units. No single example can suggest the remarkable variety of form and style, but Example 3.7 exemplifies some characteristics. The strophes are in the A–A–B form familiar from many songs of the trobadors, trouvères and Minnesänger ('Barform'). After the seven-syllable verses in the first part (A), the verses in the second part (B) include a four-syllable and two three-syllable lines. Then comes the refrain, again with mixed verse-lengths, in fact the same pattern as the B section. The refrain begins with the same notes as the B section. The strophes, too, have a refrain verse 'Cum gloria'. This is an entirely syllabic song (although many have more ornate surface detail), and it is easy to imagine it accompanying the rhythmic tread of the procession to read one of the lessons at Matins in Beauvais on New Year's Day (actually the seventh lesson – all nine are provided with a conductus).

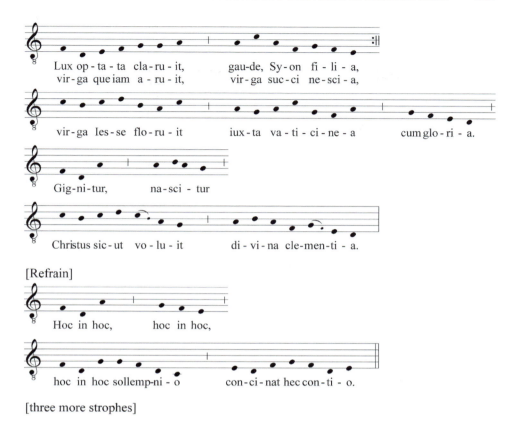

Lux op - ta - ta cla - ru - it,   gau - de, Sy - on   fi - li - a,
vir - ga que iam a - ru - it,   vir - ga suc - ci   ne - sci - a,

vir - ga Ies - se flo - ru - it   iux - ta va - ti - ci - ne - a   cum glo - ri - a.

Gig - ni - tur,   na - sci - tur

Christus sic - ut vo - lu - it   di - vi - na cle - men - ti - a.

[Refrain]

Hoc in hoc,   hoc in hoc,

hoc in hoc sollemp-ni - o   con - ci - nat hec con - ti - o.

[three more strophes]

Ex. 3.7 Conductus *Lux optata claruit*

Conductus *Lux optata claruit*
The welcome light has shone: rejoice, daughter of Sion! The rod which was dried up, the staff knowing no sap, the stem of Jesse has flowered according to the prophecy *in glory*.
   He has been brought forth, he is born, Christ, as divine clemency willed it.
   On this, this, this festival this company sings carols.

Representational or 'dramatic' ceremonies

It may seem that a good deal of the liturgy has to do with role-playing and representation, and is related to drama and play-acting. It would, however, be a mistake to draw too close a comparison. It is true that the Eucharist is in some sense a re-enactment of the Last Supper, but the greater part of the liturgy is quite static, concerned with meditation rather than representation. However, several special ceremonies of Holy Week commemorate events in the life of Christ in a way which brings them to the mind of the worshipper with exceptional force, almost in the sense of a dramatic re-enactment. (For a summary of these ceremonies, see section 1.iii above.) For example, in the processional ceremony on Palm Sunday, Christ's entry into Jerusalem, just five days before his crucifixion, is remembered. Chants are sung with texts from the biblical narrative, and in several cities, when the bishop came to the main church (as it were Jerusalem) he would sing a verse from Psalm 23 (24):

> *Tollite portas principis vestri, et elevamini portae aeternales: et introibit rex gloriae.*
> [Lift up your heads, O ye gates, and be ye lift up, ye everlasting doors: and the
>   King of glory shall come in.]

From inside the church, or from a high place above the door, was sung the question:

> *Quis est iste rex gloriae?*
> [Who is the King of glory?]

To which the bishop replied:

> *Dominus virtutum ipse est rex gloriae.*
> [Even the Lord of hosts, he is the King of glory.]

Another example of a ceremony where a biblical scene is represented, albeit in a highly stylized way, is the 'Improperia' ('Reproaches') sung during the Adoration of the Cross on Good Friday. Imagined words of Christ on the cross are sung by soloists and answered by two choirs in alternation. The ceremony begins where the priest reveals a crucifix and invites those present to regard it:

> *Ecce lignum crucis in quo salus mundi pependit.*
> [Behold the wood of the cross, on which the saviour of the world hung.]

The reproaches begin:

> *Popule meus, quid feci tibi? aut in quo contristavi te? responde mihi. Quia eduxi te
>   de terra Ægypti: parasti crucem salvatori tuo.*
> [O my people, what have I done to thee? Or in what have I afflicted thee? Answer
>   me. Because I led thee out of the land of Egypt, thou hast prepared a cross for
>   thy Saviour.]

The choirs answer:

> *Agios o Theos.* [Holy God.]
> *Sanctus Deus.* [Holy God.]
> *Agios ischyros.* [Holy strong one.]
> etc.

Although, as we shall now see, a number of other episodes from the history of man's salvation were re-enacted from the tenth century onward, these presentations never approach drama as we know it from the sixteenth century and later, with its character drawing and moral and spiritual questionings. The first examples of new representational ceremonies within the liturgy are very simple, and the more complex examples are longer principally because more scenes are included, not because persons are depicted in more depth, issues explored more fully, or conflicts resolved. We might say that the persons depicted remain 'one dimensional', just as they do in medieval painting. The important thing is to be able to recognize the persons and objects depicted and connect them to each other and to the principal theme. The artist is free to arrange things in a significant hierarchy, not 'realistically', untrammelled by any obligation to show only those things which belong together in 'real life'. The performers in a dramatic ceremony need only be recognized as indicators, pointing to an overarching web of meaning linking all parts of the story of salvation.

Text box 3.1 Amalar of Metz on the Mass

Amalar of Metz (*c.*780–850), a pupil of Alcuin, was appointed in 835 to direct the see of Lyons after the deposition of its archbishop, Agobard. His writings illuminate the necessary accommodation between Roman and Frankish liturgical practice in the early ninth century. The following extract from his *Missae expositionis geminus codex* has often been quoted as an example of his manner of thought, connecting elements of the Mass with a host of happenings in sacred history. While it may seem over-fanciful to modern ways of thinking, it is representative of the medieval penchant for seeking out associations and links between all aspects of worship and the history of man's salvation.

3

In truth the introit looks to the choir of prophets [who announced the coming of the Christ, just as the choir announces the entrance of the bishop], and it is right that we touch them here, as Augustine said: 'Moses was the minister of the Old Testament and the prophets are ministers of the New Testament'.

The Kyrieleison looks to the prophets from the time of Christ's coming, among whom were Zacharius and his son John [the Baptist].

4

Gloria in excelsis Deo looks to the host of angels who announced to the shepherds the joy of the birth of the Lord [for one sang first, then all together, just as the bishop intones the Gloria and all then join in].

The first Collect looks to that which the Lord did in his twelfth year, when he went up to Jerusalem and sat in the temple among the teachers, listening to them and questioning them.

5

The Epistle relates to the preaching of John.

The responsory [gradual] relates to the willingness of the apostles, when they were called by the Lord and followed him.

The alleluia relates to the joy in their hearts which was vouchsafed them by him or because of the miracles which they performed by him or in his name.

We shall speak elsewhere of the tract.

The Gospel relates to his preaching up until the time foreseen.

6

In truth the things which are performed next in the Office of Mass look to that time from that Sunday [Palm Sunday] onward when the boys came to meet him [and the crowds, like the congregation of the faithful bringing their gifts] up to his Ascension or Pentecost.

The prayer which the priest says from the Secret up to 'Nobis quoque peccatoribus' signifies the prayer which Jesus delivered on the Mount of Olives.

And that which is performed afterwards signifies that time when the Lord lay in the sepulchre.

7

When the bread is dipped in the wine, it shows the soul of the Lord returning to the body.

And what is celebrated afterwards signifies the greetings which the Lord gave to his disciples.

And the breaking of the gifts [bread] signifies that which the Lord did before the two in Emmaeus.

Original text edn Jean-Michael Hanssens, *Amalarii episcopi opera liturgica omnia*, vol. 1 (Rome, 1948), pp. 255–6.

Quem queritis in sepulchro?

The first new ceremony was performed on Easter morning, and was no doubt regarded as a natural addition to the many extraordinary liturgical performances of Holy Week. It is a simple dialogue between the angel (or angels in some versions) and the three women who bring spices to the tomb of Christ on Easter morning. The shortest form consists of just three 'speeches' (cited here from manuscript St Gall 484, of the second quarter of the tenth century):

[Angel]   *Quem queritis in sepulchro, Christicole?*
            [Whom do you seek in the tomb, Christians?]

[Women]   *Iesum Nazarenum crucifixum, o caelicolae.*
             [Jesus of Nazareth who was crucified, O heavenly one.]
[Angel]   *Non est hic, surrexit sicut predixerat; ite, nunciate quia surrexit de*
             sepulchro.
             [He is not here, he is risen as he had foretold; go, announce that he is
             risen from the tomb.]

Although this happening is related in three of the four gospels in different words, the sung dialogue does not correspond exactly to any of the gospels; it is somebody's invention. Composers of chant were used to adapting biblical texts to make suitable verses for singing. Yet the creation of this new ceremony, however brief, and despite its similarity to older ways of making chant, seems qualitatively significant. Other versions of the ceremony include more verses. For example, what may be the oldest of all sources, from Limoges (Paris 1240, *c.*930, therefore contemporary with or slightly older than St Gall 484), has an introductory verse:

> *Psallite regi magno, devicto mortis imperio.*
> [Sing praises to the great king, now that death's reign is overthrown!]

And, after the dialogue, concludes with an announcement of Christ's resurrection, thus carrying out the instruction of the angel:

> *Alleluia, resurrexit Dominus, hodie resurrexit leo fortis, Christus, filius Dei: Deo gratias, dicite eia.*
> [Alleluia, the Lord is risen, today the strong lion is risen, Christ, the Son of God: thanks be to God, sing eia!]

And that is the main point of the ceremony: not to re-enact a historical event but to impress upon those present that Christ is indeed risen. If one thinks of the many special ceremonies of Holy Week – including the procession with palms on Palm Sunday, the washing of feet on Maundy Thursday, the Adoration of the Cross on Good Friday, and in some churches the burial of the host, representing Christ's burial in the tomb – then a special ceremony to demonstrate the resurrection is a natural sequel.

It is disappointing that neither the precise place and time of origin of the piece, nor the original version, can be pinpointed exactly. Not only are there a number of different versions, with different numbers of verses, but the degree to which the executants are identified is also very varied, and in many cases there is no specific mention of an angel or women (sometimes identified as the three Marys). There are further differences in the liturgical function of the ceremony. Sometimes it leads straight into the introit of Mass on Easter Sunday, sometimes it forms part of a

Text box 3.2 The *Visitatio sepulchri* in late tenth-century Winchester

While the third lesson [of the Night Office] is being read, four of the brethren shall vest, one of whom, wearing an alb as though for some different purpose, shall enter and go stealthily to the place of the 'sepulchre' and sit there quietly, holding a palm in his hand. Then, while the third respond is being sung, the other three brethren, vested in copes and holding thuribles in their hands, shall enter in their turn and go to the place of the 'sepulchre', step by step, as though searching for something. Now these things are done in imitation of the angel seated on the tomb and of the women coming with perfumes to anoint the body of Jesus. When, therefore, he that is seated shall see these three draw nigh, wandering about as it were and seeking something, he shall begin to sing softly and sweetly, *Quem quaeritis*. As soon as this has been sung right through, the three shall answer together, *Ihesum Nazarenum*. Then he that is seated shall say *Non est hic. Surrexit sicut praedixerat. Ite, nuntiate quia surrexit a mortuis*. At this command the three shall turn to the choir saying *Alleluia. Resurrexit Dominus*. When this has been sung he that is seated, as though calling them back, shall say the antiphon *Venite et videte locum*, and then, rising and lifting up the veil, he shall show them the place void of the Cross and with only the linen in which the Cross had been wrapped. Seeing this the three shall lay down their thuribles in that same 'sepulchre' and, taking the linen, shall hold it up before the clergy; and, as though showing that the Lord was risen and was no longer wrapped in it, they shall sing this antiphon: *Surrexit Dominus de sepulchro*. They shall then lay the linen on the altar.

When the antiphon is finished the prior, rejoicing in the triumph of our King in that He had conquered death and was risen, shall give out the hymn *Te Deum laudamus*, and thereupon all the bells shall peal. After this a priest shall say the verse *Surrexit Dominus de sepulchro* right through and shall begin [Lauds] . . .

From Thomas Symons, *Regularis Concordia: The Monastic Agreement of the Monks and Nuns of the English Nation* (London, 1953), pp. 49–50.

procession to a special sepulchre set up in the church. That procession may then lead back to the choir for Mass. In other churches the ceremony concluded the Night Office, often following the responsory *Dum transisset Sabbatum*, which itself relates how the Marys came to the tomb.

Later ceremonies and plays

Following the typology of Karl Young, a distinction is often made between the *Quem queritis* dialogue when performed before Mass, and the *Visitatio sepulchri* at the end of the Night Office. Young believed that the latter liturgical position enabled the ceremony to 'realize' its 'dramatic potentialities'. (The term 'Visitatio sepulchri' does not actually appear until about the beginning of the thirteenth century.) While this distinction between *Quem queritis* and *Visitatio sepulchri* is liturgical and not based on content (since all *Visitatio* ceremonies include a *Quem queritis* dialogue or something like it), Young went on to divide the *Visitatio* into three subtypes according to their content. His first type has only the angel(s) and Marys, the second type brings the apostles Peter and John, while the third introduces the risen Christ. These types did not develop in chronological order. The apostles' scene was added to a recasting of the dialogue, with new melodies, and is found mostly in German and Central European sources. (It may have been made at Augsburg in the later eleventh century.) At roughly the same time, some north French and English sources contain the scene where Mary Magdalene meets Christ in the garden. This idea was also taken up in the eastern half of Europe, but was composed differently.

All these forms of the new Easter ceremony are firmly centred on the liturgy. Indeed they sometimes incorporate chants with suitable texts (antiphons and responsories) from the Easter services. But other compositions appear to have originated in a different environment, or betray non-liturgical influences. This is the case, for example, with various versions of a Magi play, in which the Three Wise Men follow the star, are questioned by Herod, and come to the stable where Christ was born. Far more persons are introduced than in the Easter ceremonies, and they may sing strings of hexameters, sometimes with enough musical differentiation (different modes, for example) to suggest a sort of musical characterization. Liturgical chants are hardly ever drawn upon.

In the first parts of this chapter, attention was drawn to the increased use of rhymed, rhythmic verse in sequences and new *historiae*. The same sorts of texts were taken up in the dramatic ceremonies as well. Some of them are actually cast in strings of four-line strophes, the same melody being repeated for each strophe in a group, or even for a whole play. Even in the more varied compositions, this means that the plays became stylistically further removed than ever from the 'classical Gregorian' of the traditional liturgy. The twelfth century also witnessed a great expansion in subject matter. For Eastertide we find a representation of the meeting of Christ with two disciples on the road to Emmaeus; they take him for a pilgrim (*peregrinus*), hence the usual appellation of this ceremony as 'Peregrinus'. Some manuscripts present grand combined versions of all the Easter episodes in succession, recast in verse. (Two famous sources from the first and second halves of the thirteenth century, respectively, are the so-called 'Fleury Playbook', Orléans, Bibliothèque Municipale, MS 201, and the manuscript of the so-called 'Carmina Burana', Munich, Staatsbibliothek, clm 4660 and 4660a.) There are also Christmas plays: the shepherds hear the good tidings from the angel and visit the stable in Bethlehem (the 'Officium Pastorum' or 'Ceremony of the Shepherds'); the lament of Rachel over the children

Ex altera autem parte erit paratum sepulchrum, ibique erit Ihesus et duo Angeli,
unus ad caput et unus ad pedes. Cum autem venerit Maria Magdalena, dicent ei Angeli:

Mu - li - er, quid plo - ras?   *Et illa:*

Qui - a tu-le-runt Dominum meum, et ne-sci-o u-bi po-su-e-runt e-um.

Hec autem cum dixerit, convertat se retrorsum, vidensque Ihesum non cognovit eum,
quia Ihesus esset. Qui dicit illi:

Mu - li - er, quid plo - ras? Quem que - ris?

Illa putabat eum esse ortulanum, et dicit illi:

Do-mi-ne, si tu su-stu-li-sti e-um, di - ci-te mi-chi, al - le-lu-ia:

et e-go e - um tol-lam, al - le-lu-ia.

Ihesus dicit illi: Ma - ri - a.   *Et illa:*   Ra - bo - ni.

Et Ihesus: No-li me tan-ge-re, nondum e-nim a-scen-di ad pa-trem meum.

Sed va - de et dic fra-tri-bus me-is   ut   e - ant in Ga-li - le-am.

I - bi me vi-de-bunt, al-le-lu-ia, al - le - lu-ia.

Ex. 3.8 Mary Magdalene and Christ in the garden

Mary Magdalene and Christ in the garden

In another part of the church will be prepared the Sepulchre, and there will be Jesus and two
Angels, one at the head and one at the foot. And when Mary Magdalene comes, the Angels shall
say:

slain on Herod's orders; and a curious procession of prophets announcing Christ's birth ('Ordo Prophetarum'). We have the Wise and Foolish Virgins awaiting the Bridegroom (*sponsus*) as in one of Christ's parables, a play about the raising of Lazarus from the dead, a set of miracles of St Nicholas. The most ambitious, original and entertaining of all is the *Ludus Danielis* of Beauvais, preserved in a manuscript of the 1220s (London, Egerton 2615). The word 'play' (*ludus*) is indeed appropriate for such pieces, for neither in subject matter nor mode of expression do they have any close link with the liturgy. (This is not to say that the play was not intended to fit into the liturgical round. The manuscript also contains a complete liturgy for New Year's Day – a song from it was quoted above, Example 3.7 – and the play itself ends with an announcement of Christ's birth and the singing of the Te Deum. Daniel appears, of course, in the *Ordo Prophetarum*, for he sees the Son of Man in the apocalyptic vision reported in Daniel 7:13–14.)

Two examples are included here in order to point up the contrast between the older style of prose verses, near to traditional Gregorian chant, and the new rhymed, rhythmic items. Example 3.8 is from one of versions of the meeting of Mary Magdalen with Christ in the garden. Example 3.9 is from the *Ludus Danielis*.

Several verses in Example 3.8 share the same tonality, the *E* mode, and even turns of phrase ('Mulier', 'Maria', 'Raboni'). Some sound rather like Gregorian antiphons, and in fact 'Domine si tu sustulisti' takes up the second half of the Easter antiphon *Tulerunt Dominum meum* (*Antiphonale Monasticum* 464). That is probably why the range of this verse is different from the rest of the piece.

Ex. 3.8 (*cont.*)
Woman, why weepest thou?
And she replies:
Because they have taken away my Lord, and I know not where they have laid him.
And when she shall have thus said, she shall turn herself back, and seeing Jesus she shall not know that it be Jesus. He saith unto her:
Woman, why weepest thou? whom seekest thou?
She shall suppose him to be the gardener and shall say unto him:
Sir, if thou have borne him hence, tell me, alleluia: and I will take him away, alleluia.
Jesus saith unto her:
Mary.
And she:
Rabboni.
And Jesus:
Touch me not; for I am not yet ascended to my Father: but go and say to my brethren that they shall go into Galilee. There they shall see me, alleluia, alleluia.

Conductus Regine venientis ad Regem

Cum doc-to-rum   et ma - go-rum   omnis ad - sit con-ti - o

Se-cum vol - vit,   ne-que sol-vit   que sit   ma-nus vi - si - o.

(3 more strophes)

Tunc Regina veniens adorabit Regem dicens:

Rex, in   e - ternum vi-ve!

Ut scribentis   nos-cas in - ge - ni-um,   Rex Bal-tha - sar,   au - di   con-si - li-um.

Rex audiens hoc versus Reginam vertet faciem suam. Et Regina dicat:

Cum Iu-de - e   cap-ti - vas   po-pu - lis   prophe-ti - e   doctum o - ra - cu-lis.
Da-ni - e-lem   a su - a   pa-tri - a   cap-ti - va-vit   pa-tris vic-to - ri - a.
Hic sub tu - o   vi-vens im - pe - ri - o,   ut mande-tur,   re-qui-rit ra - ti - o.

Er-go manda   ne sit di - la-ti - o,   nam do-ce-bit quod ce - lat   vi - si-o.

Tunc dicat Rex Principibus suis:

Vos Da-ni - e-lem que - ri - te,   et in-ventum ad-du-ci-te.

Tunc Principes, invento Daniele, dicant ei:

Vir prophe-ta   De - i,   Da-ni-el,   vien   al   Roi.
Pa-vet et tur - ba - tur,   Da-ni-el,   vien   al   Roi.
Te di - ta-bit   do - nis,   Da-ni-el,   vien   al   Roi,

Ve-ni,   de - si-de - rat   par-ler   a   toi.
Vel-let   quod nos la - tet   sa-voir par   toi.
Si scrip - ta   po-te - rit   sa-voir par   toi.

Ex. 3.9 From the *Ludus Danielis*

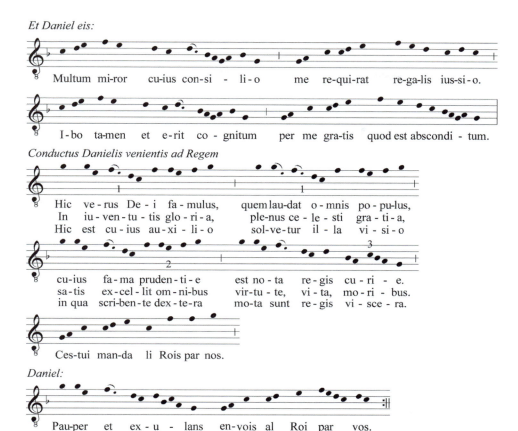

Et Daniel eis:

Multum mi-ror   cu-ius con-si - li-o   me re-qui-rat   re-ga-lis ius-si-o.

I-bo   ta-men   et   e-rit   co - gnitum   per me gra-tis   quod est abscondi - tum.

Conductus Danielis venientis ad Regem

Hic   ve - rus De - i   fa - mulus,   quem lau-dat o - mnis   po - pu-lus,
In   iu - ven-tu - tis glo - ri-a,   ple-nus ce - le - sti   gra - ti-a,
Hic   est cu - ius au-xi - li - o   sol-ve-tur   il - la   vi - si - o

cu-ius   fa-ma pruden-ti-e   est no - ta   re-gis cu - ri - e.
sa-tis   ex-cel-lit om-ni-bus   vir-tu - te,   vi - ta,   mo-ri - bus.
in qua   scri-ben-te dex-te-ra   mo-ta sunt   re-gis   vi - sce - ra.

Ces-tui man-da   li Rois par nos.

Daniel:

Pau-per   et   ex - u - lans   en-vois al   Roi par   vos.

(The verses 'Cestui manda' and 'Pauper et exulans' are sung after all three strophes.)

1 without liquescent note in first strophe
2 liquescent note in second strophe
3 b alone in first strophe

Ex. 3.9 *(cont.)*

From the *Ludus Danielis*

Conductus for the Queen as she comes to the King

While the teachers and wise men are all here in counsel,

they ponder but cannot explain the sight of the hand.

(3 more strophes)

Then the Queen, coming, will worship the King, saying:

O King, live for ever!

If you would know the nature of the writing, King Belshazzar, hear my counsel.

The King, hearing this, will turn his face towards the Queen, and the Queen shall say:

With the captive people of the Jews, one learned in the oracles of prophecy,

Daniel, was taken from his native land after your father's victory.

Living here under your rule, sense demands that he be summoned.

The extract from the Daniel play in Example 3.9 comes after the wise men of Belshazzar's court have been unable to read the writing on the wall. The Queen enters, accompanied by the lively conductus *Cum doctorum et magorum* in rhymed verses of 4 + 4 + 7 syllables. She salutes the King (*Rex in eternum vive* – a verse heard repeatedly throughout the play) and explains in a series of couplets with 4 + 6 syllables that the wise Jew, Daniel, will be able to interpret the writing. Daniel is summoned by means of a song with refrain phrases in the vernacular (*Vir propheta Dei*). He replies in verses of 4 + 6 syllables (*Multum miror*), and comes to Belshazzar's court accompanied by another conductus to which he sings a personal refrain (*Hic verus Dei famulus*). This extract is not untypical in its dazzling

---

Ex. 3.9 (*cont.*)

Therefore command that there be no delay, for he will teach what the vision conceals.

Then let the King say to his Princes:

Go ye and seek Daniel, and when found, lead him hither.

Then the Princes, having found Daniel, shall say to him:

Man of God and prophet, DANIEL, COME TO THE KING. Come, for he wishes TO SPEAK WITH YOU.

He fears and is troubled, DANIEL, COME TO THE KING. He wants TO UNDERSTAND THROUGH YOU that which is hidden.

He will give you presents, DANIEL, COME TO THE KING, if he is able TO UNDERSTAND THROUGH YOU the writing.

And Daniel, to them:

I wonder greatly by whose counsel the royal command has summoned me.

Yet I go and that which is concealed will be known freely through me.

Conductus for Daniel as he comes to the King

This is the true servant of God, whom the whole people praises,

whose reputation for prudence is known to the royal court.

THE KING HAS SUMMONED THIS MAN THROUGH US.

Daniel:

POOR AND EXILED, I GO TO THE KING WITH YOU.

In the glory of his youth, full of heavenly grace,

he greatly excels in every virtue, in his life and his ways.

THE KING HAS SUMMONED THIS MAN THROUGH US.

Daniel:

POOR AND EXILED, I GO TO THE KING WITH YOU.

This is he whose counsel will explain that vision

in which by the writing of the finger the king's bowels were troubled.

THE KING HAS SUMMONED THIS MAN THROUGH US.

Daniel:

POOR AND EXILED, I GO TO THE KING WITH YOU.

display of diverse poetic forms and alternation of strophic conductus and solo verses.

Further reading

Research into the 'neo-Gregorian' and 'post-Gregorian' types of chant has been especially vigorous in the last half century, as more and more chant has been unearthed that had not formed part of the restoration of 'classical' Gregorian chant. There are overviews of the new types of chant in Hiley, *Western Plainchant*, Ch. II, sections 22–6. For rhymed Offices, see Hughes, 'Late Medieval Plainchant for the Divine Office'. Crocker, *The Early Medieval Sequence*, and Fassler, *Gothic Song*, on earlier and later sequences respectively, are dense and specialized but rewarding. The Beauvais Office for New Year's Day has been edited by Arlt. There is an excellent essay on representational ceremonies by Rankin, 'Liturgical Drama'. There are many editions of later medieval chant – most easily located at www-musikwissenschaft.uni-regensburg.de/cantus. The editions of Offices in the series *Historiae*, and the editions of the sequences and tropes of Benevento (by Boe and Planchart) and Nonantola (by Borders and Brunner) may be mentioned.

3.iii The later Middle Ages

So far this section has concentrated on musical matters, but we should not lose sight of chronology. What about the historical context? This was set out in Chapter 2 as far as the ninth century, when the Carolingian adoption of Roman liturgy and chant had run its course. A few salient points about the high Middle Ages now need to be explained.

Many parts of the Roman-Frankish chant repertory established in the ninth century remained the same to the end of the Middle Ages and beyond. The chants of the Mass Proper were not significantly altered or added to. Only alleluias increased in numbers, and changed in style, in the later Middle Ages. The alleluia seems in any case to be a special case among the Mass Proper chants, starting from a narrow base with very few melodies, new ones then being composed from Carolingian times onwards. But the case is different for Office chants, as we have seen, with the creation of many new *historiae* for local saints well into the later Middle Ages. In many instances the cult of a local saint was enhanced liturgically by the composition of both a new Office and a new alleluia, and one more item: a new sequence. For sequences, even more than alleluias, continued to be composed in considerable numbers throughout the Middle Ages and even beyond. Especially striking is the production of new sequences for the Blessed Virgin Mary. Most of these were for the weekly (or even daily) Mass of the Blessed Virgin. The sequences were sometimes collected in alphabetic series (with multiple entries for A, *Ave* . . . . ., G, *Gaude* . . . . ., and S *Salve* . . . . .).

Tropes for Proper of Mass chants were a relatively short-lived phenomenon, reaching a peak around the turn of the millennium and fading rapidly in the twelfth century. There are no doubt theological and institutional reasons for this decline. Non-biblical texts like those of tropes were not always welcome, especially not in the Proper of Mass, and newer religious orders like the Carthusians and Cistercians turned their faces away from tropes. Furthermore, the interest of composers had shifted in favour of settings of the new rhymed, rhythmic poetry, and their creative energies went into the cultivation of sequences and songs in the new style. While the antiphons and responsories for new Offices were versified, however, the Proper of Mass chants remained sacrosanct. When the veneration of a saint was newly instituted or reformed, the traditional Mass chants from the Common of Saints continued in use. Tropes, 'neo-Gregorian' glosses on the old Proper chants, were neither as venerable as the Propers nor as colourful as the new verse compositions. Perhaps this is one of the reasons why they fell into desuetude.

The Ordinary of Mass continued to be a field for new endeavour, at least in some areas of Europe. Most churches continued to sing troped Kyries, Sanctus and Agnus chants at least into the thirteenth century. Tropes for the Gloria, however, shared the fate of tropes for the Proper of Mass. There exist some large collections as late as the twelfth century, but not later. One set of trope verses, beginning *Spiritus et alme*, for a newly composed Gloria melody, was very often sung at Masses for the Blessed Virgin Mary from the twelfth century onward and into the late Middle Ages, but this is an exception to the rule.

Taking a very broad view, it might be said that the cultivation of plainchant forms a background to the growing use of increasingly elaborate polyphony in some parts of Europe. Or, rather than speak of chant as a 'background', it would be better to say that plainchant was the principal form of worship though music, onto which polyphonic music was grafted in many progressive and ambitious centres. Desiring to praise the Lord in the best way known to man, composers in France and England, and to a lesser extent in Italy and Spain, turned increasingly to polyphony. In Germany and Central Europe this was not the case, or not to anything like the same extent, and this may be related to the fact that in the later Middle Ages some extensive new repertories of (monophonic) votive antiphons, alleluias, and Ordinary of Mass chants (especially Credos in Central Europe) were created in these lands. A large proportion of these chants were for services in honour of the Blessed Virgin Mary. They are the monophonic counterpart of the polyphonic Ordinary of Mass compositions, Magnificats and Marian antiphons common in

France and England from the fifteenth century. The great majority are still practically unknown.

New religious orders

The changing emphasis in the categories of chant to be cultivated naturally reflects changing priorities in the institutions where chant was sung. Mention was made above of the newer religious orders, the Carthusians and Cistercians. Under the Franks Benedictine monasticism had become established as the principal form of conventual life, and held undisputed sway for three more centuries. The new orders arose from the desire to recapture features of monastic life which had become obscured or difficult to maintain in the Benedictine order.

The Carthusian order was founded in 1084 by St Bruno of Cologne, who with the support of Bishop Hugo of Grenoble built a monastery in the massif of the Chartreuse (Lat. Cartusia) north of Grenoble. The number of houses increased only slowly, mostly in Western Europe, although from the middle of the fourteenth century there was a notable expansion in Germany, and by the sixteenth century there were nearly 200 monasteries. The order was strongly ascetic and in its chant practice avoided musical elaboration, so that sequences, new alleluias and Ordinary of Mass chants, and melismas in Office responsories were not used.

The Cistercian order was founded in 1098 by the Benedictine monk Robert of Molesme. It takes its name from the monastery he founded at Cîteaux. Especially through the work of Bernard of Clairvaux (1090–1153), a figure of supreme spiritual and even political importance, the order flourished spectacularly during its first century, with over 300 new foundations. By the sixteenth century there were 700 abbeys with monks, over 600 with nuns. During the twelfth century the chant repertory and way of singing it was laid down in master exemplars and defined in theoretical tracts, for the Cistercians had a very clear sense of how the liturgy should be performed and ensured that it should follow a uniform pattern throughout the order. Sequences were sung, but tropes avoided, and there was no expansion of the Office cycle. Particularly interesting is the recasting of some chants to make them more straightfoward tonally (avoiding *b-flats*, for example, or transposing passages which strayed from the mode) and simplifying elaborate melismatic phrases. Like much else in Cistercian practice, their chant was thus influenced by carefully considered ideals, a desire to reach back to a pure source. Knowing the reputation of Metz in Carolingian times, they sent singers to Metz to listen to the chant there, but were disappointed in what they heard. Knowing that St Ambrose had composed hymns, they sent singers to Milan to learn his hymns, and actually introduced many of them at Cîteaux, but later revised what was in fact a rather exotic selection.

The singing of the Cistercians influenced that of the Dominicans in the next century. The Dominicans were one of the two great new orders of friars (from Latin *fratres*) of the thirteenth century, the other being the Franciscans. Because of the high priority they accorded to work in the community, elaboration of ritual and ritual music was not of great interest. Both celebrate the Office according to the Roman, not the Benedictine cursus. The Dominican order of Friars Preachers, founded by St Dominic, was formally constituted in 1220. The form and content of its liturgical books was finalized in Paris under Master-General Humbert of Romans (1254–63) and the master-copy of the complete liturgy prepared then, including its chant, still exists. It was faithfully followed in all houses of the order.

With the Franciscans we return to the history of chant in Rome itself, since the Franciscans, founded by St Francis of Assisi in 1209, adopted a liturgy closely coordinated with that of the Roman curia. As already discussed (section 2.i and especially 2.ii above), the earliest notated chant books from the city of Rome itself, contain a type of chant usually called 'Old Roman', not 'Gregorian'. The earliest book is a gradual dated 1071. From then up to the thirteenth century we have five such books, three graduals and two antiphoners. The nature of Old Roman chant and its relation to Gregorian has been discussed at great length over the last sixty years. One view (held by the present writer) is that Old Roman chant developed from (one might say: away from) the chant heard by the Franks in the eighth and ninth centuries, while Gregorian chant is a largely faithful record of Roman chant made by Franks in the ninth century, also supplemented according to their own needs. This implies that tension must have been generated whenever Gregorian and Old Roman chant came into contact in subsequent centuries. One wonders what popes Gregory V (996–9), a German, and Sylvester II (999–1003), a Frenchman, Gerbert of Aurillac, made of the situation when they ascended the papal throne. The German protégés of Emperor Henry III, especially Leo IX (1049–54), himself a composer of neo-Gregorian chant (including the proper Office *Gloriosa sanctissimi* for his musical predecessor Gregory I), would also presumably have noticed a difference. We have evidence from another quarter that these things really did matter. In the middle of the eleventh century the great Benedictine abbey of Montecassino had two German abbots in succession, and one of these, Frederick, became Pope Stephen IX in 1057. Revisiting Montecassino in 1058, he forbade the singing of what he called 'Ambrosianus cantus'. By this he probably meant the old Beneventan chant (see section 2.iii above). The presumption is that he wanted Gregorian chant sung in its place, which is indeed what we find in later Cassinese chant books. Finally, Alexander II (1061–73) had formerly been a canon of St Fridiano, Lucca, and he brought canons to reform the monastery attached to the Lateran. It was these who would perform the services in the Lateran basilica, presumably singing Gregorian chant, although no chant books have survived to prove this.

Despite these winds of change blowing through chant practice in Rome, Old Roman chant appears to have persisted into the thirteenth century. Then Innocent III initiated a revision of the Mass and Office of the papal chapel in 1213–16. More revisions followed up to the middle of the century, with Franciscan collaboration. Nicholas III (1277–80) ordered the destruction of all books in Rome which did not conform to the revised ones. It is customary to refer to the new generation of books, missals and brevaries, graduals and antiphoners, as 'Roman-Franciscan'.

The Benedictines in the later Middle Ages

All this time chant in Benedictine monasteries continued according to old tradition, which actually means many local traditions. The uniformity insisted upon by the Cistercians was foreign to the older Benedictines. Numerically they remained the largest of the monastic orders, with many thousand houses across Europe. But they had no central organization. Often depending upon local bishops and magnates for ecclesiastical and financial support, they were frequently involved in struggles to protect their autonomy, hence many attempts to gain papal or (in Germany) imperial protection. Up until the twelfth century, many of those chant books which are richest in content (with *historiae*, sequences and tropes) come from Benedictine houses, such as St Gall and the Reichenau, St Emmeram in Regensburg, St Martial in Limoges, Nonantola and Novalesa. Later this is not so much the case.

Books of the new religious orders of monks and friars, as just said, select the same chants in the same order, and the chants display the same melodic readings (these are the two chief ways of investigating relationships between manuscripts). So it is fairly easy to 'spot' a Cistercian book. This is not the case with Benedictine books, except where a mother–daughter relationship exists, where one monastery affiliated itself to another, more powerful one, or where a monastic reform was imposed. For there were reforms within the Benedictine order itself. The Burgundian monastery of Cluny was founded in 909 independent of diocesan control, owing obedience only to the pope. It gained a reputation for excellence, many monasteries were inspired to follow its example or were instituted as priories under Cluny's authority. (That is, they were headed by a prior, acting under the abbot of Cluny.) In monasteries of the Cluniac congregation, the same pieces might be sung in the same order as at Cluny, and, less often, the musical versions of the pieces might correspond to Cluniac practice. But this is not always so. It depended on the circumstances under which the monastery had become a member of the Cluniac group.

In south Germany, the monastery of Hirsau in the Black Forest also established a high reputation during the abbacy of William (Wilhelm) (b. 1026, abbot from 1069, d. 1091), formerly a monk of St Emmeram in Regensburg. William admired the example of Cluny but did not copy its liturgical practice chant for chant. In the same way as Cluny, Hirsau became the model for a group of reformed or newly founded Benedictine monasteries following, to a greater or lesser extent, the chant practice of the fountain-head.

One could pick out several such groups of Benedictine houses. An interesting development in Italy arose from the desire to follow the example of the papal chapel. Since the format (the 'cursus') of the Benedictine services is not the same as that of Roman usage, the Roman selection of chants from season to season and day to day was adapted to the Benedictine cursus. This is what the Olivetans did, an order founded near Siena in the early fourteenth century, and so did the order of St Giustina of Padua in the early fifteenth century. Their use attained international dimensions when it was adopted by Subiaco in central Italy. Many centuries earlier, St Benedict had dwelt in a cave near Subiaco and first attracted companions to a monastic life, before moving to Montecassino in about 529. Its special connection with the great saint contributed to Subiaco's high reputation, and in the later Middle Ages it attracted monks from outside Italy as well, especially Germany. The monastery of Melk on the Danube was reformed after the model of Subiaco after the appointment in 1418 of Nikolaus Seyringer as abbot. Seyringer was born *c*.1360, appointed 1401 rector of the University of Vienna, entered the Benedictine order in 1403, was appointed Abbot of Subiaco 1412, and entrusted at the Council of Constance with the reform of Austrian monasteries. A number of south German and Austrian monasteries were reformed from Melk, and so it comes about that a 'Romanized' Benedictine usage, with a strongly Romanized selection of chants and melodic readings, became established north of the Alps. At the same time, the singing of the Night Office was shortened, so that Office chant books of the Melk type often contain only one antiphon and responsory per Nocturn, or only the texts, to be read without singing.

These developments are harbingers of greater changes to come, after the Reformation, a story which will be taken up in Chapter 5.

The end of anonymity

Gregorian chant is often thought of as impersonal, almost super-human in the literal sense of the word, something which is 'above' ordinary human beings, God-given. The legend of the dove dictating the chant to Gregory enshrines not only a desire to emphasize the great ecclesiastical-political authority enjoyed by the chant, but also a real belief that chant is a gift of the Holy Spirit. Singers did not create it, but were simply the vessels to which it was entrusted.

It is true that we know almost no composers of early medieval chant by name, but as time goes on, more and more are identifiable. A recent survey collected well over 100 names of composers whose works have survived or who are at least reputed to have written chant. The list could certainly be extended. Even if not all of these attributions are sound, they reflect the attitude that it was quite legitimate for musicians to create new melodies. The musicians might well have regarded themselves as conduits for heavenly harmonies (an attitude not restricted to the Middle Ages). At any rate, many are by now well known to music historians, and several are mentioned in the present book. Quite often the composition of a cycle of new chants for a local saint, a *historia*, as a complement to a new biography (*vita*), is the work of an identifiable musician. We have such *historiae* by Bishop Stephen of Liège (*c.*850–920), Adémar of Chabannes (*c.*988–1034) at Limoges, Bruno of Egisheim, later Pope Leo IX (d. 1054), and Abbot Udalscalc of Augsburg (d. 1150). Abbot Hucbald of St Amand (840–*c.*930), Abbot Bern of Reichenau (d. 1048) and Hermannus Contractus (1013–54) of the Reichenau composed in several genres, including *historiae*, as well as being notable music theorists.

One composer, exceptional in several senses, deserves to be singled out here: Hildegard of Bingen (1098–1179). Hildegard's compositions have survived principally in two manuscripts. One is now preserved in Wiesbaden, the so-called 'Riesencodex', and the other in Dendermonde. Both have early German staff notation. Between them they contain seventy-seven chants, including forty-three antiphons, eighteen responsories, seven sequences and four hymns. The 'Riesencodex' (so called because of its large dimensions, 46 × 30 cm, written at Rupertsberg shortly after Hildegard's death) also contains a versified morality play by Hildegard, the *Ordo virtutum*, with a further eighty-two songs. Hildegard was given by her parents to the Benedictine convent of Disibodenberg in 1112. She eventually became prioress, under the authority of an abbot. About 1150 she established her own convent at Rupertsberg near Bingen, and then, in order to accommodate yet more nuns who wished to join her, a daughter house at Eibingen near Rüdesheim. Hildegard was an inspired mystic who often described her visions in precise detail rather than ecstatic hyperbole. She was famous for her prophecies and visions, a form of religious utterance open to women, who were otherwise not allowed to teach. Other writings concern medicine and the natural world. Hildegard's music is as remarkable as her life and literary writings. Although the principal manuscripts set out her chants in thematic groups (the Trinity, the Blessed Virgin, Angels, Saints, etc.) they do not form regular liturgical groups, as for example a complete *historia* for a particular saint's day. Since they do not turn up in 'normal' liturgical books (antiphoners, graduals or whatever), and because of their remarkable musical style, they have generally been ignored in the orthodox chant literature. Yet there can be no doubt that Hildegard's chants were intended for liturgical performance, even if sung only in her own community. The melodies are often highly melismatic, which with Hildegard's often lengthy Latin texts makes them among the longest chants known. Their tonality is dominated by the *finalis*, upper fourth, upper fifth and octave, with frequent leaps between these notes and scale passages through a whole octave. This style is anticipated somewhat in the compositions of Hermannus Contractus a century earlier, and can be found

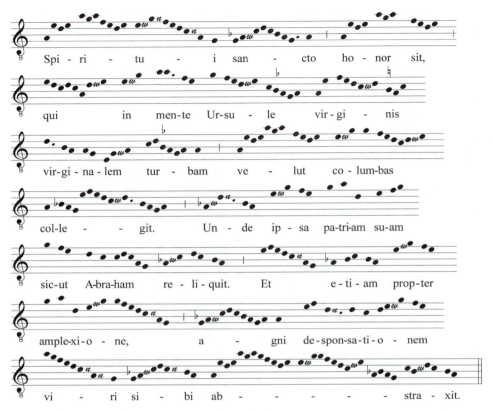

Spi - ri - tu - i san - cto ho - nor sit,

qui in men-te Ur-su - le vir-gi - nis

vir-gi - na-lem tur - bam ve - lut co - lum-bas

col-le - - git. Un - de ip - sa pa-tri-am su-am

sic-ut A-bra-ham re - li - quit. Et e - ti - am prop-ter

ample-xi-o - ne, a - gni de-spon-sa-ti-o - nem

vi - ri si - bi ab - - - - - stra - xit.

Ex. 3.10 Hildegard of Bingen, responsory *Spiritui sancto*

Hildegard of Bingen, R. *Spiritui sancto*
Honour be to the Holy Spirit, who in the soul of the virgin Ursula brought a virgin host like
doves together. Therefore she left her home, like Abraham. And thus she withdrew herself
from marriage with a man to embrace the Lamb.

in other German chant of the twelfth century, though not in pieces of such extended
average length.

Example 3.10 is one of Hildegard's chants for St Ursula and the 11,000 Virgin Martyrs of
Xanten. As well as the features just mentioned, it will be noted that the initial leaps up to
the fifth and the octave recur three times: at 'honor sit', 'velut columbas' and 'abstraxit'.
Other melodic elements recur: 'ipsa . . . Abraham' = 'propter amplexione', and 'sancto' =
'agni'. A chant with none of the traditional Gregorian idioms must create its own internal
points of reference. This is a responsory, of which only the first section but not the verse is
given here.

This chapter has included many remarks about new musical styles, particularly about the tendency to aim for the 'consonant' notes of the modal scale, the lower fourth, upper fifth and upper octave. Something will be said about this change of style in the next chapter, against the background of new music-theoretical concepts. These should help us to understand better both the old 'classical Gregorian' and the new 'pan-consonant' melodic style.

Further reading

The survey of named composers is by Kelly, 'Medieval Composers of Liturgical Chant'. There are facsimiles of both the principal manuscripts of Hildegard of Bingen's compositions, and editions of all her compositions (see Bibliography under 'Hildegard'). James Grier has written extensively about Adémar of Chabannes.

Chapter 4

Thinking about Gregorian chant in the Middle Ages, and notating it

The revival of learning under Charlemagne and his successors brought with it knowledge of the music theory of late antiquity and consequently a desire to relate Gregorian chant to that theory. Section 4.i explains what happened. An important element of the theory was the notion that the whole of creation was ordered according to harmonic principles. At the end of Chapter 3, it was suggested that some of the new chant composed in the eleventh century might have been inspired by a desire to reflect this harmony of the universe in newly composed melody, as it were composition according to theoretical principles. This idea is briefly considered in section 4.ii.

Simultaneously with the assimilation of classical music theory, musical notation was developed, in the form of the signs we call neumes. Musical theory and the notating of chant books were not at first directly linked. Neumes did not indicate precise pitch, and were thus of no use for the description of such matters as musical scales and intervals. But the ninth-century theoretical enterprise included one achievement of crucial importance, the linking of Gregorian chant to the tonal network of classical scale systems. Chant melodies could be imagined as a series of notes placed on the steps of a ladder (Latin *scalae* means 'stairs', hence our 'scale'), where the pitches at each step and the intervals between them were precisely defined. The concept remained in the domain of music theory, however, until notational signs were placed on a tonal grid, Guido of Arezzo's staff, and the notation was born which eventually led to the one we use today. Section 4.iii is about notation. Section 4.iv is a short guide to the liturgical and other books where chant is notated.

4.i Situating Gregorian chant in the harmonious universe; classical Greek music theory and Gregorian chant; the modal system

This section summarizes the chief notions of classical music theory which were taken up by Frankish writers of the ninth and tenth centuries. The political strength and relative stability of the Carolingian realm created the circumstances in which intellectual study could flourish, driven by the Franks' burning desire to recover the learning of antiquity and reshape it according to the needs of a new age and new circumstances. The great importance attached to the proper performance of the liturgy was one of the chief aims of the programme of reconstruction. To be able to read and write Latin was essential for this and much else besides. Among the many Latin texts studied by the Carolingians, at least those with the most advanced knowledge, were several concerned with music theory, the most important being those of Boethius.

Classical Greek theory; Boethius

Classical theory provided medieval musicians with scale systems and pitch names, even signs to represent steps on the scale (although these were not widely adopted). It acquainted them with the concept of the modes. It also outlined a theory of consonant intervals in a hierarchic order (octave, fifth, fourth, etc.) determined by simple arithmetical ratios, and showed how these reflected the harmonic ratios in accordance with which the universe had been created. Another aspect of classical theory, the moral influence of the modes, was conscientiously rehearsed by medieval writers, and new examples from the Christian era were adduced to support the notion, but this had little connection with chant practice. Whatever 'meaning' resided in chant was discernible in its texts.

The writers of late antiquity most influential in the Middle Ages were, in chronological order, Martianus Capella (early fifth century), Boethius (*c*.480–*c*.524), Cassiodorus (*c*.485–*c*.580) and Isidore of Seville (*c*.599–636). Boethius offers the most thorough explanation of musical proportions, scales and species. He was a member of one of the most important patrician Roman families, and served as consul and, from 522, *magister officium* at the court in Ravenna of Theodoric the Ostrogoth. He eventually fell foul of political intrigues and was executed for treason. Several of Boethius's chief works are translations and reworkings of treatises of Greek antiquity, made at a time when knowledge of the group of disciplines known as the *quadrivium* (arithmetic, geometry, astronomy and music) was suffering under a preference for the *trivium* (grammar, rhetoric and dialectic). (These subjects together comprise the 'liberal arts', worthy of study by free men; their counterpart were the 'illiberal', servile or mechanical arts, such as performing music, practised by slaves.) Knowledge of the Greek language was also deteriorating. Among Boethius's works on the *quadrivium*, his *De institutione musica* is accordingly based on Greek writings by Nicomachus and Ptolemy.

Boethius demonstrates (among other things) the correct division of the double-octave of the Greek Greater and Lesser Perfect System (*systema teleion meizon* and *elatton*). The basic scale-segment is the tetrachord (of four notes, a perfect fourth with two notes in between), and notes were named according to their position in the tetrachord (highest, next-highest, etc.), not with letters as we do today. Adding tetrachords to each other creates a full two-octave range. Using letters, this could be expressed, in descending order, as *aa–e*, *e–b*, *a–E*, *E–B*, with a low *A* standing alone to complete the lower octave. It will be seen that there are in fact two pairs of conjunct tetrachords, joined at *e* and *E*.

Different ways of arranging the notes within the tetrachord were designated according to three *genera*. In the diatonic *genus* the arrangement was the equivalent of modern *a–G–F–E*; in the chromatic *genus* it was *a–F♯–F♮–E*; in the enharmonic *genus* it was *a–F♮–∗–E*, where ∗ represents a note between *F* and *E*, a quarter-tone (though not measured to make two identical intervals). And so on for all the tetrachords in the System. The Greater Perfect System extended through two octaves, but the Lesser Perfect System had only three tetrachords, all conjunct: *d–a*, *a–E*, *E–B*, *A*; in the *diatonic* genus its highest tetrachord would be *d–c–b♭–a*.

Another important concept is that of the species of scale or scale-segment. Restricting ourselves to the diatonic *genus* (in any case the only one relevant to medieval chant), we can take perfect fourths from different places in the complete scale, as for example, *a–E*, *G–D* and *F–C*. The arrangement of full tones and semitones within these fourths is different in each case:

a–G–F–E: tone–tone–semitone
G–F–E–D: tone–semitone–tone
F–E–D–C: semitone–tone–tone

The next scale-segment down, *E–D–C–B*, would repeat the constellation of intervals of *a–G–F–E*. So there are three different species of fourth ('fourth' here meaning scale-segment between two notes a perfect fourth apart). By the same token there are four species of fifth, and seven species of octave.

These categories and definitions (and much more besides) were exemplified by Boethius by means of the monochord, a single-stringed instrument with a moveable bridge. By moving the bridge to different positions beneath the sounding string, precisely measured intervals could be produced, the positions being marked on the body of the instrument. (The divisions were made by bisecting and trisecting with a compass, not measuring with a ruler.) Medieval monochords were usually about a yard long. They frequently had two bridges, one fixed and the other moveable, and a sound-box to enhance sonority.

As is well known, the most consonant intervals are produced by string-lengths in simple proportions. A string-length half as long as another, that is, in the proportion 2:1, sounds an octave higher. String-lengths in the proportion 3:2 sound a fifth apart, 4:3 a fourth apart. Taking the latter from the former (done mathematically by multiplying the reversed numbers) produces the whole tone: $3:2 \times 3:4 = 9:8$.

The calculation of different types of semitone was also of interest. A whole tone can of course be divided into two equal halves. But a different semitone is produced if a major third is subtracted from a perfect fourth. To do this, a major third is calculated first, by adding two whole tones (done by multiplying the figures): $9:8 \times 9:8 = 81:64$. This can then be subtracted from a perfect fourth (multiplying the figures reversed): $4:3 \times 64:81 = 256:243$, known as the 'limma'. Another discrepancy in the system can be seen if we add six whole tones together. They overreach the octave by another small interval, the 'comma', $531441:524288$ (which looks rather startling when written in Roman numerals).

These are abstract schemata and measurements, setting out in an orderly and logical way the tonal possibilities open to Greek musicians. They do not help us very much to imagine the actual sound of Greek music, which in any case existed on a quite different plane, being performed by slaves. But as an intellectual resource they could, with some difficulty, serve as an abstract design against which to measure Gregorian chant.

The perfect intervals of music had a much greater significance than merely as expressions of relationships between sounds. The Greek philosopher and religious teacher Pythagoras, who lived in the second half of the sixth century BC, was credited with the recognition of the numerical ratios which governed the simple intervals. They were all derived from the simple series 1, 2, 3, 4, the 'tetractys', prolonged two ways, 1:3:9 and 1:2:4:8 to give expression to the whole tone, 9:8. The Pythagoreans invested these ratios with cosmic significance, believing them to represent the proportions by which both the universe and man's soul and body

---

Text box 4.1 The harmony of the universe

Certain features of the art of music for the adornment of ecclesiastical chant may here be set down. Certainly they bear careful study no less and just as profoundly [as the foregoing matters]. For the reason why some sounds consent to such a sweet mutual commixture with each other, while others disagree unpleasantly, unwilling to blend with each other, is at once profound and divine and in some ways one of the most deeply hidden of nature's secrets. Many writings of the ancients are in accord about this reason, into whose workings in this sphere the Lord allows us to enter. Here it is asserted with the most tried and tested arguments that the very same controlling principle which governs the concord of musical notes also moderates the natures of mortals. By the same numerical proportions through which unequal sounds concord with each other, eternal harmony unites both souls with bodies and also the conflicting elements of the whole world.

From *Musica enchiriadis*, chapter 18. Original text edn Hans Schmid, *Musica et Scolica Enchiriadis una cum aliquibus tractatulis adiunctis* (Munich, 1981), p. 56.

were governed. There is a graphic description of the creation of the world-soul in Plato's *Timaeus*, which shows how the demiurge (for Christians, God) combined and divided abstract substances according to the Pythagorean ratios. So music is an aural reflection of the principles which order the position and movement of the heavenly bodies as well as the balance between man's spiritual and physical being.

Carolingian theory

Aligning Gregorian chant with the classical tonal system was not easy. New scales and modes were defined which reflected better the hierarchy of notes in typical Gregorian melodies. Then the standard system of eight modes was used not only to classify chant in theory but also to make it more manageable for teaching.

It is not easy to think ourselves back into an age without pitch notation, but this is what we must do if we are to appreciate what the Carolingian and post-Carolingian musicians accomplished. The sounds of chant had to be coordinated with the abstract scales of classical music theory as learned from Martianus Capella, Boethius and the others. It had to be fitted into that progression of whole tones and semitones. The starting and finishing notes of the chants had to be pinpointed within the two-octave range. (For practical purposes, only the diatonic system was referred to, the chromatic and enharmonic *genera* play no significant part in chant theory.) It seems certain that not all chants fitted perfectly into the diatonic series, even when the third conjunct tetrachord with the equivalent of our *bb* was used. Several communions, for example, included what we would call *Eb*, or *F♯*, and some offertory verses shifted into tonal regions where the same extra notes would be required in modern notation. However, as far as we can tell, most chants were successfully brought into alignment with the two-octave diatonic system, and their final notes settled on the equivalent of *D, E, F* and *G*.

We can get a sense of how this was done by reading the treatise of Hucbald of St Amand (near Valenciennes in north France). Hucbald was one of a group of brilliant scholars with connections to the court of Charles the Bald (823–77). He was educated at St Amand and Auxerre and taught at St Amand, St Bertin and Reims. In his work *De musica* (also known as *De harmonica institutione*) he explains the composition of the two-octave scale, using the Greek names for the positions of each note. However, for a systematic explanation of the intervals of music he does not point to positions on the scale but recalls pieces of plainchant where the interval can be heard. In this way he makes a vital connection between what the singer knows, the plainchant melody, and the abstract concept. He does the same in another way when giving extra attention to the semitone. He cites two chants where the melody runs through the six-note scale-segment which we would notate *C–D–E–F–G–a*, once ascending and once descending. He says these six notes correspond to those of a lyre with six strings (*sex chorda*), and recommends scoring six lines to represent the strings, noting the intervals between them (tone–tone–semitone–tone–tone). Then, when an appropriate passage of chant is found which uses these six notes, the syllables of a chant text can be placed on the appropriate lines. 'In accordance, then, with these two kinds of interval, the tone and the semitone, they being set in due place and order, all the others are ranged, as fixed by calculation. A sum total of fifteen *phthongi* are arrayed thus, one above the other.' It is at this point that he presents the Greek names for the positions on the two-octave scale. But he also assigns to them letters and letter-like signs borrowed from Boethius and ultimately going back to the Greek writer Alypius (probably fourth century AD). This is because he wants to present more musical examples and 'place' them on the tonal ladder.

Hucbald then defines the tetrachords in the way which was standard in the Middle Ages but differs from the Greek arrangement. He singles out what we would call *D–E–F–G*. 'These four notes', he says, 'are called "finals" because everything that is sung [he means all Gregorian chant] ends among them'. The semitone occurs here as the middle interval, not the lowest as in Greek theory. The five tetrachords in all, all of the same intervallic species, are then as follows: *A–B–C–D*, *D–E–F–G*, *a–b–c–d*, *d–e–f–g* and *G–a–b♭–c*.

Finally Hucbald can call upon the singer's memory once again, in order to quote further pieces of chant which illustrate the theoretical concepts. For each of the four basic modes, D, E, F and G, he gives the range of notes within which they can begin and end, and cites musical examples. These are not only named but also partly notated with his special letters. In this way the singer can position the chants he knows on the two-octave scale, his anchor-point being the tetrachord of the 'finals'. Hucbald quotes eight chants for the D-mode, with starting notes *a*, *G*, *F*, *E*, *D*, *C*, *B* (for the note *B* Hucbald has to cite a phrase from within the chant, because he does not know any that begin on *B* in this mode) and *A*. After that come eight examples for the E-mode, eight for F and nine for G (from *d* down to *C*).

I have taken some time to summarize what Hucbald says, because no other treatise of the period brings us so close to the process of what I have rather grandly called above 'situating Gregorian chant in the harmonious universe'. This sort of writing, I imagine, reflects very well what a teacher would have explained to his more advanced pupils.

Other authors – there is space to mention only a few – adopted a different approach. The pitch-letters which Hucbald so judiciously introduced were not taken up elsewhere. But others recognized the usefulness of such a device. A different set of letters, the so-called *dasia* signs, was used in a group of treatises from north-west Germany, written towards the end of the ninth century. The three most important are *Musica enchiriadis* (Music handbook), *Scolica enchiriadis* (School handbook) and *Commemoratio brevis de tonis et psalmis modulandis* (Short reminder of the modes and the singing of psalms). *Musica* and *Scolica enchiriadis* set out the *dasia* signs right at the start, while *Commemoratio brevis* takes knowledge of them for

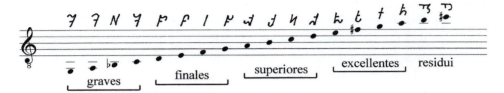

Ex. 4.1 Tetrachords and *dasia* signs from *Musica enchiriadis*

granted. From the point of view of plainchant, *Commemoratio brevis* is particularly interesting because it gives all the psalm tones in full, a most valuable record over a century before they can be found in staff notation. The series of signs takes the tetrachord of the 'finals' as its starting point, then turns the four signs upside down and back to front to generate signs for the other tetrachords (see Ex. 4.1). Curiously, none of the tetrachords are conjunct, which means that only the fifths are perfect throughout the range, while many fourths and octaves are not. This may be an indication that the notes we would call E♭, f♯ and c♯ were admitted in all octaves.

The modes

The *Enchiriadis* treatises, together with those of Hucbald of St Amand, Regino of Prüm and some other writers, can be dated to the end of the ninth century. But we can be certain that knowledge of Boethius and other classical writings, on the one hand, and thinking out the modal system, on the other, date back to the beginning of the century. This is when the first references to Boethius's theory can be found, even if copies of his treatise have only survived from later, and a list of Mass and Office chants in a manuscript of *c.*800 from St Riquier (near Abbeville in north France) divides them between the eight modes. (This sort of book is usually called a tonary: see section 4.iv below.) I give the names of the modes here as they were used in the St Riquier manuscript, by Aurelian of Réôme (a writer of the mid-ninth century), Hucbald, Regino, and in the *Enchiriadis* treatises. These names are derived from Byzantine chant practice, to which we must turn in a moment. By the end of the ninth century a different set of names was also in circulation, borrowed from classical Greek theory. (Its earliest principal witness is a treatise called *Alia musica, c.*900.) Curiously enough, in the process of adapting the modal theory and tonal system of ancient Greece to medieval chant, not only the constellation of the basic tetrachords was changed, but the Greek names were applied to different species of octave. (The error was not rectified until the humanist revival of classical Greek learning in the sixteenth century.) The range of notes most used in the different modes is not stated in these treatises and is given here as an approximation based on chant practice (see Table 4.1).

Why was it important to assign chants to one of eight modes? In several of the Eastern churches chants in the eight modes (*oktōēchos*) were organized calendrically,

Table 4.1 *Modes in the early Middle Ages*

	tonaries, Aurelian, Hucbald, etc.	*Alia musica*	*finalis*	conventional range
1	*protus authentus*	Dorian	*D*	*C–c*
2	*protus plagalis**	Hypodorian	*D*	*A–a*
3	*deuterus authentus*	Phrygian	*E*	*D–d*
4	*deuterus plagalis**	Hypophrygian	*E*	*C–c*
5	*tritus authentus*	Lydian	*F*	*F–f*
6	*tritus plagalis**	Hypolydian	*F*	*C–d*
7	*tetrardus authentus*	Mixolydian	*G*	*F–f*
8	*tetrardus plagalis**	Hypomixolydian	*G*	*C–d*

*or *plagis*

those in one mode being sung one Sunday, in the next mode the next Sunday and so on (see section 2.iv above). That would encourage the categorization of chants across the repertory. In the West no such calendric system was applied. Here, as perhaps originally in the East, the assignments were applied to melodies already existing. Old Roman and Ambrosian chant apparently managed perfectly well without categorizing their melodies according to mode. The earliest Western witness, incidentally, the St Riquier tonary mentioned above, is hardly a century later than the earliest eastern evidence for the *oktōēchos*.

A need to regularize or introduce order into modal assignations may well have to do with the connections between psalm verses chanted to a standard formula and the antiphons or responsories which frame them. The number of verse formulae is limited and they are easy to learn. But which was the right one to use with a particular antiphon or responsory? In medieval practice, for psalm-singing in the Office there was one tone for each mode (and a few extras such as the *tonus peregrinus*) and a number of alternative cadences, and for the verses of responsories sung after the lessons of the Night Office there was again one tone for each mode. (Other chants also used tones like the psalm tones: for example, the psalm verses for introits and communions, the Benedictus and Magnificat.)

It is usually assumed that when learning a chant such as an antiphon or responsory the singer should also fix in his/her mind its modal assignation, so that there should be no doubt as to which tone should be used for the psalm or psalm verse. This explanation has some plausibility. When antiphons (sometimes other chants as well) are listed in tonaries, they are not usually set out in alphabetical order so that the user can quickly check the mode (as in a telephone directory, where the user needs to find the number to ring). Instead, the antiphons for mode 1 are listed, then those for mode 2, and so on. That is, the antiphons requiring psalm tone 1, then those requiring tone 2, etc. And within each modal group there are further subdivisions according to the *cadence* to be applied to the psalm tone in question. What actually results are sets of chants with similar melodies. Antiphons in the same melodic family will require the same psalm tone and the same cadence. One can imagine a cantor rehearsing the *schola* in singing melodies of a particular family, two or three perhaps, then reminding them that other antiphons with the same melody would take the same psalm tone and cadence.

The cantor had other means at his disposal for instilling a sense of the melodic character of chants in a particular mode. Both Byzantine and Gregorian chant knew short vocalizations which contained the melodic essence, as it were, of chants in each of the modes, moving through its typical range and incorporating one or two typical turns of phrase. In Byzantine chant these *ēchēmata*, as they were known, seem to have been intoned before a chant, to remind the choir of the range and idiom of what was to be sung. In the Gregorian tradition they appear in tonaries, where they were presumably part of the rehearsal material of the cantor. The Byzantine melodies were sung to texts such as 'ananeanes', 'neanes', the Gregorian ones to 'noannoeane', 'noeane', etc. Aurelian of Réôme (writing *c*.850) says the Latins borrowed them from the Greeks. But in the West they were also added as festal extensions, 'neumae', to the antiphons for the Magnificat, Benedictus and other antiphons. Many Western tonaries also record 'typical' antiphons, one for each of the eight modes, which also capture something of the melodic character of melodies in each mode. The arrangement in several tonaries is therefore: (i) model antiphon for mode 1, (ii) 'noeane' melisma for mode 1, (iii) list of antiphons for mode 1, divided into sets according to cadence. These three items are then set out for each mode in turn.

It is one thing to provide examples of chants in a particular mode, but quite another to compose a technical definition of it. A treatise written in dialogue form in north Italy at the end of the millennium, the *Dialogus de musica* (formerly attributed to Odo of Cluny) gives ranges for the chants in each mode, but these are elementary rules of thumb and there are inevitably very many exceptions. Guido of Arezzo cites the model antiphons, saying: 'we learn the mode of the chant from the way it fits these, just as we often discover from the way it fits the body which tunic is whose'. That is another purely practical answer. Some south German theorists, however, adopted a more intellectual approach, suggesting that the nature of the mode was bound up with what we might call characteristic scale-segments. Here is a brief account of these two different approaches, focused on two famous music theorists.

Guido of Arezzo

Guido of Arezzo was born at the beginning of the 990s and died some time after 1033. He trained as a monk at Pomposa, then about 1025 went to Arezzo, where

Bishop Theodaldus deputed him to train the cathedral singers. A few years later he was called to Rome by Pope John XIX (1024–33) to explain the new notation he had used in an antiphoner. Some of his principal writings concern his new staff notation (see section 4.iii below): these are the so-called *Prologus in antiphonarium* and *Regulae rhythmicae* (because written in verse). The *Epistola de ignoto cantu* or *Epistola ad Michaelem* ('Letter about a chant not known' or 'Letter to Michael') are about the six syllables assigned to the notes of a hexachord as a reference point in learning to notate a melody and reading from notation. This is the technique known today as 'solmization'. The so-called 'Guidonian hand', where the solmization syllables are assigned to points on an open (left) hand, was credited to Guido by a contemporary writer, but does not appear in his authentic writings. Hands of a similar sort were known before Guido, and he may well have used the idea in teaching.

The hexachord with a semitone as the central interval had already been singled out by Hucbald (see above). As a reference against which to test pieces of chant it is less ambiguous than the narrow tetrachord and more compact than the unwieldy octave. What is crucial is that it complements Guido's staff notation perfectly. The hexachord was transposable to three pitches and their octaves: *C–D–E–F–G–a* (the *hexachordum naturale*), *G–a–b–c–d–e* (the *hexachordum durum*, the 'hard hexachord' with *b♮*, written as a square b), and *F–G–a–b♭–c–d* (the *hexachordum molle*, the 'soft hexachord' with *b♭*, written as a round b). The singer has to hear the set of notes in his/her mind, or test them by singing, and mark the position of the semitone. In Guido's staff notation the *F* and *c* lines are marked by a clef or coloured red and yellow respectively, and these are just where the semitone occurs.

Guido proposed a simple hymn melody, to the words *Ut queant laxis* for St John the Baptist, as a memory aid (Ex. 4.2). Not only does the melody as a whole fit into the hexachord, the starting notes of each the six verses are, in order, *C–D–E–F–G–a*. (It is possible Guido composed this tune specially, for the hymn was usually sung to other melodies.)

Guido then took the first syllable of each verse to designate the pitches of the hexachord. They were applicable in any position of the hexachord. Combining them in one diagram which covers the whole of the usual range of chant, and adding the alphabetic letters which Guido also used, we have Figure 4.1, found in many medieval books. (The word 'gamut' derives from the first note, *gamma+ut*, and is commonly used to mean the complete range of available notes. It is frequently used nowadays in a transferative sense, for example: 'Saunders ran through the whole gamut of ecclesiastical malpractices in St. David's.')

Finally, Figure 4.2 shows a 'Guidonian hand', also very common in medieval books.

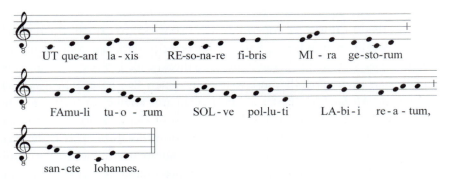

Ex. 4.2 *Ut queant laxis*, Guido's hexachord hymn melody

Hymn *Ut queant laxis* (text by Paul the Deacon? *c.*720–799)
So that they may be able to tell forth with loud voices the wonders of thy deeds, set free from sin the polluted lips of thy servants, O holy John.

ee							la
dd						la	sol
cc						sol	fa
♮ ♮							mi
♭ ♭						fa	
aa					la	mi	re
g					sol	re	ut
f					fa	ut	(durum)
e				la	mi	(molle)	
d			la	sol	re		
c			sol	fa	ut		
♮				mi	(naturale)		
♭			fa				
a		la	mi	re			
G		sol	re	ut			
F		fa	ut	(durum)			
E	la	mi	(molle)				
D	sol	re					
C	fa	ut					
♮	mi	(naturale)					
A	re						
Γ	ut						
	(durum)						

Figure 4.1 The medieval gamut

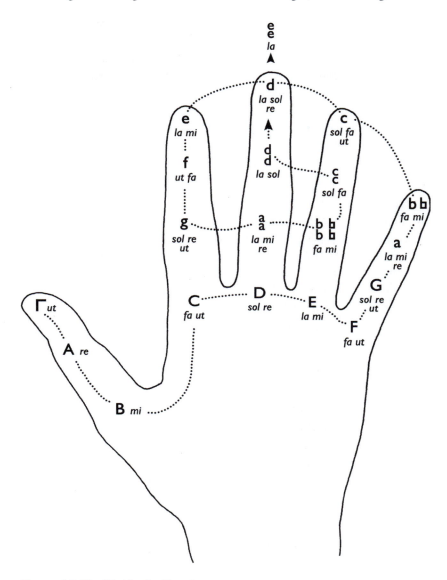

Figure 4.2 The 'Guidonian' hand

Hermannus Contractus

Hermannus bore the nickname 'Contractus' because he was a cripple from child-hood, hardly able to speak or write, who had to be carried by his brethren on a small litter. But he was one of the greatest scholars of his age. He was born in 1013 and died in 1054. He entered the famous Benedictine monastery on the Reichenau (an island in Lake Constance, now joined to the mainland by a causeway) in 1020. Since 1008 the abbot of the monastery had been Bern (*c.*978–1048: also known

Text box 4.2 Guido of Arezzo

In his *Prologus in antiphonarium*, a short essay explaining how he came to notate an antiphoner with his new staff notation, and how the notation works, Guido begins by complaining about the incompetence of singers of chant. He continues:

Who does not bewail this also, which is at once a grave error and a dangerous discord in Holy Church, that when we celebrate the Divine Office we are often seen rather to strive among ourselves than to praise God? One scarcely agrees with another, neither the pupil with his master, nor the pupil with his colleague. It is for this reason that the antiphoners are not one, nor yet a few, but rather as many as there are the masters in the various churches; and that the antiphoner is now commonly said to be, not Gregory's, but Leo's, or Albert's, or someone one's else. And since to learn one is most difficult, there can be no doubt that to learn many is impossible.

Since the masters, then, change many things arbitrarily, little or no blame should attach to me if I depart only in the slightest from common use so that every chant may return uniformly to a common rule of art. And inasmuch as all these evils and many others have arisen from the fault of those who make antiphoners, I strongly urge and maintain that no one should henceforth presume to provide an antiphoner with neumes unless he understands this art and knows how to do it according to the rules laid down here. Otherwise, without having first been a disciple of truth, he will most certainly be a master of error.

Therefore I have decided, with God's help, to write this antiphoner in such a way that hereafter any intelligent and studious person may learn the chant by means of it; after he has thoroughly learned a part of it through a master, he will unhesitatingly understand the rest of it by himself without one. Should anyone doubt that I am telling the truth, let him come to learn and see that small boys can do this under our direction, boys who until now have been beaten for their gross ignorance of the Psalms and vulgar letters. Often they do not know how to pronounce the words and syllables of the very antiphon which they sing correctly by themselves without a master, something which with God's help, any intelligent and studious person will be able to do if he tries to understand with what great care we have arranged the neumes.

In a letter to a fellow monk, Michael, Guido mentions how quickly chant can be learned by means of the new staff notation, then relates how he was summoned to Rome by John XIX (1024–33) to show and explain his antiphoner:

For if at present those who have succeeded in gaining only an imperfect knowledge of singing in ten years of study intercede most devoutly before God for their teachers, what do you think will be done for us and our helpers, who can produce a perfect singer in the space of one year, or at the most in two? And even if such benefits meet with ingratitude from the customary miserliness of mankind, will not a just God reward our labours? Or, since this is God's work and we can do nothing without him, shall we have no reward? Forbid the thought. For even the Apostle [Paul], though whatever is done is done by God's grace, sings none the less: 'I have fought a good fight, I have finished my course, I have kept the faith. Henceforth there is laid up for me a crown of righteousness' [2 Timothy 4:7–8].

Confident therefore in our hope of reward, we set about a task of such usefulness; and since after many storms the long-desired fair weather has returned, we must felicitously set sail.

But since you in your captivity are distrustful of liberty, I will set forth the situation in full. John, holder of the most high apostolic seat and now governing the Roman Church, heard of the fame of our school, and because he was greatly curious as to how boys could, by means of our antiphoner, learn songs which they had never heard, he invited me through three emissaries to come to him. I therefore went to Rome with Dom Grunwald, the most reverend abbot, and Dom Peter, provost of the canons of the church of Arezzo, a most learned man by the standards of our time. The Pope was greatly pleased by my arrival, conversing much with me and inquiring of many matters. After repeatedly looking through our antiphoner as if it were some prodigy, and reflecting on the rules prefixed to it [the Prologue quoted above], he did not give up or leave the place where he sat until he had satisfied his desire to learn a verse himself without having heard it beforehand, thus quickly finding true in his own case what he could hardly believe of others.

Cf. Oliver Strunk, *Source Readings in Music History*, rev. edn, ed. Leo Treitler (New York, 1998), pp. 212, 215 (translations by Oliver Strunk, revised by James McKinnon. Used by permission of W. W. Norton & Company, Inc.). Original texts ed. J. Smits van Waesberghe, Divitiae Musicae Artis A.III, 62 and Gerbert, Scriptores 2, 43. Cf. editions and translations by Dolores Pesce, *Guido of Arezzo's Regule rithmice, Prologus in antiphonarium, and Epistola ad Michaelem* (Ottawa, 1999), pp. 410, 445.

as Berno or Bernhardus), previously monk and probably master of the school at Prüm. This was a royal appointment, for Bern had been called to office by the Emperor Henry II. The abbacy of a monastery like the Reichenau was, after all, of importance at the highest level. Bern was, among other things, a composer of chant and one of the leading music theorists of his time. Hermannus was these things and more. Three complete *historiae* composed by him have survived (for St Afra of Augsburg, St Wolfgang of Regensburg and St Magnus of Füssen), and five liturgical sequences. As well as a comprehensive treatise on music theory, he was author of didactic chants for learning the rudiments of music. He invented a set of signs which indicated not pitches on a scale but the intervals between notes (or a note repetition); this is described in section 4.iii below. He composed treatises on astronomy and mathematics, a chronicle of the history of the world, and made musical instruments and chronometers.

Bern's music treatise had taken the form of a prologue to a comprehensive tonary. (The tonary is ordered alphabetically, like an earlier one from the Reichenau; such an arrangement is exceptional.) Drawing on the writings of an earlier theorist known as 'Pseudo-Bernelinus', Bern defines the modes in terms of their constituent species of fifths and fourths. The doctrine of the 'species', as was explained above,

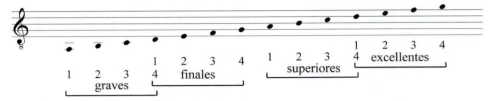

Ex. 4.3 Tetrachords in mainstream chant theory

1	2	3		4	5			6	7		8
mode		lower scale segment with 4 notes (characteristic of the plagal modes)			central scale segment with 5 notes (shared by the authentic and plagal modes)				upper scale segment with 4 notes (characteristic of the authentic modes)		
tetrardus (G)	D	E	F	G	a	h	c	d	e	f	g
tritus (F)	C	D	E	F	G	a	h	c	d	e	f
deuterus (E)	B	C	D	E	F	G	a	b	c	d	e
protus (D)	A	H	C	D	E	F	G	a	h	c	d

Figure 4.3 The principal notes in the modal scales according to Hermannus Contractus

is a feature of classical Greek theory, and refers to the constellation of intervals within a scale-segment. This is one of the things which Hermannus takes up and develops further. Interestingly, between Bern's prologue and Hermannus's treatise, knowledge of Guido's writings must have reached the Reichenau, for Hermannus refers to Guido, without, however, reproducing his teaching.

Guido's 'definition' of a mode is rather like saying: 'it ends on such and such a note and goes something like this (quotation of a model antiphon)'. But Hermannus wants to define its melodic substance more scientifically. He associates the finals of the modes with the (medieval) tetrachords and with particular notes within the tetrachords. The first mode is associated with the first note of each tetrachord, the second mode with the second note of each tetrachord, and so on. And it is these notes which give the mode its defining quality. Example 4.3 sets out the medieval tetrachords, numbering each note in each tetrachord from 1 to 4.

Figure 4.3 sets out the finals and scale-segments according to Hermannus's teaching. For ease of reference I have numbered the columns 1 to 8. Column 1 gives the mode, D, E, F and G. Columns 2, 4, 6 and 8 give the defining notes, derived from their position in the tetrachords of Example 4.3. So the bottom line, for the D mode, picks out the first note of each tetrachord; the second lowest line, for the E mode, picks out the second note of each tetrachord; and so on. These notes are printed in bold. The other notes are less important. Columns 4–6 then comprise the notes common to both the authentic and plagal forms of the mode; columns 2–4 comprise the notes characteristic of the plagal form of the mode; columns 6–8 comprise the notes characteristic of the authentic form of the mode.

Hermannus describes all this almost obsessively. Here is what he says about the first mode:

> The Protus with its Plagal mode, since they are the first, by necessity require all [notes and species] which are first,
>
> - the first letters in all the tetrachords, that is, A, D, a, d,
> - the first species of the octave, that is, A–a and D–d,
> - the first species of the fifth, that is, D–a,
> - the first species of the fourth, that is, A–D.
>
> Of the four letters above, the authentic mode takes three for itself, that is, D, a and d, and the octave is D–d. On one of these the mode attains its highest note according to the rule, it ends on the other, and in the middle is the note upon which 'seculorum amen' is sung [that is, the tenor of the psalm tone]. It has the fifth D–a, and the fourth a–d, the *superiores*.

Turning to a chant actually composed by Hermannus, one expects to see these principles put into practice. And so they are. *Invicta Christi testis* (Ex. 4.4) is the first antiphon at Lauds from his Office in honour of St Afra of Augsburg. Since the chants follow the numerical order of the modes, the antiphon is in mode 1. All four verses end on D or a, and most of the individual words end on D, a or d. (Only 'Christi' and 'Gaio' end on G instead.) Most of these endings are driven home by the sub-tonal ending, C–D–D, G–a–a or c–d–d (see 'testis Afra', 'iudice', 'attempta', 'agnite', 'veritatis', 'potuit' and 'ratione').

In this section more theorists could have been mentioned, and their chronological and geographical distribution could have been traced in more detail. But enough has been said to bring home the most important concerns of medieval thinkers about chant. Two matters still need consideration. The most important is musical notation, so far alluded to but not described at length. That is the subject of section 4.iii. But first I include a short digression about the significance of the sort of music composed by Hermannus and some contemporaries, and its relation to music theory. Is this chant composed according to some sort of theoretical prescription?

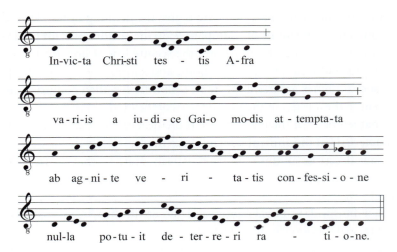

Ex. 4.4 Hermannus Contractus, Antiphon *Invicta Christi testis Afra* (St Afra)

Hermannus Contractus, A. *Invicta Christi testis Afra*
Afra, the invincible witness to Christ, tried in various ways by the judge Gaius,
could not be deterred by any argument from delivering a confession of the truth.

Further reading

There is comprehensive coverage of medieval music theory in volumes of the German
series *Geschichte der Musiktheorie.* There are articles in *NG2* and *MGG2* on all the
writers mentioned here, with information about modern editions. Several texts are
available in translation, for example, *Hucbald, Guido, and John on Music*, trans.
Babb. The chapters by Bower and Cohen in the *Cambridge History of Western Music
Theory* are useful summaries. See also Hiley, *Western Plainchant*, ch. V. As the present
book was going to press, a fine new synthesis by Atkinson appeared: *The Critical
Nexus.*

4.ii Medieval theory and medieval chant: composition according to theoretical principles?

The theoretical definition of the modes, and its subsequent refinement and enlarge-
ment by medieval writers, was a considerable intellectual achievement in itself, but
it had further consequences, for it seems possible that it affected the Gregorian
melodies themselves. Theory ('musica') put the chants to the test and found that
not all of them met adequate standards of perfection. Medieval writers frequently

speak of correcting melodies, and the chant books themselves provide plenty of evidence of it. The chant reform of the Cistercians (see section 3.iii above) was inspired by such ideas, in the belief that the original melodies had been corrupted. Such things could happen to the most perfect creations when entrusted to the leaky vessel of human memory. New melodies were also composed which matched theoretical prescriptions more exactly.

The aim of the Frankish singers had been to follow Roman practice, buttressed by the authority of St Gregory. We have just seen in section 3.iii how the Gregorian chant repertory was enlarged in a variety of ways and for a variety of reasons. To a music historian, one of the most interesting things about this is that a lot of the new music is in a different melodic style from the 'classical Gregorian' manner. But how could composers justify breaking fresh ground in this way, when the Gregorian repertory had such authority, a quasi-divine authority in fact? The newness is most apparent in the quite new types of chant such as sequences and Christmas songs. But the melodic style of the old categories was also transformed, especially the antiphons and responsories of the *historiae*, for example the antiphon by Hermannus Contractus quoted above (Ex. 4.4) or the chants composed about 150 years later for St Thomas of Canterbury (Exx. 3.2–3). For these saints' Offices it would have been possible to go on using the traditional melody types and formulae. But composers did not do so. Why not?

One of the reasons for composing antiphons and responsories in this new style was a heightened consciousness of modal quality and propriety. Specialists have discovered many examples where in some manuscripts even the most venerable chants of all, those for the Proper of Mass, are adjusted to remove details which contradict a clear and unambiguous modal character. Another interesting detail may be observed in the way responsory verses are sometimes adjusted to end on the final of the mode. Not all the old, traditional tones do this. Ending the verse on a note other than the *finalis* does not really disturb the tonal propriety of the responsory as a whole, because after the verse there will be a repeat of the last part of the respond, naturally closing on the *finalis* of the mode. But some musicians evidently felt that the verse, too, should end on the *finalis*, and made a corresponding modification of the traditional tone.

It is not surprising, therefore, that newly composed melodies should aim for the key notes, as we may call them, in the respective modes. This change of direction in chant style can be seen as early as the ninth century. The movement gathers momentum in the tenth century and reaches full strength in compositions like those of Hermannus. Not all new works are equally 'progressive', but the general trend is clear. Practically all the music discussed in section 3.ii above is affected by it.

Composers seem to have had few inhibitions about striking out on these new paths. One might think that reverence for St Gregory as the creator of plainchant would have ensured continued use of the old style, but this was not the case. It is symptomatic that medieval writers on chant hardly ever mention Gregory as the creator of chant. Bern and Hermannus, for example, never speak of him, and nor do the writers of the *Enchiriadis* treatises. Guido says in *Micrologus* that Gregory loves the *tritus* more than all other notes (he is thinking of the repeated *F*s and *c*s in introits, graduals and other chants), which is a sort of acknowledgement of Gregory's authorship of all the chant. And in the *Regulae rhythmicae* he names Gregory as the author of the rules which govern properly composed chant.

Hermannus, as already mentioned, is one of several theorists who treat the lower fourth, the *finalis*, the upper fifth and the octave as the pillars of a chant melody, fundamental to its modal character. These are the notes embodied in the harmonic series 1:2:3:4, which will hardly have escaped the mathematician and astronomer Hermannus and his contemporaries, for it is no more than a rudimentary element of the general knowledge of the time. Admittedly, Hermannus does not say outright, 'these are the harmonies which hold creation together, as laid down when God ordered all things in measure and number and weight (Wisdom 11:20). Therefore it is right that we should dispose our melodies accordingly.' But as a justification for writing his treatise he states that 'the whole intent of musical reasoning bears upon the establishment of the science of composing melody rationally, of judging it according to the rules, and of singing it properly' (§15, Ellinwood p. 47). The words 'reasoning' (*musicae ratio*) and 'rationally' (*rationabiliter*) refer, of course, to the harmonic bases of what he has explained, and which are set out in the very first paragraph of his treatise.

4.iii Representing Gregorian chant in written signs; neumes, the invention of the staff

Beginning in the ninth century, a few dozen examples of musical notation have survived, which show that a need had arisen to support the oral tradition with written aids. Since chant had been performed and taught to successive generations of singers for centuries without the aid of musical notation, we may wonder why notation was invented at all. A number of reasons can be suggested, and we shall come back to these at the end of the section. First, however, the basic characteristics of the notational system should be explained.

From the end of the ninth century three completely notated books with the chants for Mass have survived. The places they come from (Brittany, Laon, St Gall) are widely separated geographically, and the appearance of their notation signs, the neumes, is quite distinct, although the principle behind them is always the same. Other styles of neumes are also known from the ninth and tenth centuries. So the need to write down the melodies was obviously widespread, while the manuscripts

---

Text box 4.3 Neume

The word 'neume' comes from Greek and Latin *neuma*, meaning 'gesture'. In a transferred sense, a melodic gesture would be the movement of the voice while delivering a syllable of text. This might be a single note, a short phrase, or even a long melisma. An analogy, even a deliberate amalgamation, was made with Greek *pneuma*, meaning breath, life and soul, spirit, the Holy Spirit. The usual word for a written sign in the ninth and tenth centuries was 'nota'. We find 'neuma' for the written sign only later, in the later tenth century.

'Neuma' or 'pneuma' meaning a melodic phrase is widely documented, for instance as the term for the melody of a sequence, certainly a melisma of striking proportions and character. Another example, more complicated to explain, concerns melismas added to Office antiphons. The story goes like this. Tonaries, in which the cadences for psalm tones, long lists of antiphons according to the different modes, and other useful didactic materials are included, often set out 'model' antiphons which contain as it were the melodic essence of antiphons in each of the eight modes. The model antiphons are often followed by short melismas with the same purpose. From about the twelfth century the melismas made the transition from teaching aid to liturgical use, when they were added as a festive extension to the last antiphon of Vespers and Lauds and to the Magnificat and Benedictus antiphons. In this form the melismas are often called 'neumae'.

---

which resulted look different from place to place, their notations differing at least on the surface much more than the writing of the Latin text in them.

At this point the signs of most of the main musical scripts could be set out in a comparative table. But this would take up a great deal of space, since one would have to take account not only of the different scripts used in different areas of Europe but also of the changes they underwent over the centuries. (The tables in article 'Notation, III.1, Plainchant' in *NG2* are a case in point, with three tables for three different periods, displaying up to eighteen different signs in twenty-four different scripts.) We shall concentrate on just eight scripts here, six early ones and two later ones. That is enough to demonstrate the principles and give some idea of the variety. (See Table 4.2.)

Notation where pitches are not indicated precisely is called 'adiastematic', the opposite of 'diastematic' (from Greek *diastēma*, 'interval') where we can read the intervals accurately. As already stated several times, neumes do not indicate pitch precisely, nor do they communicate measurable rhythmic values. Since we nowadays expect notation to do these two things before all else, it takes some stretching of the imagination to understand the actual function of the signs. There are a few signs for single notes, many more for groups of notes. The signs indicate, first and foremost, the direction of the melodic flow, always with reference to a syllable of Latin text. That is easy to visualize in the case of note-groups, for example, a sign for three notes

Table 4.2 *Eight medieval types of signs for notating chant*

name	modern	Breton c.900	Laon c.900	St. Gall c.900	Winchester 11th century	Toulouse 11th century	Benevento 12th century	Paris 13th century	gothic 13th century
virga									
punctum									
pes									
clivis (flexa)									
torculus									
porrectus									
scandicus									
climacus									
oriscus									
quilisma									
epiphonus									
cephalicus									

in ascending order, another for three notes in descending order. The relation of the notes to one another is indicated in the sign itself, the marks of the pen moving upward or downward. (The question of how the notion of 'up' and 'down' arose, in both script and musical pitches, is an interesting one but would burst this chapter at the seams.) For a single note the case is different, for it has no internal 'direction'. Instead the sign is interpreted in relation to the preceding and succeeding notes, as being relatively higher or lower than these.

Common neumes

The first column in Table 4.2 gives the customary name for the signs. In the second column, note-heads as in a modern transcription (for example, in this book) are given. There follow the signs themselves in eight different scripts. The first three are

Ex. 4.5 Examples of liquescence

the signs in the manuscripts already mentioned above, the earliest books containing the Proper chants of Mass for the whole year, from Brittany, Laon and St Gall, respectively. These are from roughly 900. After that come two eleventh-century scripts, from Winchester and Toulouse. The pitches of the latter can already be read accurately, once one knows which note to start on, although it does not use a staff. The same is true of the next manuscript from Benevento in south Italy, from the twelfth century. Finally come two staff notations: square or quadratic notation as standardized in Paris in the thirteenth century; and one of the varieties of 'Gothic' notation used in Germany from the thirteenth century onwards. This selection means that Italy gets very short shrift and Spain is omitted entirely, while the many interesting staff notations from Central Europe (Hungary, Bohemia, Poland) are also missing. Several comprehensive surveys are available which fill these gaps (see 'Further reading' below).

The meanings of most of the signs are self-evident. Sometimes alternatives are given, since several of the early scripts make subtle distinctions, mostly of a rhythmic nature, between different ways of singing the same note or melodic progression. More is said about these below, under 'Rhythm'. But some signs have a special meaning. Two are connected with the pronunciation or delivery in singing of the Latin text. They are found when the liquid or sonant consonants occur, 'l', 'm', 'n' and 'r', and also diphthongs in words such as 'alleluia' and 'eius'. A word like 'alleluia' will often have two of these special signs, known as 'liquescents', the first to get from 'al-' to '-le-', and the second to get from '-lu-' to '-ia'. Probably the singer anticipated the following note while singing the consonant or double-vowel in question (see Ex. 4.5).

Two other signs are more difficult. The *oriscus* was frequently used to indicate a repeat of the previous note, although it must have been something more than a simple repeat, otherwise the special sign would have been superfluous. The *quilisma* appears as the penultimate element of three notes in ascending order. (The first note can be the end of the previous note-group.) Again, some special mode of delivery must have been involved. One school of interpretation believes that a rhythmic nuance is involved in both the *oriscus* and *quilisma*. While the signs might indeed have had an effect on the rhythm, it is difficult to escape the impression that more must have been involved in the employment of such striking graphic shapes. They often occur at the semitone step in the scale, yet this is not invariably the case, so that a 'warning' function of that sort does not fully explain their use. A vocal ornament of some sort should not be completely ruled out, for such things are common enough in Christian religious chant outside the Latin tradition. No medieval writers give clear explanations of the signs.

Note that the intervals within the note-group and between one note or note-group and the next are not specified. Evidently the notation conveyed enough to the teacher for instructing the singers, who would sing from memory. For early notated books were used by teachers, as a record and reminder of the right way to sing the sacred melodies. They were not read from during the liturgy.

To see the notation in use, the facsimiles given in this book may be compared with Table 4.2. The front cover has Winchester neumes. Figures 4.4–7 have examples of Laon, St Gall, Aquitainian and Beneventan notation, while Figures 4.8–9 are examples of English staff notation of the late twelfth and mid-thirteenth centuries, respectively. Example 4.6 below shows in more detail how the signs were used in practice.

Rhythm

The rhythmic interpretation of Gregorian chant is a difficult matter, and the last word on the subject has certainly not been said. Chant notation does not indicate precise rhythmic note-values. As we shall see in a moment, when Example 4.6 is discussed, some early scripts indicate a lot of rhythmic differentiation, but we do not know exactly what was intended. Note-values in a metrical relationship, such as 2 shorts = 1 long? Or a subtle rhythmic nuance of some sort? Most singers today adopt the latter position. At least the early sources show incontrovertibly that in the ninth and tenth centuries notes were not equally long throughout. But was it only a matter of fine shading? One might posit the following analogy. In the ninth and tenth centuries (and longer in many places) chant was notated without precise pitch information, yet no one supposes that singing in tune was first practised (or at least attempted) in the eleventh century. Could not one argue in the same way about the length of the notes? If chant notation does not indicate precise note-values, does this necessarily mean they were never employed?

Medieval writings on music do not describe musical notation in terms of precise pitches or rhythms. How should they? Imagine trying to describe a *porrectus*: 'This sign signifies that the voice first descends and then reascends. The second note may

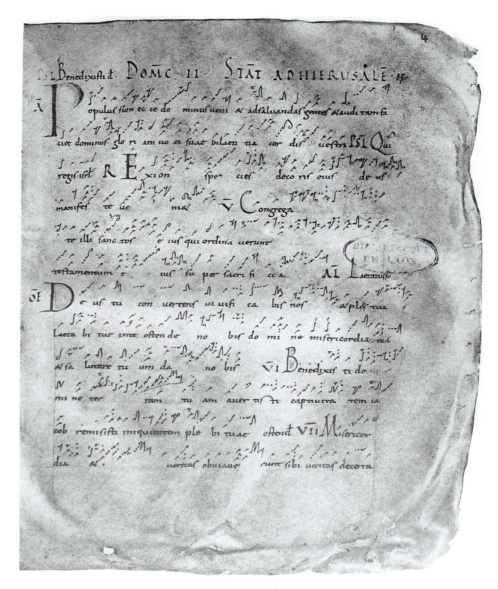

Figure 4.4 Laon, Bibliothèque Municipale, MS 239, p. 9 (fol. 4r)

be lower than the first by any interval sanctioned by St Gregory, as also the third note may be higher than the second by the same intervals.' Any more specific information about the intervals would be most cumbersome. But the basic nature of the *porrectus* can be grasped in the twinkling of an eye. Similarly for rhythm. Only rarely do we read hints that chant may have been rhythmically differentiated, and only in two instances are there remarks about the choir singing in strict proportional rhythms.

Figure 4.5 St Gall, Stiftsbibliothek, MS 359, p. 7–27

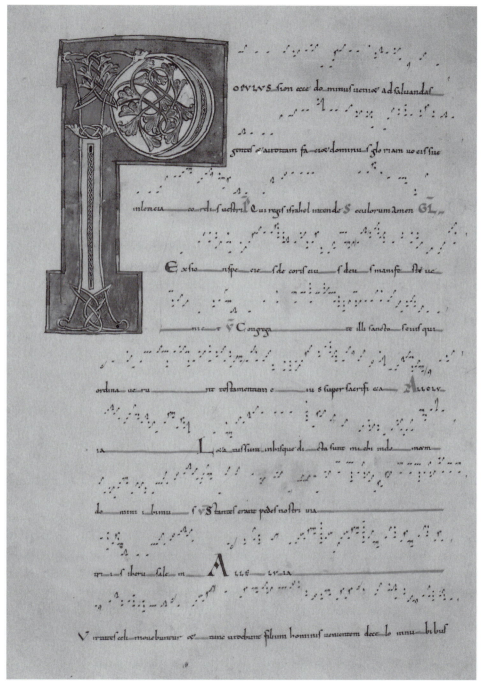

Figure 4.6 London, British Library, MS Harley 4951, fol. 124v.

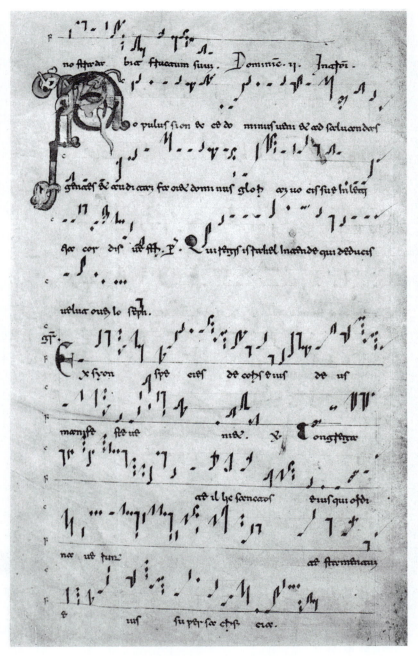

Figure 4.7 Benevento, Biblioteca Capitolare, MS 34, fol. 2v

Figure 4.8 Worcester Cathedral, Chapter Library, MS F 160, fol. 294r

Sometimes silence may speak volumes, but an *argumentum ex silentio* is weak for all that.

This is obviously not the place to expound a theory of the rhythmical performance of chant. It has been done before, by Wagner and Vollaerts among others, and

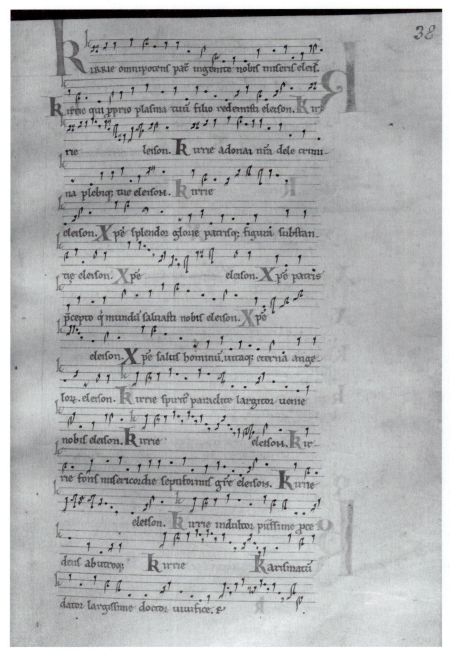

Figure 4.9 London, British Library, Cotton MS Caligula A.xiv, fol. 38r

Ex. 4.6 Gradual *Ex Sion species* in three notations

opposed or ignored by the majority of writers and practitioners. Example 4.6 will show what the controversy is about.

In Example 4.6 the first section (respond) of the gradual *Ex Sion species* is transcribed into modern notation from the manuscript London Harley 4951, from Toulouse in the eleventh century. The corresponding page in the manuscript is given in Figure 4.6; the signs used in the manuscript are in column no. 5 of Table 4.2. The signs in manuscripts Laon 239 and St Gall 359 (both from about 900) are copied over the transcription. The complete page from Laon 239 is in Figure 4.4, the signs are in column no. 2 of Table 4.2; for St Gall 359 see Figure 4.5 and column no. 3 of Table 4.2. In what follows I refer to the note-groups 1–26, all written thus in London 4951. (The other manuscripts divide some of these further.)

There are very few substantial discrepancies between the transcription from London 4951 on the staff and the signs from the other manuscripts. At the end of the first line London 4951 has two notes more than the others. At the start of 26 London 4951 lacks a *G* which is usual here; the other manuscripts begin with a *torculus*, *GAG*. Other differences concern the presence or absence of the *quilisma* and *oriscus*. (There are no liquescent neumes in this piece.)

For single notes, Laon 239 uses a little hook-shaped sign, usually referred to nowadays as the *uncinus*. St Gall differentiates between higher-lying single notes, written with a *virga*, and lower-lying ones, written with a short horizontal bar, the *tractulus*. Two notes in descending order, written with a *clivis*, can be seen at 18. Note that the St Gall *clivis* has a small letter 'c'. This is short for *celeriter* or *cito*, 'quickly'. Laon has a short upstroke joined to a longer downstroke, and the fact that this sign is joined up is significant. Immediately afterwards, at the start of 19, we can see a contrasting way of writing the *flexa*. Laon separates the two notes into two *uncini* and puts the letter 'a' – *augete*, 'increase' – between the two for good measure. St Gall has a *flexa* with a bar across the top, the so-called *episema*, signifying a lengthening. The same signs can be seen at the start of 3 and 5, and at 12, and there is something similar at 10. This time, instead of the lengthening *episema*, St Gall uses the letter 't' – *trahere* or *tenete*, 'drag, hold' – while Laon has two separate *uncini*.

Already in these few instances some of the capabilities for rhythmic differentiation will have become clear. Notes can be separated or joined, the small letters and (in St Gall) extra strokes can be added. The letters are described in a letter of the monk Notker of St Gall at about the time this manuscript was copied. A later St Gall writer, Ekkehard IV (d. 1036), called them 'litterae alphabeti significativae' and said that a Roman singer, appropriately called Romanus, had added them to an authentic antiphoner of St Gregory in the abbey's possession. Some of these 'significative' or 'Romanian' letters refer to pitch, warning of a particular step up or down, or the letter 'e' for *equalis*, most useful as indicating that the next sign starts on the same note as the last has ended on. The most frequent rhythmic one beside 'c' and 't' is 'x' for *expectare*, 'wait'. Laon has a partly different vocabulary. We have seen 'a', *augete*, 'increase', in Laon, whereas in St Gall this would be short for *altius*, 'higher' (in pitch). Laon has 'h', *humiliter*, 'low' and 'n', *nectere*, 'join', not found in St Gall.

Other instances of rhythmic differentiation can be seen as follows:

  2 Shorter *pes*.

13 *Pes* with a longer second note, with an *episema* in St Gall and 't' in Laon.

12 Longer *pes*, written angled instead of rounded in St Gall, separate *uncinus* and *virga* in Laon.

14 Shorter form: two normal *puncta* followed by a normal *clivis*, emphasized by 'c' in St Gall.

21 Longer *scandicus*: three bars (*tractuli*) instead of *puncta*, followed by a *virga* with *episema* in St Gall; separate *uncini* instead of *puncta*, and *virga* in Laon.

23 In St Gall there are two *puncta*, then two *tractuli*, indicating two shorter followed by two longer notes; in Laon the third note is marked 'a', and separated from the final *uncinus* (marked 'h'), so the same rhythmic effect is indicated in both manuscripts.

24 In both manuscripts the first note is separated from the other three. See also 9, where Laon emphasizes the separation with 't'.

26 The *G* lacking the start in London 4951 was mentioned above. The two other manuscripts have two normal *torculi* one after the other. The second of these has an *oriscus* added on. The piece ends with yet another *torculus*, this time written in the longer form, like a *ritardando*. In Laon there are three *uncini*, supplemented by 'a'. St Gall uses a sign like a rather angular 'S'. As in other cases, the actual writing of the sign, more deliberate, taking longer than the usual round *torculus* immediately preceding it, is analogous to the slower delivery.

One could pick out several more details such as these, but the main point has been made. The careful attention to such detail on the part of the early notators in these and a few other early sources is extremely impressive. There are hundreds of chants in the Laon and St Gall manuscripts, thousands in the antiphoner of Hartker of St Gall. I do not know how many times the scribe of St Gall 359 placed an *episema* on a *clivis*, but the Dutch scholar Joseph Smits van Waesberghe counted the numbers of supplementary letters (*litterae significativae*) in the principal sources: 4,156 in St Gall 359; 12,987 in Hartker's antiphoner (St Gall 390–391); and a staggering 32,378 in the tenth-century gradual Einsiedeln 121.

We must not forget the *oriscus* and *quilisma*. The transcription on the staff, from London 4951, shows that the Toulouse manuscript has an *oriscus* near the end of 12 and near the end of 26, both times where a note is repeated – at least, that is what most manuscripts with staff notation indicate. Toulouse has a *quilisma* in 6, 8 and 11, in rising-third formations. The other sources sometimes differ from Toulouse. In Laon and St Gall, the *oriscus* with repeat function, or something of the sort, is the penultimate note in 4, the antepenultimate in 13 (like Toulouse) and the antepenultimate in 26 (again like Toulouse). In addition, Laon has it at the start of 15. Laon and St Gall have no *quilisma* at 8.

Pitch

Music theorists from the ninth century onward sometimes employed pitch-names and pitch-signs to explain concepts such as consonant intervals and steps in a scale. Such things were not applied to chant books until the early eleventh century, when alphabetic letters were in a few cases written instead of or alongside the traditional

Text box 4.4 Chanting in rhythm

Two writings about chant from the late ninth century mention chanting in strict measured rhythm. These are *Scolica enchiriadis* and *Commemoratio brevis de tonis et psalmis modulandis*. They are related to each other by their common use of *dasia* pitch-notation and the fact that they are usually found next to each other in medieval manuscripts, preceded by another related treatise, *Musica enchiriadis*. Toward the end of *Commemoratio brevis*, after general recommendations about disciplined psalm-singing, we read the following:

All notes which are long must correspond rhythmically [*numerose concurrant*] with those which are not long through their proper inherent durations, and any chant must be performed entirely, from one end to the other, according to this same rhythmic scheme. In chant which is sung quickly this proportion [*ratio*] is maintained even though the melody is slowed towards the end, or occasionally near the beginning (as in chant which is sung slowly and concluded in a quicker manner), for the longer values consist of the shorter, and the shorter subsist in the longer, and in such a fashion that one has always twice the duration of the other, neither more nor less [*ut nec maiore nec minore sed semper unum alterum duplo superet*].

Terence Bailey, *Commemoratio brevis de tonis et psalmis modulandis: Introduction, Critical Edition, Translation* (Ottawa, 1979), pp. 102–3.

The master also recommends tapping with the hand or foot to keep the choir in time. At the end of Part I of *Scolica enchiriadis* the antiphon *Ego sum via* is cited, with the instruction to sing the last syllable of each of the three phrases long, the others short. That is probably what any singer would do anyway. The interesting thing is that the author twice refers to durations in the ratio of two to one, and also to beating time in the manner of metrical feet [*metricis pedibus cantilena plaudatur*].

(See Hans Schmid, *Musica et Scolica Enchiriadis una cum aliquibus tractatulis adiunctis* (Munich, 1981), p. 86; Raymond Erickson, *Musica enchiriadis and Scolica enchiriadis*, trans., with introduction and notes (New Haven, 1995), p. 51.)

neumes. The system of pitch-notation which was eventually used everywhere was the staff-notation promulgated by Guido of Arezzo (around 1030). The traditional signs, modified if necessary, could now be placed on the staff. The earliest surviving complete book where this was done is a gradual from Rome dated 1071 (Bodmer 74, facsimile edn Lütolf). Guido recommended using a staff of four lines. The lines for *F* and *c* should be indicated, for these are the notes above the semitone steps in the diatonic scale. This could be done either with coloured lines, red for *F* and yellow for *c*, or with little letters against the lines. With four notes on the lines and five above, between and below the lines, most chants could be notated comfortably without too many changes of clef.

Different notators in different areas often used modifications of the Guidonian system. For example, we find green instead of yellow for *c*, or some other colour

Figure 4.10 Clefs in London, British Library, Cotton MS Caligula A.xiv

scheme, and different clefs. Pieces with extremely low passages might use a gamma sign for the *G* a seventh below *F*, and a high *g*-clef for the highest passages is fairly common. Several south German manuscripts placed letter-clefs against every staff-line. Another interesting variant can be found in several twelfth-century manuscripts from the British Isles and Scandinavia. In these the clefs most used are *D*, *a*, *b* (our *b♭*) and *h* (our *b♮*). This makes sense if we imagine a situation where red *F*-line and yellow *c*-line are used. The *D*- and *a*-clefs cover the other lines, but can easily stand alone even when the lines are not coloured. The *b♭* and *b♮* signs make the tonality clear but, once in place, can be regarded as clefs in their own right. If a purist ever objected to this turning inside out of the Guidonian system, his voice has remained unheard over the centuries. Figure 4.8 shows a page from a Worcester manuscript of the late twelfth century, a Kyrie with trope verses, using only *h*-clefs. Figure 4.10 shows the clefs on other pages of the same manuscript, *D*, *b♭* and a double *b♮*, actually two *h*s one on top of the other (single *b♮* would be an octave lower).

The fine detail of the notation in Laon 239 and St Gall 359 (and a few more manuscripts: Hartker's antiphoner St Gall 390–391, Einsiedeln 121, Bamberg 6 from Regensburg) is rare and gradually disappears in the course of the eleventh century. The *oriscus* and the *quilisma* persisted longer, into the twelfth century, liquescent neumes even longer. The adoption of staff notation did not necessarily hasten their demise, although it happened at roughly the same time. Many twelfth-century sources are still written with *oriscus* and *quilisma*. On Figure 4.8, in line 3, notes 3, 12 and 16 are *oriscus*-repeat notes. The third sign on line 12 is a *pes+oriscus* (called *pes stratus*), *FGG*. Many syllables have a liquescent sign, for example in line 5 *eleison* (for the diphthong) and *splendor* ('n' before another consonant), or line 6 *mundum* and *eleison* again.

The origins of chant notation

The notation in Laon 239 and St Gall 359 is, as we have just seen, highly detailed and sophisticated, never surpassed since. The musical notation in earlier manuscripts, going back into the first half of the ninth century, is by no means as complex, but practically all the essential signs (in whatever script) were in place. We have examples from north-east France, Brittany, the Loire (but not southern France), Spain (but not Italy) and south Germany. England would no doubt have used them but for the wholesale cultural destruction which followed the Danish invasions. It is possible that redatings and new discoveries may alter the picture. Although the oldest books with a complete cycle of chants for the year are from the end of the ninth century, the skills needed for making such books were already established fifty years earlier, perhaps even further back. Perhaps notated books existed and have been lost. We don't know. From the diversity of the musical scripts it looks very much as if the general principles were widely understood but that different ways of executing the signs established themselves in different areas. That accords with what we can see in the melodies themselves. They are basically the same from one source to another, but small differences can be found again and again. This suggests that different cantors notated them from memory, not from copying some authoritative exemplar. The same could then be true of the musical scripts. They seem to have developed independently of any central model.

The 'invention' of one musical script eventually proved unsuccessful, at least in the long run. A small number of manuscripts from north-east France (St Amand seems to have been especially interested in it) contain a notation somewhat different from all the others. This is the so-called 'paleofrankish' (that is, ancient and Frankish) notation – once thought to have been the ancestor of other types, but this cannot be proven. If we look again at Table 4.2 we can see that the *pes* is made of two elements: a starting stroke or curve and then an upward stroke. Similarly the *clivis*, which starts with an upward stroke of some sort, to get to the initial higher-lying note, as it were, then a downstroke. On the same principal, the *torculus* and *porrectus* contain three elements, the pen moves in three directions. In paleofrankish or St Amand notation there is one element less, at least when the *pes* and *clivis* are not split into two dots (see Table 4.3).

Table 4.3 *St Amand or paleofrankish neumes*

	St. Amand	Breton	French
pes	⌡	⌐	⌐
clivis	⌐	⌐	∧
torculus	⌒	⌒	⌒
porrectus	Y	⋎	⋎

The significance of this notation is twofold. Whether or not it is a predecessor of other types, it was, like them, the result of an independent initiative. Ultimately it fell out of use, but so did all neumatic notations sooner or later. The other point is more curious. As Charles Atkinson has pointed out, three of the four basic signs shown above correspond to the prescriptions of writers on prosody. The word 'prosody' comes from Greek *prosōdia* (Latin *accentus*), and is concerned with *tonos*, vocal inflection. Grammar being another prime concern of the Carolingian 'renaissance' of the ninth century, the writings on prosody by Donatus, Isidore of Seville and Martianus Capella were studied, and the use of prosodic accents certainly understood, though not often employed in documents of the time. But one writer on chant, Aurelian of Réôme (*c*.850), draws a parallel between some melodic elements in chants which he cites and the accents of the grammarians. He says that, in the chant he describes (in words, though not with musical notation), a syllable with two notes in ascending order (a *pes*) is 'enunciated according to an acute accent'. At another place, where a syllable is given a *torculus* in chant manuscripts, Aurelian says it is 'circumflexed' (*circumflectetur*). So there is a correspondence between the vocal gesture which Aurelian hears, the prosodic accent which he names, and the signs in paleofrankish or St Amand notation. But the signs in all the other scripts do not correspond in this way.

This may seem a rather complicated matter, and hardly worth explaining at such length, were it not for the fact that prosodic accents have been seen as the *fons et origo* of all chant notation. A treatise of the late tenth or early eleventh century also says as much: 'De accentibus toni oritur nota quae dicitur neuma' (From the accents of tone arises the sign which is called a neume). (The author was particularly concerned to relate chant-singing as a whole to grammar, to both prosody and metrics.) Yet, while knowledge of the accent signs was certainly on hand, it can only have formed a very narrow base, hardly more than a suggestion as to how a musical notation might function. After all, more than a dozen different basic signs were necessary for chant, and a great many more combinations of them. There had simply been nothing in the history of writing anything like the continuous stream of signs over a chant text.

Another idea about the origin and nature of the musical signs is the so-called 'cheironomic' theory. Cheironomy (from Greek *cheir*, 'hand' and *nomos*, 'rule') is the art of directing precise details of singing with hand signs. It has been practised in both Christian and non-Christian religious worship, for example in Hindu ritual, in Jewish biblical cantillation, and in Coptic Christian chant. Particular hand gestures remind the singers of the melodic inflections to be executed. Early neumatic notations have often been seen as the written counterpart of these cheironomic gestures. No medieval statement to this effect has actually come down to us, but that does not necessarily mean it did not happen that way. It is certainly possible to imagine the St Gall or Laon neumes as the counterparts in writing of hand gestures, although the speed of the gestures would have to be disturbingly fast if the neumes were to be reproduced exactly in performance (at least, at what seems a reasonable singing pace). However, hand gestures to aid the performance of chant, reminding singers of the contours of the melody and some significant details such as ornaments, breaks and cadences, is one thing. A fully evolved system of hand gestures which was subsequently transformed into the written signs of chant notation is another. Attractive though the theory is, in the absence of firm evidence it has to remain a hypothesis. The development of the wonderfully subtle notations of the end of the ninth century no doubt drew ideas from many sources.

If generations of singers had managed without it, why was notation invented at all? Learning and teaching the vast chant repertory was an enormous task, of course, and the Carolingian ambition to sing the services properly was powerful. That would be a reason for inventing a written aid and would seem to be a natural extension of the Carolingian educational programme, even though no contemporary document mentions it specifically as part of that programme. Opinions differ on this matter. My own view is that, while notation itself is an invention of the early ninth century, it was not applied to complete service books until the later ninth century. The three earliest books with Mass Proper chants (Chartres 47, Laon 239 and St Gall 359) were written around the end of the century. Earlier books of this sort might, of course, have been lost. But it is surely significant that from the close of the eighth century and the first half of the ninth we have no fewer than six books with all the texts to be sung, *but no notation*. No doubt the argument will continue.

While the notation of the full cycle of chants for the Proper of Mass had been accomplished during the second half of the ninth century, if not before, the codification of the Office chants seems to have been undertaken rather later. At least, the first surviving sources are a century later than those for the Mass chants. And once again, we have a number of earlier sources with the texts alone, which suggests that notation was not yet needed for supporting performance and for passing on knowledge of the melodies to the next generations. Some pages from at least one notated antiphoner from the ninth century (Vienna 3645) survive, and it may well be that only accidents of history have deprived us of others. The number of different chants sung at the Office hours increased substantially during the tenth and eleventh centuries, and this may well have led to the scrapping of older books and their replacement with more comprehensive notated ones.

The need for pitch-notation

Around the beginning of the new millennium musical notation which gave exact pitches seems to have become more urgently needed. In his music theory treatise of about 900, Hucbald of St Amand had already said that signs denoting pitches on the musical scale would be useful adjuncts to neume notation, but his idea was not taken up in practice. Shortly before the end of the tenth century, however, another writer – anonymous, writing in north Italy – composed a treatise in dialogue form (known as the *Dialogus de musica*) which recommended notating a complete antiphoner with alphabetic letters *A–G* for the lower octave, *a–g* for the higher, and *aa–cc* for the highest notes. Only a few manuscripts have survived where this is done, and only one antiphoner, or rather, a couple of pages from it, later used as flyleaves for a thirteenth-century breviary of Hereford Cathedral. They are the remains of what would have been a complete book, presumably superseded by the later one, which has square notation on the staff. The most important book with alphabetic and neume notation in parallel is a remarkable manuscript from the Benedictine abbey of St-Bénigne at Dijon in Burgundy (Montpellier H159). This book contains all the Proper chants of Mass, but not in liturgical order like a normal gradual. Instead, it divides them into their liturgical categories, first all introits, then all the communions, all the alleluias, and so on. And within each category the chants are arranged by mode. This is a reference book without parallel. If a normal chant book such as a gradual is one step removed from the liturgical performance, being used in the song-school rather than the choir, then Montpellier H159 is two steps away, a sort of musicologist's or music theorist's manual. But extremely important, for it is one of the earliest of all chant books where the pitches can be read unequivocally.

Montpellier H159 dispenses with the two-octave system of the *Dialogus de musica* and goes straight through the alphabet from *a* to *p*. So *A–G* in the *Dialogus* is *a–g* in Montpellier H159, *a–g* in the *Dialogus* is *h–o* (with *i* for *b♭* and i for *b♮*; there is no j), with *p* for the highest *a*. The system made its way from St.-Bénigne to Normandy and thence to England. This interesting journey is connected with the history of monasticism in those lands. William of Volpiano (d. 1031), an Italian who became abbot of St-Bénigne in 990, came to Normandy in 1001 to revive monastic life after the destruction perpetrated by the Northmen. His reforms, and knowledge of musical practice in his monasteries, subsequently spread to England as well.

Guido of Arezzo and staff notation

But then came Guido of Arezzo's staff notation. He tells how he invented it and demonstrated it to Pope John XIX (1024–33) in a letter to a fellow monk, Michael (*Epistola ad Michaelem*), and describes it in what is usually called a *Prologus ad antiphonarium*. We have grown so accustomed to staff notation that it is difficult to appreciate what a stroke of genius it was. True, in older writings on music theory we occasionally find lines on which syllables of text are placed, to show the pitch at which the syllables should be sung. But to use just four lines (because no more are needed) and simply to place the usual notational signs (neumes) upon them, this was new, brilliantly simple and effective.

Staff notation was good for not one but two things. Firstly, once you know which line is which (through the clefs or coloured lines, because these show you where the semitone steps are), you can sing straight from the staff notation, instead of having to memorize the chant beforehand. Guido says the time needed to learn all the chant was reduced from ten to two years. To learn how to use the notation you have to have something like an aural matrix in your head, a scale-segment such as *D–E–F–G* or, better still, *C–D–E–F–G–a*. You do not need to know the letters, the sound of the segment is what is vital. If you can hear that, and relate it to the staff by means of the clefs or coloured lines – that semitone step! – then you can 'hear' your way up and down the staff. But the converse is equally important. If you have learned a chant by the traditional method of hearing the teacher sing it, then you can place it in writing on the staff, by checking in your mind where the semitone steps are. It would be important to check the last phrase of the chant first, so that it would end on one of the usual final notes, *D, E, F, G*. (The exceptions to that rule could be dealt with by more experienced singer-notators.)

The question arises, as usual, as to why it was necessary to change to staff notation. Not everyone did. There are many manuscripts from the thirteenth, fourteenth, even fifteenth centuries with adiastematic notation, showing that the old methods were still functioning adequately. We should also not forget that for most singers, performance by memory remained the rule for centuries to come. The early books with staff notation – they are preserved from the later eleventh century onward – are still books for the cantor, not for the choir. Be that as it may, was there a reason why cantors should need pitch-accurate notation? One reason might be that in the course of the tenth century, and even more in the eleventh, many new melodies of non-traditional melodic character were composed. Trope-verses, some sequences, but above all new chants for the Office hours. As explained in Chapter 3, more and more saint's days were supplied with proper chants, made for that saint and no other, instead of drawing upon the pool in the Common of Saints (*Commune sanctorum*). For these new pieces, the singer would not be able to rely on his experience and

Table 4.4 *The interval notation of Hermannus Contractus*

ϵ	equalis (unison)	⌇	semiditonus (minor third)	Δ	diapente (perfect fifth)
s	semitonus (semitone)	⌇	ditonus (major third)	Δ̃	diapente cum semi- tono (minor sixth)
τ	tonus (whole tone)	d	diatessaron (perfect fourth)	Δ̃	diapente cum tono (major sixth)

knowledge of the old, 'classical' melodic patterns in antiphons and responsories. The new pieces are individuals, unique. It must have been important to see the unexpected twists and turns, the unorthodox leaps, in clear staff notation.

This hypothesis is supported by the way in which some very difficult melodies, composed by Hermannus Contractus of the Reichenau (1013–54) in honour of St Afra of Augsburg, were copied in a manuscript from the Benedictine monastery of Prüfening near Regensburg in Bavaria. They are found in a notated breviary, where alongside the prayers and lessons for the Office hours through the year the chants are recorded in the neumes typical for that part of the Germany – until Hermannus's extravagant melodies for Afra are reached, where the scribe switches to staff notation.

As it happens, Hermannus was the inventor of another type of pitch-notation, which might have helped ensure that his Afra chants (and many more like them) survived intact. His idea was to specify the intervals between notes, indicated by letters alongside the neumes. The intervals were understood to be ascending unless a dot was placed underneath the letter, indicating a descending interval. The letters are given in Table 4.4.

As already explained, the varieties of script used in the Middle Ages are very numerous. Getting to know their idiosyncrasies is one of the great pleasures of chant research, and there is great satisfaction to be had from being able to 'place' a script on the notational map of Europe. Music printing changed all this.

The invention of music printing for chant

The invention of music printing in the late fifteenth century (a *Missale* printed in 1476 in Rome by Ulrich Han of Ingolstadt is the first example) led both to a simplification (because of the limited number of characters) and a standardization (because handwritten books were influenced by printed ones). In the late nineteenth century, hand in hand with the restoration of the melodies to their medieval forms, a music type was created by the monks of Solesmes, in collaboration with the firm of Desclée in Tournai, based on the square notation in Parisian manuscripts of the thirteenth to fourteenth centuries. This is the basis of the font used

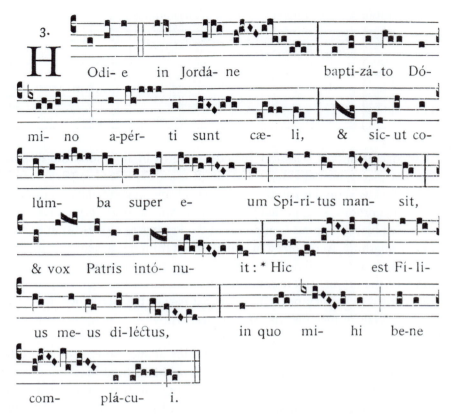

Figure 4.11 *Hodie in Iordane*, from *Liber responsorialis* (Solesmes, 1895), p. 71

in nearly all modern chant books. German or 'gothic' fonts were also occasionally revived. Nowadays, variety has returned, in a way, to the printing of chant, through the development of fonts for the computer, for Solesmes-type notation and many others.

Figures 4.11–12 show two examples from Solesmes publications. In both cases the Epiphany responsory *Hodie in Iordane* is illustrated (only the first part, the respond; the verse is omitted here). Figure 4.11 is from the *Liber responsorialis* of 1894. Special signs such as the liquescent at 'in' and the *quilisma* at '-ne' are to be seen. Figure 4.12 shows the same chant from the *Liber antiphonarius*, vol. 1 (2005). The neumes of the Hartker antiphoner are drawn (in red in the publication) over the staff. The third note at 'in' is liquescent, but the second is now given as an *oriscus*. There is another *oriscus* fourth note from the end of 'Iordane'. At '[a-]per[-ti]' there are three *strophas*, and another as fourth note of 'cae[-li]'. A careful comparison will reveal that several pitches are different between the two versions.

Figure 4.12 *Hodie in Iordane*, from *Liber antiphonarius* (Solesmes, 2005), p. 112

Transcribing chant

Obviously, melodies are best appreciated when actually sung. Representing them on a page is a poor substitute. In the case of chant the manner of transcription is somewhat controversial. It is generally considered important that the note-groupings of neume notation should be reflected in any modern transcription, and I certainly subscribe to this view. It is largely achieved in the printed notation developed by Solesmes. The *Graduale triplex* of 1979 goes one better. This is the *Graduale Romanum* of 1974, with the Solesmes notation, into which neumes from two early manuscripts were drawn by hand, the best of both worlds, one might say, since both the pitches to be sung and the intricate detail of the early staffless neumes can be seen simultaneously. At the same time, Solesmes notation is often preferred for less objective reasons. It has become so closely associated with Gregorian chant as to form its visual identity, so to speak; using it is almost like an article of faith which separates the true believer from the sceptic.

Music fonts are nowadays available which enable anyone with a computer to make transcriptions with square notation. Nevertheless, square notation is not universally known, and it would have been a barrier for many readers of the present plain and easy introduction, needing a further act of translation, when the musical examples should be taken in at a glance. If a transcription into note-heads (the hated 'eggs' of the square-notation party) respects the note-groupings of the original manuscripts (and reproduces any special signs of the old notation), then the most important thing is achieved. Transcriptions where all notes are equally widely spaced, on the other hand, without regard even for syllable- or word-breaks, are a sad distortion of medieval practice and block appreciation of melodic structure. In this book therefore, groups of round note-heads are used, with a few extra signs for liquescence, the *quilisma* and the *oriscus*.

Further reading

There is neither a comprehensive nor a handy introduction to chant notation in English. The best short survey is by Hiley and Szendrei in *NG2*, 'Notation, §III,1, Plainchant'. See also Hiley, *Western Plainchant*, ch. IV. For more extensive treatment see Suñol, *Introduction à la paléographie musicale grégorienne*, Stäblein, *Schriftbild der einstimmigen Musik*, and Corbin, *Die Neumen*. Cardine, *Gregorian Semiology*, is the standard work on the interpretation of St Gall notation.

4.iv Medieval chant books

Chant notation is found in a great variety of medieval books, principally in those for the liturgy but also in books for teaching chant and in writings on music theory.

Books for chants of the Mass

The book with chants for the Mass is known as the gradual. A few books with the texts to be sung at Mass have survived from the ninth century, without notation, then from about 900 most graduals are notated. Up to the end of the first millennium, and sometimes beyond, it was usual to make separate books for the chants, the prayers and the lessons at Mass. The book with the prayers is known as the sacramentary, that with the lessons is the lectionary. Quite often these three parts were bound together in one book. But it became increasingly usual to set out all items in their liturgical order, 'fusing' the three types of material into a continuous series of items as they would have been performed in the liturgy. This book is called a missal. Many missals contain just the chant texts, not their music. But other missals have the melodies as well. In this case one speaks of a 'noted' or 'notated' missal. The missal is a reminder that these liturgical books are first and foremost records of the approved practice of a certain church, for consultation. This applies not only to chant books, the performance of whose contents was divided between a choir and different soloists. They could hardly all read from the one book alone. So also the missal: it would hardly have been practical for it to be passed from singer to priest to deacon, for performance of the chants, the prayers, the lessons, and so on.

Books for chants of the Office

Office chants were notated in the antiphoner. Since the word 'antiphoner' was used in the eighth and ninth centuries to mean any chant book, a distinction is sometimes made between 'Mass antiphoner' (that is, the gradual) and 'Office antiphoner' (the antiphoner in the narrower sense, applied only to chants of the Office). The combination of all the things needed for the Office hours in one book is the breviary, which may be 'noted' or 'notated'. Some writers use the term 'choir breviary' to designate the notated breviary.

The materials needed for performing the Office hours are very extensive indeed, and some of them were regularly set out in separate books. The most common of these are the Psalter and the hymnal.

The Psalter, if designed for liturgical use, will contain more than just the 150 psalms of the Old Testament book. The psalms will be divided up, with rubrics, according to the days of the week and the hours of the day, and quite often the antiphons for the weekly round will be entered, either in full or by incipit (the first few words). As well as the psalms, the canticles (Te Deum, Benedictus, Magnificat, etc.) will often be included. We are speaking here of the texts only of the psalms and canticles: they would be performed by means of the psalm tones.

Hymns were also frequently collected separately, or perhaps put together with a Psalter, leaving the great cycles of antiphons and responsories for the antiphoner.

Other books with chant

Some early books with Mass chants are restricted to those performed by a soloist, rather than the choir. Such a book is referred to as a cantatorium (the book of the cantor). Later books with solo chants tend to concentrate on sequences, tropes, and Ordinary of Mass melodies and their tropes. The usual name for a book with these chants is the troper. But the contents of tropers vary considerably. Before they were recorded in a more or less systematic fashion and bound into a book for reference, the chants must often have circulated in collections of loose leaves – collections of sequences, collections of tropes, and so on. How they were eventually brought together was a matter for the individual cantor to decide.

Some books with chant are for teaching rudiments and theory. The materials for use in the song school include typical antiphon melodies for teaching the common melodic contours of Office antiphons (*Primum querite regnum Dei* for mode 1, *Secundum autem simile est huic* for mode 2, and so on), and of course the psalm tones and tones of responsory verses. Such things are commonly attached to the book known as a tonary (sometimes 'tonale'). The principal contents of a tonary are lists of antiphons grouped according to mode and, within the mode, the psalm-tone ending which should be used with the antiphon. Antiphons, it will be recalled, are chants framing the singing of a psalm. In a tonary the first group of antiphons will be those in mode 1 requiring the psalm to be sung to the first psalm one with its first ending. Then come antiphons requiring the second ending of the first psalm tone, and so on. Very few tonaries attempt a complete listing of all antiphons through the church year. Most content themselves with a small selection of typical items, enough to cover the main melodic families of antiphons. A very few list the antiphons in alphabetical order.

Further reading

See Huglo, *Les Livres de chant liturgique*, and, more briefly, Hiley, *Western Plainchant*, ch. III. Hughes, *Medieval Manuscripts for Mass and Office*, is extremely detailed. There are catalogues of liturgical books in the series *Répertoire internationale des sources musicales* by Husmann, *Tropen- und Sequenzenhandschriften*, and Huglo, *Les Manuscrits du Processional*.

The research project CANTUS makes full inventories of antiphoners available on-line at http://publish.uwo.ca/~cantus. Articles on individual books can be found through key-word search at www-musikwissenschaft.uni-regensburg.de/cantus.

Over the years a large number of chant books have been published in facsimile. Well-known examples are the volumes in the series *Paléographie musicale*, edited by the monks of Solesmes. Others include Walter Howard Frere's editions of the graduale and antiphoner according to the use of Salisbury, *Graduale Sarisburiense* and *Antiphonale Sarisburiense,* and the gradual, antiphoner and processional of York use. Increasing numbers can now be seen on the internet, for example the manuscripts of St Gall on-line at http://www.cesg.unifr.ch/de/index.htm. If they have the chance, readers should try to see the colour facsimiles of manuscripts St Gall 381 and 484 edited by Rankin and Arlt, and *The Winchester Troper* edited by Rankin.

Chapter 5

New chants for new times: from the sixteenth century to the present; aspects of performance

In this chapter the historical narrative continues roughly from the point where it was left at the end of section 3.iii. We are mostly concerned here with the cataclysm of the sixteenth century and the attempted restoration of medieval chant in the nineteenth. The restoration had a practical aim, that of improving the standard of music and performance in the Roman church. But the great fund of musicological knowledge which it created also provided the foundations of modern academic chant scholarship, much of which is not concerned with the practicalities of church worship at all. At the same time, Gregorian chant has also moved outside the church, or at least been co-opted for non-religious purposes. Because of its special associations it has often been used in modern non-sacred music, for example, opera and orchestral music in the nineteenth century, film music in the twentieth, and latterly even pop music.

The final section of this book is not, however, about the modern uses of chant but offers some observations on the difficulties in performing it. For not only the notes of medieval chant had to be restored, a way of performing it had to be reconstructed – or, rather, constructed, since no 'hard' evidence exists about matters like medieval voice production, tempo and dynamic exists.

5.i Chant in the age of humanism; the 'Editio Medicaea'; neo-Gallican chant

In the early sixteenth century most of the Gregorian repertory from the early Middle Ages was still being sung. It is true that some liturgical reforms of more or less local significance cut down the length of the Night Office, and some types of chant like tropes had fallen out of general use. But a good proportion had survived.

In the course of the Counter-Reformation a revision of the Roman liturgy was undertaken at the highest level, with the intention of making it binding throughout the Roman Catholic church. (Exceptions were made for local uses which had a documented history at least two centuries old.) In the aftermath of the Council of Trent (1545–63) a new Roman breviary was published in 1568 and a new missal in 1570. In these revised books (laying down texts, but without music) the great majority of the chant texts were left unaltered, and it would have been perfectly possible to continue singing them to the old Gregorian melodies. However, the latter were no longer thought acceptable, for ideals of text-setting in monophonic, as in polyphonic music, were by now radically different from those of the early Middle Ages. In 1577 Giovanni Pierluigi da Palestrina (1525–94), choirmaster of the Cappella Giulia in Rome, and Annibale Zoilo (c.1537–92), from the Cappella Sistina, were commissioned to produce new chant books. The letter of commission by Pope Gregory XIII speaks of 'barbarisms, obscurities, contrarities and superfluities' which it will be Palestrina's and Zoilo's task to 'purge, correct and reform'. The two did not complete the work, and in 1608 a new six-man committee took up the work. Felice Anerio (c.1560–1614), closely associated with the Congregation of Oratorians, and Francesco Soriano (c.1549–1621), *maestro* of the Cappella Giulia, were appointed in 1611 to finish the task. A new gradual was finally published in two volumes: *Graduale de Tempore. Iuxta ritum Sacrosanctae Romanae Ecclesiae. cum cantu* in 1614, and *Graduale de Sanctis . . .* in 1614–15. The Medicaea press published the books, hence the usual references to the 'Medicaean Gradual'. No sister books for Office chants were produced. However, even before the appearance of the Medicaean Gradual, the papal chaplain Giovanni Guidetti, who was a pupil of Palestrina and a singer in the papal chapel, published a series of handbooks in small format in the years 1582 to 1588 containing the recitation formulae for prayers and lessons, including the prefaces of Mass and the passion tones of Holy Week, also the psalm tones, versicles and their responses, hymns and short responsories. The most important of these handbooks was the *Directorium chori* of 1588. Whereas the Medicaean Gradual uses a very simple, square musical type, Guidetti used a mensural notation with four note values –

Ex. 5.1

– which could be transcribed as crotchet, minim, dotted minim, semibreve (quarter-note, half-note, dotted half, whole note). These were sometimes taken up in other chant books in the coming centuries. Most chant books used a very restricted set of signs, partly for ease of printing: the square, the square with a downstroke to the right, and the diamond (both for descending groups and standing alone on an unaccented syllable).

In the Medicaean Gradual the medieval melodies suffered a drastic revision. The alterations chiefly concerned two things:

(i) The relationship between text and music. Syllables which according to classical principles were short were not allowed to carry too many notes. The melismas on unaccented syllables at the ends of verses in graduals suffered particularly.

(ii) The tonality of the chants. Many modal melodic inflections were restyled to sound more straightforwardly minor or major. This is a particularly interesting matter. Chants in D, F and G were not generally altered very drastically, since they fitted fairly well the tendency of the time towards what we would call D-minor, F-major and G-major tonality. But several chants in mode 4, the lower E-mode, were more difficult. Example 5.1 gives an example of this, the offertory for the First Mass on Christmas Day, *Laetentur caeli*. 4. In medieval manuscripts the melody displays a characteristic tendency to hover around *F*, sometimes reached by a step up from *D*. The figure *DGFE* is also prominent. The higher pivotal note is *a*, with *b♭*s as upper auxiliary notes of *a*. Only the final cadence falls in *E*. The 'Medicaea' uses *E* for intermediate cadences as well, eliminates *b♭*, and reduces the small melismas on 'terra', 'Domini' and 'venit' to one or two notes. Most striking is the emphasis on the trichord *CEG* and the swing up through to *a* to *c*. In the medieval version there is only one *C*, at the start, and no *c* at all.

The new melodies have been variously regarded as a disaster (which they obviously were for the superseded Gregorian chants) or a practical and timely replacement. Which version of Example 5.2 do you prefer? The new melody is certainly more straightforward tonally. It seems to have been conceived in something like *a* minor

Graduale Romanum 1908

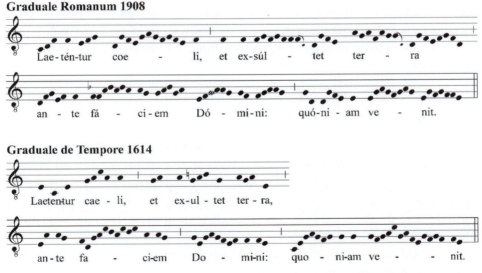

Ex. 5.2 Offertory *Laetentur caeli* from the *Graduale Romanum* 1908 and the Editio Medicaea 1614

Off. Laetentur caeli
Let the heavens rejoice, and let the earth be glad before the face of the Lord, for he cometh. (Ps. 95:11, 13)

with an ending on the dominant, fairly common in polyphony of the time. (Palestrina's offertory setting *Posuisti Domine* is a good example.) Although not medieval, it is not at all clumsy or misshapen.

During the next two centuries the new, official Roman chant made its way into a number of dioceses, though by no means all. Just as disastrous for Gregorian chant as the Roman revision, however, was the message clearly coming out from Rome itself that revision and replacement were legitimate and necessary. The lead was taken up in France, for example, at the church of the Oratorians in the rue St Honoré in Paris, the royal chapel of the Louvre; a *Brevis psalmodiae ratio* with the new chant was published in 1634, and this set the pattern for a host of modernizing chant publications.

In France there were additional, political reasons for discarding Roman books and Gregorian chant: the independent stance of the French church regarding Roman ecclesiastical legislation during the reign of Louis XIV. The movement which resulted, with Jacques-Bénigne Bossuet (1627–1704) as its chief apologist, is known as 'Gallicanism'. While the form of the Roman liturgy was maintained, large numbers of new texts were composed, with new melodies, and many traditional texts also received new melodies. In the seventeenth and eighteenth centuries well over half of all French dioceses adopted books which contained new chants, and of these more than a third copied the books of Paris. 'Neo-Gallican' is the name usually given to this chant. The French term most used seems to have been 'plain-chant musicale', as for example in the *Leçons de Ténèbres en plain-chant musical composé dans le goût de M. Nivers* published by Ballard in Paris in 1665 (the reference is to the composer Guillaume-Gabriel Nivers, *c.*1632–1714), and the *Cinq messes en plein-chant* (1669) by Henri du Mont. (The *Messe royale* from this set was still being performed in the twentieth century.) Some of the newly composed chant went so far as to borrow the expressive style of contemporary French operatic recitative, with metrical note-values and signs for ornaments. This type of chant, known as 'chant figuré', is described in such books as the *Méthode nouvelle pour apprendre parfaitement les règles du plain-chant et de la psalmodie, avec des messes et autres ouvrages en plain-chant figuré et musical* (Poitiers, 1748, reprinted many times) by François de la Feillée (d. *c.*1780)

New chant books were also published in Italy, Spain, Germany, Austria, the Netherlands, Poland and several other countries, all showing greater or lesser divergence from medieval tradition. In time, however, the pendulum would swing again.

5.ii A phoenix rising from the ashes? The attempt to recover medieval chant

In the nineteenth century, after the upheavals of the French Revolution, the secularization of the monasteries and confiscation of church property in many areas of Catholic Europe, there was a conservative reaction on many fronts. Part of the reaction was a desire to return to the liturgical practice of the Roman church in the 'Age of Faith'. Old chant books were studied and transcribed with increasing expertise, particularly at the French Benedictine monastery of Solesmes. In 1903 Pope Pius X issued an edict in favour of the restored Gregorian chant. Published editions sanctioned by the Vatican appeared soon afterwards.

The revival of the medieval versions of the melodies is indissolubly associated with the monks of Solesmes, and rightly so, but they were not alone in the work of restoration, nor the earliest. Even before the restoration of the old political order in Europe in 1814, the French teacher and writer on music Alexandre Choron (1771–1834) published a tract entitled *Considerations sur la nécessité de rétablir le chant de l'Église de Rome dans toutes les églises de l'Empire*. But at the same time as Choron and others were advocating the replacing of neo-Gallican chant with Roman, questions were being asked about the Roman chant itself. One option followed was to adopt the Medicaean gradual and one of the printed Italian books of Office chants of the late sixteenth century, such as those printed by Peter Liechtenstein in Venice. However, knowledge of medieval chant sources was increasing, in the wake of scholarship in other fields of medieval studies. The famous codex Montpellier H159, notated with both neumes and alphabetic letters (see section 4.iii above), was discovered by J.-L.-F. Danjou in 1846 and used soon afterwards as the partial basis for new graduals in France. Louis Lambillotte published a hand-drawn copy of manuscript St Gall 359 in 1851. An important step towards full-scale restoration of the medieval melodies was taken by Michael Hermesdorff in Trier (1833–85) in his *Graduale ad normam cantus S. Gregorii* (Trier, 1876–82). Here the chants were restored to their form in medieval manuscripts from Trier, and over the staves were printed small neumes modelled on the notation of the original manuscripts.

In the meantime the French Benedictine Dom Prosper Guéranger (1805–75) had refounded the Abbey of Solesmes, near Le Mans. His three-volume work *Institutions liturgiques* (1840–51) was a leading document in the campaign to restore Roman liturgical practice in France, and set out principles for the scholarly restoration of chant. Work on this began in the late 1850s, with Dom Joseph Pothier as the leading figure. Manuscripts were copied and photographed, compared and transcribed. Pothier's book on chant, *Mélodies grégoriennes*, appeared in 1880 and a gradual, the *Liber gradualis*, in 1883. These were landmark publications. *Mélodies grégoriennes* explained the nature of neumatic notation and its evolution to staff notation, the principles of correct Latin pronunciation, the constituent elements of chant melodies, the nature of 'Gregorian rhythm', and the different genres of chant. The *Liber gradualis* was the direct forerunner of the *Graduale Romanum* eventually approved by the Vatican and published in 1908, the two being in many respects identical. In 1875 Dom André Mocquereau had joined the community, and it was his idea to publish a series of facsimiles of important early chant manuscripts. This became the series *Paléographie musicale*. The first volume, a reproduction of manuscript St Gall 339, was published in 1889. Up to the First World War ten more volumes had been published, mostly with chants for Mass (Einsiedeln 121, Montpellier H159, Laon 239 and Chartres 47) but also the Office antiphoner Lucca 601, and the earliest comprehensive Ambrosian chant book (London 34209). Just as important were two volumes with over 200 reproductions of the same chant (or a similar one) from multiple sources, the gradual *Justus ut palma*. The point of this was to show the near-unanimity of medieval manuscripts as against the much altered version of the Medicaean gradual.

For the Medicaean Gradual had by no means been driven from the field. Quite the contrary. The printing firm of Friedrich Pustet in Regensburg had engaged the scholar and church music teacher Franz Xaver Haberl to make a modern edition of the *Graduale Romanum* based on the Medicaean Gradual, which appeared in 1871 (octavo size and the first volume of a large folio edition) and 1873 (second folio volume). They were followed in 1878 by an *Antiphonale* based on printed editions originally published in Venice in 1585 and Antwerp in 1611, and in 1889 by a *Directorium Chori* based on Guidetti's publication of 1588. The whole enterprise was supported by an official declaration by Pope Pius IX and the Sacred Congregation of Rites, already delivered in 1868 and coming into effect in 1871, which granted to the Pustet gradual a monopoly, which eventually lasted thirty years.

During the 1890s support for the melodies as restored by Solesmes, and published in several books for the Mass, Office and processions, gained in strength. On St Cecilia's Day (22 November) 1903 the famous *motu proprio* 'Tra le sollecitudini' was issued by Pius X sanctioning the restored chant. In 1904 a commission was appointed under Pothier's leadership to prepare a new Graduale and Antiphonale. These appeared in 1908 and 1912 respectively. The most important independent Solesmes publication was the compendium *Liber Usualis* of 1895, which contains chants for both Mass and Office.

The production of any new chant book is a complicated and expensive undertaking, not least because special music fonts have to be developed. The splendid Pustet folio volumes are a reminder of this, and make Pustet's anxiety to secure a monopoly understandable. (He was also awarded the title of official Typographer to the Sacred Congregation of Rites in 1870.) Solesmes went to great lengths to devise a font which would reproduce as much of the subtlety and variety of medieval manuscripts as possible, developed in collaboration with the firm of Desclée of Tournai in Belgium. It was based on the square notation of French manuscripts of the thirteenth and fourteenth centuries, including liquescent signs, with the addition of the quilisma that had fallen out of use by that epoch. The result was certainly a great improvement on any previous edition from both a practical, historical and visual point of view.

Text box 5.1 The *Motu proprio* of Pius X

From the *Motu proprio* ['on his (the pope's) own initiative'] *Tra le sollecitudini* of Pope Pius X of 22 September 1903. The first part of the document has emphasized that sacred music must possess the qualities of holiness, beauty and universality. It continues as follows. (The phrases referring to the restoration of medieval chant by the monks of Solesmes are printed here in bold.)

These qualities are found most perfectly in Gregorian chant, which is therefore the proper chant of the Roman Church, the only chant which she has inherited from the ancient Fathers, which she has jealously kept for so many centuries in her liturgical books, which she offers to the faithful as her own music, which she insists on being used exclusively in some parts of her liturgy, and which, lastly, **has been so happily restored to its original perfection and purity by recent study.**

For these reasons Gregorian chant has always been looked upon as the highest model of Church music, and we may with good reason establish as a general rule that the more a musical composition for use in church is like Gregorian chant in its movement, its inspiration, and its feeling, so much the more is it right and liturgical, and the more it differs from this highest model so much the less is it worthy of the house of God.

Wherefore **this ancient Gregorian chant should be largely restored in divine worship**, and it should be understood that a service of the Church loses nothing of its solemnity when it is accompanied by no other music than Gregorian chant. Especially should this chant be restored to the use of the people, so that they may take a more active part in the offices, as they did in former times.

Robert F. Hayburn, *Papal Legislation on Sacred Music, 95 AD to 1977 AD* (Collegeville, Minn., 1979), pp. 224–5. (Quoted with the permission of Roman Catholic Books, PO Box 2286, Fort Collins, CO 80522, 970-490-2735.)

Solesmes publications since the beginning of the twentieth century have typically included rhythmic signs as well (dots and bars for longer notes, accents to indicate the 'ictus', that is, for the note in a group which the singer should understand to be the most important, though it does not receive a dynamic stress). These were not adopted in the Vatican editions. Although Pothier was well aware of the rhythmic elements in the early neumed manuscripts he regarded them as a local phenomenon and unsuitable for a practical edition to serve the whole church. Since the 1980s further refinements and new signs have been added in Solesmes books, including the *oriscus*.

The restoration of the medieval melodies was certainly a magnificent achievement, but looked at from a medieval perspective it was only partial. The Roman liturgy of the twentieth century was not that of St Gall in the tenth. The pieces to be sung were not always exactly those found in medieval books (which in any case differ among themselves), and some medieval chants were adapted to fit new texts (for example, for new feast days). Much later medieval chant was not restored if it no longer had a place in the liturgy: most sequences, for example. The Night Office was by this time rarely sung and its great repertory of antiphons and responsories was therefore left aside. The vast repertory of Offices for local saints was ignored. (Not surprisingly, these areas have therefore proved a happy hunting-ground for modern scholars.)

The core, in fact the greater part, of what was restored was constituted by the Proper chants of Mass, most of which are among the earliest notated chants and are generally considered to have the best claims to antiquity. Not surprisingly, there arose a tendency to regard later chant as 'decadent' and inauthentic. More sympathetic discussion by modern scholarship has done much to redress an imbalance here and open ears and minds to the real achievement of later medieval musicians.

Taking a critical view of the restoration, it cannot be denied that it was in many respects a compromise. The overwhelming need was felt to be the provision of improved books for the use of the church, recovering the music of an 'Age of Faith', returning to the pure, original sources of Christian worship. But decisions were necessary on matters where no perfect, single solution existed. The readings of medieval manuscripts are not always in perfect agreement. The chant fonts developed by Solesmes and Desclée are not like any single medieval manuscript and combine features of chant books from different centuries. And even when the latest chant books come as near as seems practically possible to the versions in the earliest manuscripts, there remains the question of performance, the actual vocal delivery of the melodies. The next section considers some of the problems involved.

A phoenix rising from the ashes? In some ways yes, but it was a bird of very different hue which rose from the ashes of medieval chant.

5.iii Performing monophonic chant

Neither neumatic notation nor staff notation is intended to communicate every element of performance practice. The notated manuscript was not used during actual performance, though it might be carried by the singer as a symbol of his office, or placed on an altar because of its venerable contents. Its principal use was to aid the cantor – who had often written it himself – in teaching chant. The notation reminded him of just enough to uphold the tradition securely, enough for teaching the singers, which he did by singing the melodies to them as often as was necessary for them to learn the melodies by ear. This basic situation did not change when staff notation was used instead of neumes. The information communicated by the book was partly different but the function of the book as a memory aid did not alter. Guido of Arezzo (see section 4.i above) said that the use of his new staff notation reduced dramatically the time needed for a singer to learn the repertory, since the melodies need not be learned from hearing only. That is certainly true, but the goal is still the memorization of chant and its performance in the liturgy from memory, not from a book.

Since no unbroken tradition of performance links us to the Middle Ages we have to rely on intuition and sense to sing Gregorian chant, with obvious consequences. During the explanations about chant notation in section 4.iii above it should have become clear that the significance of several early signs is not precisely known. But even the majority of signs which are easy to understand leave many things open to interpretation: dynamics and tempo, for example. Several of the significative letters in the sophisticated early St Gall notation have to do with rhythm or tempo (for example: $c = celeriter$, quickly; $p = pressio$, driving forward; $t = trahere$, drag), or with dynamic ($f = cum fragore$, with hard attack; $k = klange$, with ringing tone). These and the numerous ways of modifying the basic signs, for example by adding short strokes (*episemata*) to the neumes to indicate lengthening, all show that chant was by no means sung in an undifferentiated fashion. The question is, how much differentiation? How much more quickly (*celeriter*) or slowly (*trahere*)? Were there fixed proportional relationships between long and short notes, like modern quavers, crotchets and minims? How much dynamic?

At the time when the French Benedictines began to work on the restoration of chant, it was sung slowly, with instrumental reinforcement, usually a serpent or ophicleide, by all accounts a ponderous and depressing manner of performance. The monks of Solesmes (Dom André Mocquereau was a leading figure) developed a way of singing in which most notes have equal length, with plenty of expressive dynamic, sung in a flowing tempo. Many recordings in particular from the long period when Dom Joseph Gajard was choirmaster, as well as books on the Solesmes 'method' by Gajard and others, have acquainted generations of singers and worshippers with this way of singing chant. The freedom from a regular beat imparts a timelessness, the free-ranging melodic arches seem to have a weightlessness which at the beginning of the twentieth century must have been a revelation, a new world of church music. It was certainly a potent factor in the success of the restoration. One should not, however, overlook the fact that it was in effect a new creation. There was no unbroken line between the twentieth century and the Middle Ages, but a gap of centuries where different or at least revised melodies were sung, and no memory persisted of how medieval chant was performed. The aesthetic bases of Solesmes' performance style are rather to be sought in nineteenth-century France, the period of Viollet-le-Duc and the Gothic revival in church architecture, of César Franck's music and the Schola Cantorum of Paris.

Later research (especially that of the late Dom Eugène Cardine) has refined the Solesmes method and introduced much fine rhythmic nuancing (the so-called 'semi-ological' school of research and performance). Where possible, performances use the

---

Text box 5.2 Singing chant in the early twentieth century

In his introduction to the centennial reprint in 1990 of Pothier's *Les mélodies grégoriennes,* the French musicologist Jacques Chailley (1910–99) remembered how chant was performed when he was a child:

I still remember from my Burgundian childhood in Seignelay where, despite the objurgations of the senior priest, abbé Villetard (the well-known Gregorian expert), an old cantor called Father Besse persisted in hammering out every 'E' in the 'Kyrie', one by one, panting for breath between each, in an invincible, stentorian voice, defying his adversary across the top of his steel-rimmed spectacles. I see again the High Mass in Pourain (Yonne), whither Paul Berthier had taken me with the sculptor Charlier and the poetess Marie Noël, and in particular the unforgettable procession of the *Asperges* there. Trotting behind the priest came a sacristan in a surplice too long for him, blowing into an ophicleide. That was how he accompanied this thunderously resonant chant, according to ancient practice, in which one sought in vain the 'delicate nuances of the ictus' dear to the Solesmes school. (12)

Graduale Triplex, which is an edition of the *Graduale Romanum* of 1974, in which the neumes of one of the St Gall manuscripts have been added under the staff, those of Laon 239 over the staff. But recent decades have witnessed an almost bewildering proliferation of singing styles. Strongly rhythmicized interpretations have been developed, with metrical values for longer and shorter notes. At the other end of the scale come performances which dwell upon or bring out important structural tones in the melody, delivering subsidiary note-groups as rapid ornamental flourishes. A debate about the possibility of microtonal intervals has also sprung up from time to time.

Modern culture encourages this diversity. Modern listeners experience chant in concerts ('staged' in an appropriately atmospheric ecclesiastical setting) or from recordings, quite as often as in a liturgical church service. Secular vocal ensembles wish to establish their own recognizable way of presenting chant, while church choirs are more concerned to follow an established norm. Behind both as far as the actual performance is concerned, in front of them (sometimes) in the matter of investigating old manuscripts, are the researchers. The work of producing chant books for the modern church still continues (the latest Solesmes publications are for the Divine Office: the *Psalterium monasticum* (1981), the *Liber hymnarius cum invitatoriis & aliquibus responsoriis* (1982), and the first volume of the *Liber antiphonarius pro diurnis horis* (2005)). The shelves of (some) university libraries fill with a continuous stream of new facsimiles of medieval chant books and scholarly editions of selected repertories.

Never before has so much chant been available to perform and to hear, in circumstances which are, however, vastly different from those of the time when it was composed. Plainchant has always been adapted to circumstances, as this book has tried to show. If there is one impression with which I would wish to leave the reader, it is of the enormous variety of chant. Beneath its seemingly simple surface is a multitude of forms and styles. The chief aim of this book has been to show something of that variety, and explain the circumstances which called it into being. That is, I believe, the best way to help us appreciate the creative powers of men and women in the Middle Ages, and ultimately of all ages.

Further reading

Hiley, *Western Plainchant*, chs. X–XI. The reforms after the Council of Trent are described by Molitor, *Die nach-Tridentinische Choralreform zu Rom*. Karp, *An Introduction to the Post-Tridentine Mass Proper*, presents numerous examples of revised Mass chants. The Solesmes story is told in Combe, *The Restoration of Gregorian Chant* (Washington, 2003). The aesthetic background is explored by Bergeron, *Decadent Enchantments: the Revival of Gregorian Chant at Solesmes*.

Map of places from which important medieval chant manuscripts are preserved

Chronological table

313	Edict of Milan, by which the emperors Constantine and Licinius granted Christianity equal status with other religions
c.475–524	Anicius Manlius Torquatus Severinus Boethius, theorist
c.480–c.550	Benedict of Nursia, author of the monastic rule named after him, known as the 'Patriarch of Western monasticism'
c.540–604	Gregory the Great, pope from 590
c.700	approximate date of *Ordo Romanus I*, describing papal Mass
c.735–804	Alcuin of York, Charlemagne's adviser on educational and liturgical matters
747–814	Charlemagne, King of the Franks from 768, emperor from 800
754	visit of Pope Stephen II to the Frankish king Pippin
end of 8th cent.	approximate date of oldest preserved book with cycle of Mass chant texts, the 'Blandiniensis'
c.830	earliest datable example of neumatic notation, from Regensburg, alleluia prosula *Psalle modulamina*
c.840–912	Notker Balbulus, monk of St Gall, author of sequence texts
c.840–930	Hucbald of St Amand, composer and theorist
c.850–920	Stephen, from 901 Bishop of Liège, composer
c.900	approximate date of three earliest notated books with full cycle of Mass chants: Chartres 47, St Gall 359 and Laon 239
909	foundation of the Benedictine monastery of Cluny in Burgundy; Odo, abbot 926–44, composed chant

923–4	date of MS Paris, Bibliothèque nationale de France, MS lat. 1240, earliest preserved troper from St Martial in Limoges
10th cent., second quarter	date of MS St Gall 484, earliest preserved troper from St Gall
972	council led by King Edgar and Ethelwold of Winchester to lay down guidelines for the English church
c.978–1048	Bern, abbot on the Reichenau, composer and theorist
end of 10th cent.	date of MS St Gall 390–391, earliest preserved notated antiphoner, copied by Hartker, monk of St Gall
c.992–after 1033	Guido of Arezzo, theorist and music teacher
early 11th cent.	date of 'Winchester Troper' (Cambridge, Corpus Christi College, MS 473)
1002–54	Bruno of Egisheim, from 1049 Pope Leo IX, composer
1012–54	Hermannus Contractus, monk of the Reichenau, composer and theorist
c.1030	approximate date of MS Montpellier H159, with neumes and alphabetic notation
c.1030–91	Wilhelm of Hirsau, Abbot of Hirsau from 1069, music theorist
1034	† Adhémar of Chabannes, monk of St Martial in Limoges, composer
1058	Pope Stephen IX forbids the singing of 'Ambrosianus cantus' at Montecassino
1071	date of the earliest preserved Old Roman chant manuscript, the gradual Bodmer C.74
1085	capture of Toledo from Muslim rulers of Spain by Alfonso VI, symbolic date in the introduction of Roman liturgy and Gregorian chant in Spain
1098	foundation of Cistercian monastic order
1098–1179	Hildegard of Bingen, composer
late 11th cent.	earliest chant books written in Hungary, taken to Zagreb c.1094 on foundation of diocese
first half of 12th cent.	earliest preserved gradual from Hungary, MS Graz 211
c.1146	† Adam, Precentor of Notre-Dame in Paris, composer of sequences (associated also with St Victor in Paris)
mid-12th cent.	approximate date of earliest preserved Irish chant manuscript, the gradual Oxford, Bodleian Library, Rawl. C892

1152	foundation of the Archdiocese of Nidaros (modern Trondheim) in Norway
*c.*1160	date of 'Jacobus' ('Codex Calixtinus', 'Liber Sancti Jacobi') with liturgy for the feast of St James
1219	foundation of new Salisbury Cathedral by Bishop Richard Poore; the earliest chant books of Salisbury use date from the succeeding decades
1220	official constitution of Dominican Order of Friars Preachers; the MS Rome, Santa Sabina XIV lit.1, a record of all the Dominican liturgy and its chant, is dated 1259–62
*c.*1230	date of MS London, British Library, Egerton 2615, from Beauvais, containing liturgy of the Feast of Fools and the *Ludus Danielis*
1243–4	revision of the Roman-Franciscan breviary and missal by Haymo of Faversham, General of the Franciscan Order, at request of Pope Innocent IV
1397–1474	Guillaume Du Fay of Cambrai, composer of plainchant and polyphony
1487	earliest book with printed plainchant, *Obsequiale* of Augsburg
1545–63	Council of Trent, convened to reform the Roman church
1614–15	*Graduale Romanum* published by the Medici Press in Rome
1720–93	Martin Gerbert, Prince-Abbot of St Blasien in the Black Forest, scholar of liturgy and chant
1835–1923	Joseph Pothier, monk of Solesmes, Abbot of Saint-Wandrille, chant scholar
1837	constitution of the Benedictine abbey of Solesmes
1863–1938	Walter Howard Frere, Bishop of Truro, scholar of liturgy and chant
1865–1931	Peter Wagner, chant scholar
1871	*Graduale Romanum* published by firm of Pustet in Regensburg
1889	vol. 1 of *Paléographie musicale* (Solesmes), facsimile of MS St Gall 339
1903	*Motu proprio* 'Tra le sollecitudini' of Pope Pius X sanctioning the chant restored by Solesmes
1908	*Graduale Romanum* with restored chant

Statistical table of chant categories by mode

Proportions are given to the nearest per cent

	mode 1	mode 2	mode 3	mode 4	mode 5	mode 6	mode 7	mode 8	total
Office chants									
antiphons in edition by Dobszay and Szendrei	602 23%	204 8%	181 7%	332 13%	151 6%	198 8%	322 12%	590 23%	2,580
antiphons in the Worcester antiphoner	473 24%	165 8%	118 6%	248 12%	78 4%	115 6%	259 13%	554 28%	2,010
invitatory antiphons in the Worcester antiphoner	–	11	3	30	4	23	7	–	78
great responsories in the Worcester antiphoner	186 20%	119 13%	72 8%	101 11%	50 5%	37 4%	158 17%	198 21%	921
Mass chants									
introits in Laon 239*	25	17	24	19	10	11	19	12	137
graduals in Laon 239*	11	20	10	2	42	–	9	3	97
alleluias in catalogue by Schlager***	melodies in D: 163	(40%)	melodies in E: 51	(12%)	melodies in F: 16	(4%)	melodies in G: 180	(44%)	410
tracts in Laon 239	–	6	–	–	–	–	–	15	21
offertories in Laon 239	13	14	11	17	7	8	2	21	93
communions in Laon 239**	24	17	10	16	14	19	11	20	131

* 2 not identified

** 3 not identified

*** the repertory in Laon 239, as in many early sources, is in a state of flux. Of the 106 alleluias, several attained only local circulation, and twenty-four were added by later scribes.

*Mass chants common to Old Roman and early
Gregorian sources (figures taken from
McKinnon,* The Advent Project*)*

introits	144 (McKinnon p. 198)
graduals	105 (McKinnon p. 227)
tracts	15 (McKinnon p. 283)
offertories	92 (McKinnon p. 298)
communions	141 (McKinnon p. 328)

Original manuscript sources for musical examples

Most examples are transcribed from the manuscript Worcester Cathedral, Chapter Library, F 160, here designated as 'W'. Unless otherwise indicated (by the use of the designation 'fol.'), page numbers are given for the facsimile in *Paléographie musicale* vol. 12.

ex.	chant	source
1.1	Antiphons *Deprecamur te Domine* and *Crux fidelis inter omnes*	W 227, 370
1.2	Antiphon *Hodie celesti sponso*	W 56
1.4	Antiphon *Confortatus est*	W 415
1.6	Eighth-mode responsory verses *Dum lucem habetis* and *Nonne ecce omnes isti*	W 411, W 155
1.7	Antiphons *Omnis spiritus, Cito euntes, Descendit angelus, Non enim misit filium* and *Apparuit caro suo*	W 438, 129, 325, 155, 39
1.8	Antiphons *Veni Domine et noli tardare* and *Ecce veniet propheta magna*	W 20
1.9	Responsories *Ecce ego mitto vos* and *Facta autem hac voce*	W 411, 155
1.1	Gradual *Benedicite Dominum*	W fol. 343r
1.1	Introits *Gaudete in Domino semper* and *Ego autem in Domino speravi*	W fols. 294v, 311r
1.1	Communions *Servite Domino, Quis dabit ex Sion* and *Adversum me exercebantur*	W fols. 304r, 310v, 317v
1.1	Offertory *Iusticie Domini recte*	Montpellier, Bibliothèque de l'Université, H159, facsimile in *Paléographie musicale* vol. 8, 251
1.1	*Alleluia Oportebat pati Christum*	W fol. 323r
1.2	Hymns *Christe, qui lux es, A solis ortus cardine* and *Sanctorum meritis*	W 2*, 3*, 10*
1.2	*Kyrie Clemens rector*	W fol. 287r
1.2	*Gloria in excelsis Deo*	W fol. 292r
1.2	*Sanctus*	W fol. 349r
1.2	Trope *Quem Iohannes in deserto. Agnus Dei*	W fol. 350v

(*cont*).

(cont.)

ex.	chant	source
2.1	Short responsory *Veni ad liberandum nos*	W 7
2.2	Responsories *Magi veniunt* and *Omnes de Saba venient* in Gregorian and Old Roman versions	W 53; Rome, Biblioteca Apostolica Vaticana, San Pietro B 79, fol. 40v
2.3	Transitorium *Corpus Christi accepimus*	after Bailey, *Transitoria*, p. 12
3.1	Responsory *Celestium minister donorum*	W 294
3.2	Responsory *Mundi florem*	Aberystwyth, National Library of Wales, 20541 E, fol. 22r
3.3	Antiphons *Granum cadit* and *Opem nobis*	Cambridge, Magdalene College, F.4.10, fol. 34r
3.4	Sequence *Celica resonent*	London, British Library, Cotton MS Caligula A. xiv, fol. 45v
3.5	Sequence *Ecce dies triumphalis*	London, British Library, Cotton MS Caligula A. xiv, fol. 90r
3.6	Trope *Dicite nunc pueri*, introit *Ex ore infantium*	London, British Library, Cotton MS Caligula A. xiv, fol. 8v; W fol. 299r; Provins, Bibliothèque Municipale, 12, fol. 24r; Utrecht, Bibliotheek der Rijksuniversiteit, 406, fol. 45r
3.7	Conductus *Lux optata claruit*	London, British Library, MS Egerton 2615, fol. 29v
3.8	Mary Magdalene and Christ in the garden	Madrid, Biblioteca Nacional, V.20–4, fol. 106v
3.9	From the *Ludus Danielis*	London, British Library, MS Egerton 2615, fol. 97v
3.1	Hildegard of Bingen, responsory *Spiritui sancto.*	Wiesbaden, Hessische Landesbibliothek, 2, fol. 471v
4.4	Hermannus Contractus, A. *Invicta Christi testis Afra*	Munich, Bayerische Staatsbibliothek, Clm 4305, fol. 141r

Glossary

Advent | Period from the fourth Sunday before Christmas to Christmas Eve, originally a time of fasting and penitence.

Agnus Dei | Chant of the Ordinary of Mass, originally sung at the breaking of bread (fraction), but for many centuries between the fraction and communion.

Alleluia (*Alleluia*) | Chant of the Proper of Mass, sung before the Gospel outside Lent.

Ambrosian chant | Latin liturgical chant of Milan, named after St Ambrose (*c*.340–397).

Antiphon (*Antiphona*) | Short chant framing the singing of a psalm, or group of psalms, or a canticle, in the Office. Also applied to the introit and communion chant of Mass. 'Free-standing' antiphons (without a psalm) were frequently sung in honour of the Blessed Virgin Mary and in processions.

Antiphoner | Book containing the chants of the Divine Office. In the early Middle Ages it might refer to any chant book.

Ascension Day | Celebration of the ascension of Christ to heaven.

Ash Wednesday | Day when the faithful are marked with ashes as a symbol of repentance and sorrow, the start of Lent.

Authentic | (See 'mode'.)

Benedicamus Domino | Versicle and response sung at the end of the Office hours.

Benedictus | Canticle of Lauds, *Benedictus Dominus Deus Israel* (Luke 1:68–79). Not to be confused with *Benedictus qui venit in nomine Domini*, part of the Sanctus at Mass.

Beneventan chant | Latin liturgical chant found in books from Benevento and neighbouring areas of south Italy, from the eleventh and twelfth centuries.

Breviary | Book containing the texts of everything to be performed in the Divine Office, including prayers, lessons and chants. In a noted breviary (choir breviary) the chants are notated.

Cantatorium ('cantor's book') | In the early Middle Ages, a term sometimes used to denote the book containing the chants sung by soloists as opposed to the full choir.

Canticle | Biblical (or partly biblical) song other than from the Book of Psalms, sung during the Office.

Chapter (*Capitulum*) | Short lesson in the Divine Office.

Christmas | Celebration of the birth of Christ (25 December).

Clef | Sign placed at the beginning of a staff to indicate the pitch of one of the lines, in the Middle Ages taking the form of an alphabetic letter.

Commune sanctorum | Chants which can be sung for more than one saint. They constitute groups suitable for either apostles, or martyrs, or confessors, or virgins, etc.

Communion (*Communio*) | Chant sung during the administration of bread and wine within the Eucharist. The term is used in a wider sense to mean the act of reception of the bread and wine.

Compline (*Ad completorium*) | Evening service of the Divine Office, sung at nightfall.

Corpus Christi | Feast day on Thursday after Trinity Sunday, celebrated from the second half of the thirteenth century onwards in honour of the body and blood of Christ.

Credo in unum Deum | Chant of the Ordinary of Mass sung between the Gospel and the offertory.

Doxology | (See *Gloria.*)

Easter Sunday | Day of Christ's resurrection from the dead.

Eastertide | Period extending from Easter Sunday to the Saturday after Whitsunday.

Ember Days | Days of penitence on Wednesday, Friday and Saturday in four weeks of the year, one for each season.

Epiphany | Celebration of the visit of the Magi to the newborn Christ (6 January), also the baptism of Christ and the wedding feast at Cana.

Epistle (*Epistola*) | Lesson of Mass drawn from the letters of the apostles, especially Paul, or the Acts of the Apostles.

Eucharist | The part of Mass where bread and wine are administered to the faithful (from Greek *eucharistia*, 'thanksgiving').

Feria (ferial day) | A weekday where no special feast occurs.

Gallican chant | Chant of the churches in Gaul before the establishment of Gregorian chant in the late eighth and ninth centuries.

Gamut | In medieval chant theory, the lowest note of the scale, *G*, written with a Greek *gamma* and solmized *ut*.

Gloria in excelsis Deo | Chant (or hymn) of the Ordinary of Mass, sung on Sundays and feast days after the Kyrie. Referred to as the 'greater doxology' (from Greek *doxa*, 'praise') as distinct from the 'lesser doxology' *Gloria Patri et Filio*. In the Middle Ages often designated 'laudes'.

Gloria Patri et Filio | Verse praising Father, Son and Holy Spirit sung at the end of psalms and canticles. Referred to as the 'lesser doxology' (from Greek *doxa*, 'praise') as distinct from the 'greater doxology' Gloria in excelsis Deo.

Good Friday | Friday of Holy Week, when Christ was crucified and buried.

Gospel (*Evangelium*) | Lesson of Mass drawn from one of the four gospels.

Gradual (*Graduale*) | 1. Chant of the Proper of Mass, sung after the Epistle. 2. The book containing the chants of the Proper of Mass, often also the chants of the Ordinary and sequences.

Hexachord | Scale-segment of six notes. Most commonly associated with the technique of solmization (q.v.) invented by Guido of Arezzo, based on a segment forming the intervals tone–tone–semitone–tone–tone.

Hosanna in excelsis | (See *Sanctus.*)

Hymn (*Hymnus*) | In a general sense, a song of praise. Hymns of the Divine Office are typically metrical, with several strophes of four or more lines.

Hymnal | Book containing the hymns of the Divine Office.

Introit (*Introitus*) | Chant of the Proper of Mass, the first chant, sung at the entrance of the priest and his assistants.

Ite missa est | Chant of the Proper of Mass intoned by the celebrant and answered by the choir, to dismiss the congregation.

Kyrie | Chant of the Ordinary of Mass with Greek text (meaning 'Lord, have mercy, Christ, have mercy', etc.) sung at the beginning of Mass after the introit.

Lauds (*Ad laudes*) (also *Ad matutinas laudes*) | Morning service of the Divine Office, sung before dawn.

Lectionary | Book containing lessons to be read in the Divine Office or at Mass.

Lent | Period of penitence and fasting before Easter.

Litany | From Greek *litaneia*, 'entreaty', Latin *letania* or *litania*. Prayer asking for help from the Trinity, angels and saints, where typically a deacon or other official chants the saint's name and the people respond singing 'Ora pro nobis' ('Pray for us').

Magnificat | Canticle (Luke 1:46–55) sung towards the end of Vespers.

Mass | The religious service at whose centre is the Eucharist, the administration of the bread and wine in memory of and in thanksgiving for Christ's sacrifice on the cross.

Matins (*Ad matutinas*) (Vigils, Night Office, Nocturns) | Night service of the Divine Office, sung before Lauds.

Maundy Thursday | Thursday of Holy Week,

Missal | Book recording the texts of everything to be performed at Mass, including prayers, lessons and chants. In a noted missal the chants are notated.

Mode | Tonal quality of a chant, commonly defined by its final note, typical range and the arrangement of intervals within the range. In medieval chant theory, there were four finals, D, E, F and G. Nearly all chants moved through a 'diatonic' pitch series, that is, without chromatic notes except for bb. The range extending roughly up to an octave above the final was characteristic of the 'authentic' form of the mode; the range extending from roughly a fourth below the final to a fifth above it was characteristic of the 'plagal' form of the mode. Hence a total of eight modes.

Mozarabic chant (Hispanic, Old Spanish chant) | Latin liturgical chant found in books of the Iberian peninsula, from the tenth and eleventh centuries.

Neume | From Greek *neuma*, meaning 'gesture', in terms of chant, a vocal gesture, the vocal movement made upon a syllable of text. Hence, the notational sign or signs for such a movement, from a single note to a complete phrase or melody. The term is most commonly used to refer to a single sign in medieval chant notation.

Nocturn | One of the sections of the Night Office (Matins), one Nocturn being performed on less important days, three on high feast days. Each Nocturn consists of a group of psalms, with framing antiphons, and a group of lessons, each followed by a responsory.

None (*Ad nonam*) | Afternoon service of the Divine Office, sung at the ninth hour of day.

Nunc dimittis | Canticle (Luke 2:29–32) sung towards the end of Compline.

Invitatory (*Invitatorium*) | Psalm 94 and the antiphon (invitatory antiphon) which
     frames it, sung at the beginning of the Night Office (Matins).
O antiphons | Antiphons framing the singing of the Magnificat at Vespers on the seven
     days before Christmas Eve, each beginning with the word 'O'.
Offertory (*Offertorium*) | Chant of the Proper of Mass sung while the bread and wine for
     the Eucharist were brought forward and prepared for distribution.
Office (Divine Office) | Cycle of services forming the daily prayer of the church.
Oktōēchos | The eight-mode system of Byzantine chant, sometimes applied to the
     eight-mode system of Gregorian chant.
Old Roman chant | Latin liturgical chant found in the first notated books from the city of
     Rome, from the late eleventh to the thirteenth centuries.
Ordinary of Mass chants | Chants of Mass – Kyrie, Gloria in excelsis Deo, Credo, Sanctus,
     Agnus Dei, Ite missa est – whose text does not vary from occasion to occasion,
     though their melodies may do so. The Ordinary of Mass in a wider sense also
     includes invariable prayers.
Palm Sunday | Sunday one week before Easter Sunday, celebration Christ's entry into
     Jerusalem, the start of Holy Week.
Passion Sunday | Sunday two weeks before Easter Sunday, the start of Passiontide.
Pentecost (Whitsunday) | Celebration of the bestowal of the Holy Spirit on the apostles,
     on the seventh Sunday after Easter Sunday (fifty days after Easter Sunday).
Plagal | (See 'mode'.)
Postcommunion (*Postcommunio*) | Prayer said at the end of the communion ritual.
Prime (*Ad primam*) | Morning service of the Divine Office, sung at daybreak.
Proper chants | Chants whose Latin text and music changes with each liturgical occasion.
     The word 'proper' means 'appropriate', 'fitting' or 'special to', and can be applied
     also to prayers and readings. The chants of Mass in this category – introit, gradual,
     offertory, etc. – are referred to as the *Proprium missae*. Proper chants for the Sundays
     and feasts of the Lord such as Christmas and Easter form the *Proprium tempore* or
     Temporale. Proper chants for saints' days form the *Proprium sanctorum* or *Sanctorale*.
Prosa, prosula | Text made for a previously existing melody, for example, for a vocalized
     melisma in an alleluia, offertory or responsory. Term also used in the Middle Ages
     for the texted form of a sequence (by contrast with its form as an untexted melody).
Psalter | Book containing the texts of the psalms, often set out in liturgical order as
     performed during the week in the Divine Office.
Quadragesima Sunday | Sunday six weeks before Easter Sunday.
Quinquagesima Sunday | Sunday seven weeks before Easter Sunday.
Requiem | Mass for the Dead, so called because of the first word of the introit *Requiem
     aeternam dona eis Domine*.
Respond (*responsum*) | Choral response to a solo versicle. May also refer to the first
     section of a responsory.
Responsory (*Responsorium*) | Chant of the Divine Office. A Short Responsory
     (*responsorium breve*) was sung at most hours except the Night Office, when a Great
     Responsory (*responsorium prolixum*) is sung after each lesson. The gradual at Mass

is also a type of responsory, sometimes called the *responsum gradale*. A responsory consists of a first part (sometimes called 'respond' (*responsum*)) and a verse (*versus*), followed by a partial repat of the respond.

Rubric | Instructions about the performance of services.

Sacramentary | Book containing prayers, typically the yearly cycle of Proper prayers of Mass.

Sanctus – Benedictus | Part of the eucharistic prayers. While the prayers are mostly intoned by the priest, the Sanctus, with continuation *Benedictus qui venit in nomine Domini* and *Hosanna in excelsis Deo*, is sung by the congregation or choir, a quasi-dramatic reference to the angels who sing these words in Isaiah 6:3.

Sarum | Word derived from the medieval abbreviation of 'Sarisburiense', meaning 'of Salisbury'. Used to refer to the liturgical practice of Salisbury, including its chant, widely adopted throughout medieval Britain.

Septuagesima Sunday | Sunday nine weeks before Easter Sunday.

Sexagesima Sunday | Sunday eight weeks before Easter Sunday.

Sequence (*Sequentia*) | Chant of the Proper of Mass, sung as a festal extension of the alleluia.

Sext (*Ad sextam*) | Morning service of the Divine Office, sung at the sixth hour of day.

Significative letters | Small letters placed by the neumes of some early medieval notations indicating rhythmic, agogic or dynamic features of delivery.

Solmization | In medieval chant instruction, the application of the syllables *ut, re, mi, fa, sol* and *la* to notes of a six-note scale-segment ('hexachord') forming the intervals tone–tone–semitone–tone–tone, that is *C–a*, *F–d* (with *b♭*) or *G–e*. The system was invented by Guido of Arezzo (*c*.992–after 1033).

Te Deum laudamus | Canticle at the end of Matins.

Tenebrae ('shadows', 'darkness') | The Night Office and Lauds on Maundy Thursday, Good Friday and Holy Saturday, during which the lessons were drawn from the Lamentations of Jeremiah and the candles (typically fifteen on a special stand) were successively extinguished after each psalm.

Terce (*Ad terciam*) | Morning service of the Divine Office, sung at the third hour of day.

Tetrachord | Scale-segment of four notes.

Tonary (*tonale*) | List of antiphons in modal order, grouped according to the psalm-tone cadence to be used in each case. The term is also used for a book containing such a list. It may contain other chants listed in tonal order. (Alphabetic listings are very rare.) Some tonaries contain other items for the instruction of singers.

Tract (*Tractus*) | Chant of the Proper of Mass, sung before the Gospel during Lent.

Trinity Sunday | Sunday one week after Pentecost, celebrated from the ninth century in honour of the Holy Trinity.

Troper | Book containing tropes. Often used to designate a book also containing other festal chant such as sequences.

Venite exsultemus | Psalm 94, sung at the beginning of the Night Office (Matins).

Versicle | Short verse typically sung by a soloist, to which a choir responds.

Vespers (*Ad vesperas*) | Evening service of the Divine Office, sung before nightfall.

Bibliography

This bibliography brings together the literature cited in the 'Further reading' paragraphs, together with the few other items cited by author's name in the main text. Like those references, it is mostly restricted to publications basic to the study of chant, while also including some examples of more specialized research in selected areas.

Comprehensive bibliographies may be found in Hiley, *Western Plainchant*, and the article 'Plainchant' by John Emerson and others for *The New Grove Dictionary of Music and Musicians*, 2nd edn, ed. Stanley Sadie (London, 2001), vol. 19, 825–86.

There is an on-line bibliography searchable by author, keyword, etc. at www-musikwissenschaft.uni-regensburg.de/cantus. Annual bibliographies are published in the journal *Plainsong and Medieval Music*.

Facsimiles

Arlt, Wulf, and Susan Rankin, ed., *Stiftsbibliothek Sankt Gallen. Codices 484 & 381: I Kommentar; II Codex Sangallensis 484; III Codex Sangallensis 381* (Winterthur: Amadeus, 1996)

Das Graduale von Santa Cecilia in Trastevere (Cod. Bodmer 74), ed. Max Lütolf, 2 vols. (Cologny-Geneva: Fondation Martin Bodmer, 1987)

Hildegard von Bingen, Symphonia harmoniae caelestium revelationum. Dendermonde, St.-Pieters & Paulusabdij, Ms. Cod. 9, ed. Peter van Poucke, Facsimile Series I/A.8 (Peer: Alamire, 1991); *Hildegard von Bingen. Lieder. Faksimile. Riesencodex (Hs. 2) der Hessischen Landesbibliothek Wiesbaden fol. 466–481v*, ed. Lorenz Welker, commentary by Michael Klaper (Wiesbaden: Reichert, 1998)

Paléographie musicale: Les principaux manuscrits de chant grégorien, ambrosien, mozarabe, gallican [premier série, deuxième série] (Solesmes: Abbaye-Saint-Pierre, 1889–; vols. I/18–20 Berne: Lang, 1969–83)

I/1 (Solesmes, 1889) – *Le Codex 339 de la Bibliothèque de Saint-Gall (Xᵉ siècle): Antiphonale missarum sancti Gregorii*

I/2 (Solesmes, 1891) – *Le Répons-graduel Justus ut palma, réproduit en fac-similé d'après plus de deux cents antiphonaires manuscrits du IXᵉ au XVIIᵉ siècle*

I/3 (Solesmes, 1892) – *Le Répons-graduel Justus ut palma: Deuxième partie*

I/4 (Solesmes, 1894) – *Le Codex 121 de la Bibliothèque d'Einsiedeln (IXᵉ–XIᵉ siècle): Antiphonale missarum sancti Gregorii*

I/5 (Solesmes, 1896) – *Antiphonarium Ambrosianum du Musée Britannique (XIIe siècle), Codex Additional 34209*

I/6 (Solesmes, 1900) – *Antiphonarium Ambrosianum du Musée Britannique (XIIe siècle), Codex Additional 34209: Transcription*

I/7 (Solesmes, 1901) – *Antiphonarium tonale missarum, XIe siècle: Codex H. 159 de la Bibliothèque de l'École de Médecine de Montpellier*

I/8 (Solesmes, 1901–5) – *Antiphonarium tonale missarum, XIe siècle: Codex H. 159 de la Bibliothèque de l'École de Médecine de Montpellier. Phototypies*

I/9 (Solesmes, 1906) – *Antiphonaire monastique, XIIe siècle: Codex 601 de la Bibliothèque Capitulaire de Lucques*

I/10 (Solesmes, 1909) – *Antiphonale missarum sancti Gregorii, IXe–Xe siècle: Codex 239 de la Bibliothèque de Laon*

I/11 (Solesmes, 1912) – *Antiphonale missarum sancti Gregorii, Xe siècle: Codex 47 de la Bibliothèque de Chartres*

I/12 (Solesmes, 1922) – *Antiphonaire monastique, XIIIe siècle: Codex F. 160 de la Bibliothèque de la Cathédrale de Worcester*

I/13 (Solesmes, 1925) – *Le Codex 903 de la Bibliothèque Nationale de Paris (XIe siècle): Graduel de Saint-Yrieix*

I/14 (Solesmes, 1931) – *Le Codex 10673 de la Bibliothèque Vaticane fonds latin (XIe siècle): Graduel Bénéventain*

I/15 (Solesmes, 1937–57) – *Le Codex VI. 34 de la Bibliothèque Capitulaire de Bénévent (XIe–XIIe siècle): Graduel de Bénévent avec prosaire et tropaire*

I/16 (Solesmes, 1955) – *Le Manuscrit du Mont-Renaud, Xe siècle: Graduel et antiphonaire de Noyon*

I/17 (Solesmes, 1958) – *Fragments des manuscrits de Chartres, réproduction phototypique: Présentation par le Chanoine Yves Delaporte*

I/18 (Berne, 1969) – *Le Codex 123 de la Bibliothèque Angelica de Rome (XIe siècle): Graduel et tropaire de Bologne*

I/19 (Berne, 1974) – *Le Manuscrit 807, Universitätsbibliothek Graz (XIIe siècle): Graduel de Klosterneuburg*

I/20 (Berne, 1983) – *Le Manuscrit VI-33, Archivio Arcivescovile Benevento: Missel de Bénévent (début du XIe siècle)*

I/21 (Solesmes, 1992) – Thomas Forrest Kelly: *Les témoins manuscrits du chant Bénéventain*

II/1 (Solesmes, 1900) – *Antiphonaire de l'office monastique transcrit par Hartker: MSS. Saint-Gall 390–391 (980–1011)*

II/2 (Solesmes, 1924) – *Cantatorium, IXe siècle: N° 359 de la Bibliothèque de Saint-Gall*

Salisbury (Sarum) chant books in facsimile

• *Antiphonale Sarisburiense: A Reproduction in Facsimile of a Manuscript of the Thirteenth Century*, ed. Walter Howard Frere (London: Plainsong & Mediaeval Music Society, 1901–24)

- *Graduale Sarisburiense: A Reproduction in Facsimile of a Manuscript of the Thirteenth Century, with a Dissertation and Historical Index Illustrating its Development from the Gregorian Antiphonale missarum*, ed. Walter Howard Frere (London: Quaritch,1894)
- *Processionale ad usum Sarum (London: Richard Pynson, 1502)* (facsimile, Clarabricken: Boethius, 1980)

York chant books in facsimile

- *Lambeth Palace Sion College MS. L1. The Noted Breviary of York (Olim Sion College ms Arc.L.40.2/L.1)*, ed. Andrew Hughes (Ottawa: Institute of Mediaeval Music, 2000)
- *Oxford Bodleian Library MS. Lat. liturg. b. 5*, ed. David Hiley (Ottawa: Institute of Mediaeval Music, 1995)
- *Oxford, Bodleian Library MS. e Mus. 126 (The York Processional)*, ed. David Hiley (Ottawa: Institute of Mediaeval Music, 1998)

Editions of music

(i) Vatican and Solesmes books for use in church

Antiphonale monasticum pro diurnis horis (Tournai: Desclée, 1934)

Antiphonale sacrosanctae Romanae ecclesiae (Rome: Typis Polyglottis Vaticanis, 1912)

Graduale sacrosanctae Romanae ecclesiae (Rome: Desclée, 1908)

Graduale Romanum . . . restitutum et editum Pauli VI (Solesmes: Abbaye Saint-Pierre, 1974)

Graduale triplex, ed. Marie-Claire Billecocq and Rupert Fischer (Solesmes: Abbaye Saint-Pierre, 1979)

Liber antiphonarius pro diurnis horis, I: De tempore [Antiphonale monasticum I] (Solesmes: Abbaye Saint-Pierre, 2005)

Liber hymnarius cum invitatoriis & aliquibus responsoriis (Solesmes: Abbaye Saint-Pierre, 1983)

Liber responsorialis pro festis I. classis et communi sanctorum juxta ritum monasticum (Solesmes: Abbaye Saint-Pierre, 1894)

Liber usualis missae et officii pro dominicis et festis I. vel II. classis (Tournai: Declée, 1921)

Processionale monasticum ad usum congregationis gallicae ordinis Sancti Benedicti (Solesmes: Abbaye Saint-Pierre, 1893)

Psalterium monasticum (Solesmes: Abbaye Saint-Pierre, 1981)

(ii) Other editions

Arlt, Wulf, *Ein Festoffizium des Mittelalters aus Beauvais in seiner liturgischen und musikalischen Bedeutung*, 2 vols. (Cologne: Arno Volk, 1970)

Bailey, Terence, *The Ambrosian Alleluias* (Englefield Green: Plainsong & Mediaeval Music Society, 1983)

   The Ambrosian Cantus (Ottawa: Institute of Mediaeval Music, 1987)

The Transitoria of the Ambrosian Mass Edited from Three Sources (Ottawa: Institute of Mediaeval Music, 2002)

Bailey, Terence, and Paul Merkley, *The Antiphons of the Ambrosian Office* (Ottawa: Institute of Mediaeval Music, 1989)

Beneventanum Troporum Corpus, ed. John Boe and Alejandro Planchart, Recent Researches in the Music of the Middle Ages and Early Renaissance 16–26 (Madison: A-R Editions, 1989–96)

Early Medieval Chants from Nonantola, ed. James Borders and Lance Brunner, Recent Researches in the Music of the Middle Ages and Early Renaissance 30–33 (Madison: A-R Editions, 1996–9)

Hansen, Finn Egeland, *H 159 Montpellier* (Copenhagen: Dan Fog, 1974)

Hildegard von Bingen. Lieder, ed. Pudentiana Barth, Immaculata Ritscher and Joseph Schmidt-Görg (Salzburg: O. Müller, 1969); *Symphonia armonie celestium revelationum*, ed. Marianne Richert Pfau, 8 vols. (Bryn Mawr: Hildegard Pub. Co., 1997–8)

Monumenta monodica medii aevi (Kassel: Bärenreiter, 1956–) – includes the following editions:

MMMA 1 (1956): *Hymnen I. Die mittelalterlichen Hymnenmelodien des Abendlandes*, ed. Bruno Stäblein, reprint 1995 with extra appendix

MMMA 2 (1970): Bruno Stäblein (introduction) and Margareta Landwehr-Melnicki (edition), *Die Gesänge des altrömischen Graduale Vat. lat. 5319*

MMMA 3 (1970): *Introitus-Tropen I. Das Repertoire der südfranzösische Tropare des 10. und 11. Jahrhunderts*, ed. Günther Weiss

MMMA 5 (1999): *Antiphonen*, ed. László Dobszay and Janka Szendrei

MMMA 7 (1968): *Alleluia-Melodien I, bis 1100*, ed. Karlheinz Schlager

MMMA 8 (1987): *Alleluia-Melodien II, ab 1100*, ed. Karlheinz Schlager

MMMA 13 (2001): *Das Repertoire der normanno-sizilischen Tropare I: Die Sequenzen*, ed. David Hiley

MMMA 19 (2006): *Melodien zum Ite missa est und ihre Tropen*, ed. William F. Eifrig and Andreas Pfisterer

MMMA *Subsidia* 1 (1995): Andreas, Haug *Troparia tardiva. Repertorium später Tropenquellen aus dem deutschsprachigen Raum*

Nocturnale Romanum: Antiphonale Sacrosancte Romanae Ecclesiae pro nocturnis horis. Editio princeps, ed. Holger Peter Sandhofe (Heidelberg: Hartker, 2002)

Literature

Andrieu, Michel, *Les Ordines Romani du haut moyen âge*, 5 vols. (Louvain: Spicilegium Sacrum Lovaniense, 1931–61)

Apel, Willi, *Gregorian Chant* (Bloomington: Indiana University Press, 1958)

Atkinson, Charles M., 'De Accentibus Toni Oritur Nota Quae Dicitur Neuma: Prosodic Accents, the Accent Theory, and the Paleofrankish Script', in *Essays on Medieval Music in Honor of David G. Hughes*, ed. Graeme M. Boone (Cambridge, Mass.: Harvard University Press, 1995), 17–42

The Critical Nexus: Tone-System, Mode, and Notation in Early Medieval Music (Oxford: Oxford University Press, 2009)

Bailey, Terence, *The Processions of Sarum and the Western Church* (Toronto: Pontifical Institute of Mediaeval Studies, 1971)

Commemoratio brevis de tonis et psalmis modulandis: Introduction, Critical Edition, Translation (Ottawa: University of Ottawa Press, 1979)

'Ambrosian Chant', *NG2*

Baker, Nigel, and Richard Holt, *Urban Growth and the Medieval Church: Gloucester and Worcester* (Aldershot: Ashgate, 2004)

Bergeron, Katherine, *Decadent Enchantments: The Revival of Gregorian Chant at Solesmes* (Berkeley: University of California Press, 1998)

Bower, Calvin M., 'The Transmission of Ancient Music Theory into the Middle Ages', in *The Cambridge History of Western Music Theory*, ed. Thomas Christensen (Cambridge: Cambridge University Press, 2002), 136–67

Bradshaw, Paul, *Early Christian Worship: A Basic Introduction to Ideas and Practice* (London: SPCK, 1996)

CANTUS – website http://publish.uwo.ca/~cantus

Cardine, Eugène, *Gregorian Semiology* (Solesmes: Abbaye Saint-Pierre, 1982) [trans. from the original Italian edn of 1968]

Carruthers, Mary, *A Book of Memory* (Cambridge: Cambridge University Press, 1990)

Cohen, David E., 'Notes, Scales, and Modes in the Earlier Middle Ages', in *The Cambridge History of Western Music Theory*, ed. Thomas Christensen (Cambridge: Cambridge University Press, 2002), 307–63

Combe, Pierre, *The Restoration of Gregorian Chant: Solesmes and the Vatican Edition* (Washington: Catholic University of America, 2003) [trans. from the original French edn of 1969]

Corbin, Solange, *Die Neumen*, Palaeographie der Musik 1/3 (Cologne: Arno Volk, 1977)

Crocker, Richard L., *The Early Medieval Sequence* (Berkeley: University of California Press, 1977)

An Introduction to Gregorian Chant (New Haven: Yale University Press, 2000)

Crocker, Richard L., and David Hiley, eds., *The Early Middle Ages to 1300*, New Oxford History of Music 2 (Oxford: Oxford University Press, 1989)

The Cambridge History of Western Music Theory, ed. Thomas Christensen (Cambridge: Cambridge University Press, 2002)

Davril, Anselme, and Eric Palazzo, *La vie des moines au temps des grandes abbayes X^e–XIIIe siècles* (Paris: Hachette littératures, 2000)

Doig, Allan, *Liturgy and Architecture: From the Early Church to the Middle Ages* (Aldershot: Ashgate, 2008)

Dyer, Joseph, 'Monastic Psalmody of the Middle Ages', *Revue Bénédictine* 99 (1989), 41–74

'The Singing of Psalms in the Early-Medieval Office', *Speculum* 64 (1989), 535–78

'The Schola Cantorum and its Roman Milieu in the Early Middle Ages', in *De musica et cantu. Studien zur Geschichte der Kirchenmusik und der Oper. Helmut Hucke zum*

60. Geburtstag, ed. Peter Cahn and Ann-Katrin Heimer (Hildesheim: Olms, 1993), 19–40

'Prolegomena to a History of Music and Liturgy at Rome in the Middle Ages', in *Essays on Medieval Music in Honor of David G. Hughes*, ed. Graeme M. Boone (Cambridge, Mass.: Harvard University Press, 1995), 87–115

'The Desert, the City and Psalmody in the Later Fourth Century', in *Western Plainchant in the First Millennium. Studies in the Medieval Liturgy and its Music*, ed. Sean Gallagher, James Haar, John Nádas and Timothy Striplin (Aldershot: Ashgate, 2003), 11–43

'The Roman Offertory: An Introduction and Some Hypotheses', in *The Offertory and its Verses: Research, Past, Present and Future. Proceedings of an International Symposium at the Centre for Medieval Studies, Trondheim, 25 and 26 September 2004*, ed. Roman Hankeln (Trondheim: Tapir, 2007), 15–40

'Gregor I.' and 'Schola cantorum', *MGG2*

Eliade, Mircea, *Patterns in Comparative Religion* (London: Sheed & Ward, 1958) [trans. from original French edn of 1949]

Engberg, Gudrun, 'Ekphonetic Notation', *NG2*

Engel, Ute, *Worcester Cathedral: An Architectural History* (Chichester: Phillimore, 2007)

Fassler, Margot, *Gothic Song: Victorine Sequences and Augustinian Reform in Twelfth-Century Paris* (Cambridge: Cambridge University Press, 1993)

Geschichte der Musiktheorie – vol. 3: Michael Bernhard *et al.*, *Rezeption des antiken Fachs im Mittelalter*, Geschichte der Musiktheorie 3 (Darmstadt: Wissenschaftliche Buchgesellschaft, 1990); vol. 4: Thomas Ertelt and Frieder Zaminer, eds., *Die Lehre vom einstimmigen liturgischen Gesang* (Darmstadt: Wissenschaftliche Buchgesellschaft, 2000)

Grier, James, *The Musical World of a Medieval Monk. Adémar de Chabannes in Eleventh-century Aquitaine* (Cambridge: Cambridge University Press, 2006)

Hannick, Christian, and Dali Dolidze, 'Georgia, II. Orthodox Church Music', *NG2*

Harper, John, *The Forms and Orders of Western Liturgy from the Tenth to the Eighteenth Century: A Historical Introduction and Guide for Students and Musicians* (Oxford: Clarendon Press, 1991)

Harrison, Frank Ll., *Music in Medieval Britain* (London: Routledge and Kegan Paul, 1958; 2nd edn 1963)

Harting-Corrêa, Alice L., *Walahfrid Strabo's* Libellus de exordiis et incrementis quarundam in observationibus ecclesiasticis rerum: *A Translation and Liturgical Commentary* (Leiden: Brill, 1996)

Hesbert, René-Jean, *Antiphonale missarum sextuplex* (Brussels: Vromant, 1935; rpt. Rome: Herder, 1967)

Corpus antiphonalium officii, 6 vols. (Rome: Herder, 1963–79)

Hiley, David, *Western Plainchant: A Handbook* (Oxford: Clarendon Press, 1993)

Hornby, Emma, *Gregorian and Old Roman Eighth-Mode Tracts. A Case Study in the Transmission of Western Chant* (Aldershot: Ashgate, 2002)

Hucbald, Guido, and John on Music, trans. Warren Babb (New Haven: Yale University Press, 1978)

Hughes, Andrew, *Medieval Manuscripts for Mass and Office: A Guide to their Organization and Terminology* (Toronto: University of Toronto Press, 1982)

'Late Medieval Plainchant for the Divine Office', in *Music as Concept and Practice in the Late Middle Ages*, ed. Reinhard Strohm and Bonnie J. Blackburn, The New Oxford History of Music 3/1 (Oxford: Oxford University Press, 2001), 31–96

Husmann, Heinrich, *Tropen- und Sequenzenhandschriften*, Répertoire internationale des sources musicales B/V/1 (Munich: Henle, 1964)

Huglo, Michel, *Les Livres de chant liturgique*, Typologie des sources du Moyen Âge occidental 52 (Turnhout: Brepols, 1988)

Les Manuscrits du Processional, Répertoire internationale des sources musicales B/XIV/1–2 (Munich: Henle, 1999 and 2004)

'Gallican Chant', *NG2*

Huglo, Michel, and Olivier Cullin, 'Gallikanischer Gesang', *MGG2*

Jeffery, Peter, 'Jerusalem and Rome (and Constantinople): The Musical Heritage of Two Great Cities in the Formation of the Medieval Chant Traditions', in *International Musicological Society Study Group Cantus Planus. Papers Read at the Fourth Meeting, Pécs, Hungary, 3–8 September 1990*, ed. László Dobszay, Ágnes Papp and Ferenc Sebő (Budapest: Hungarian Academy of Sciences, Institute for Musicology, 1992), 163–74

'Oktoechos', *NG2*

Karp, Theodore, *Aspects of Orality and Formularity in Gregorian Chant* (Evanston: Northwestern University Press, 1998)

An Introduction to the Post-Tridentine Mass Proper, Part I: Text, Part II: Music Examples; CD: Selected Post-Tridentine Chants, performed by the Schola Antiqua of Chicago, directed by Calvin Bower, Musicological Studies and Documents 54 (Middleton: American Institute of Musicology, 2005)

Kelly, Thomas Forrest, *The Beneventan Chant* (Cambridge: Cambridge University Press, 1989)

'Medieval Composers of Liturgical Chant', *Musica e storia* 14/1 (2006), 95–125

Kerovpyan, Aram, 'Armenia, II. Church Music', *NG2*

Knowles, David, *Christian Monasticism* (London: Weidenfeld and Nicolson, 1969, 2/1977)

Lawrence, C. Hugh, *Medieval Monasticism: Forms of Religious Life in Western Europe in the Middle Ages* (London: Longman, 1984)

Levy, Kenneth, *Gregorian Chant and the Carolingians* (Princeton: Princeton University Press, 1998)

Levy, Kenneth, and Christian Troelsgård, 'Byzantine Rite, Music of the', *NG2*

'Divine Liturgy (Byzantine)', *NG2*

Maloy, Rebecca, *Inside the Offertory* (Aldershot: Ashgate, 2009)

Martimort, Aimé-Georges, ed., Matthew J. O'Connell (trans.), *The Church at Prayer, New Edition*, 4 vols. (Collegeville, Minn.: Liturgical Press, 1987, 1987, 1988 and 1986)

McKinnon, James, *Music in Early Christian Literature* (Cambridge: Cambridge University Press, 1987)

The Advent Project: The Later-Seventh-Century Creation of the Roman Mass Proper (Berkeley: University of California Press, 2000)

'Christian Church, Music of the Early', *NG2*

MGG2 – Die Musik in Geschichte und Gegenwart, 2nd edn, ed. Ludwig Finscher (Kassel: Bärenreiter, 1994–2007)

Molitor, Raphael, *Die nach-Tridentinische Choralreform zu Rom*, 2 vols. (Leipzig: Leuckart 1901–2)

The New SCM Dictionary of Liturgy and Worship, ed. Paul F. Bradshaw (London: SCM Press, 2002)

NG2 – The New Grove Dictionary of Music and Musicians, 2nd edn ed. Stanley Sadie (London: Macmillan, 2001)

Nowacki, Edward, 'The Gregorian Office Antiphons and the Comparative Method', *Journal of Musicology* 4 (1985), 243–75

The Oxford Dictionary of the Christian Church, ed. Frank L. Cross and Elizabeth A. Livingstone, 2nd edn (Oxford: Oxford University Press, 1974)

Pesce, Dolores, *Guido of Arezzo's Regule rithmice, Prologus in antiphonarium, and Epistola ad Michaelem: A Critical Text and Translation* (Ottawa: Institute of Mediaeval Music, 1999)

Randel, Don, and Nils Nadeau, 'Mozarabic Chant', *NG2*

Robertson-Wilson, Marian, 'Coptic Church Music', *NG2*

Rankin, Susan K., 'Liturgical Drama', in *The Early Middle Ages to 1300*, ed. Richard L. Crocker and David Hiley, New Oxford History of Music 2 (Oxford: Oxford University Press, 1989), 310–56

'Carolingian Music', in *Carolingian Culture: Emulation and Innovation*, ed. Rosamund McKitterick (Cambridge: Cambridge University Press, 1993), 274–316

The Winchester Troper, Early English Church Music 50 (London: Stainer and Bell, 2007)

St. Wulfstan and his World, ed. Julia Barrow and Nicholas Brooks (Aldershot: Ashgate, 2005), incl. Susan Rankin, 'Music at Wulfstan's Cathedral', 219–29

Senn, Frank C., *Christian Liturgy: Catholic and Evangelical* (Minneapolis: Fortress Press, 1997)

Shelemay, Kay Kaufman, Peter Jeffery and Ingrid Monson, 'Oral and Written Transmission in Ethiopian Christian Chant', *Early Music History* 12 (1993), 55–117

Shelemay, Kay Kaufman, 'Ethiopia, II. Orthodox Church Music', *NG2*

Shelemay, Kay Kaufman, and Peter Jeffery, eds., *Ethiopian Christian Liturgical Chant: An Anthology* (Madison: A-R Editions, 1993–7)

Strunk, Oliver, *Source Readings in Music History*, rev. edn, ed. Leo Treitler (New York: Norton, 1998)

Stäblein, Bruno, *Schriftbild der einstimmigen Musik*, Musikgeschichte in Bildern 3/4 (Leipzig: Deutscher Verlag für Musik, 1975)

The Study of Liturgy, ed. Cheslyn Jones, Geoffrey Wainwright and Edward Yarnold, rev. edn (London: SPCK, 1992)

Suñol, Grégoire M., *Introduction à la paléographie musicale grégorienne* (Tournai: Desclée, 1935)

Treitler, Leo, *With Voice and Pen: Coming to Know Medieval Song and How It Was Made* (Oxford: Oxford University Press, 2003)

Troelsgård, Christian, 'Psalm, III. Byzantine Psalmody', *NG2*

Velimirović, Miloš, and Leonora DeCarlo, 'Russian and Slavonic Church Music', *NG2*

Wagner, Peter, *Einführung in die gregorianischen Melodien*, vol. 3: *Gregorianische Formenlehre* (Leipzig: Breitkopf & Härtel, 1921)

Wright, Craig, *Music and Ceremony at Notre Dame of Paris, 500–1500* (Cambridge: Cambridge University Press, 1989)

Index